Social theory and applied
health research

Understanding Social Research

Series Editor: Alan Bryman

Published titles

Qualitative Data Analysis: Explorations with NVivo
Graham R. Gibbs

Advanced Quantitative Data Analysis
Duncan Cramer

Ethnography
John D. Brewer

Biographical Research
Brian Roberts

Postmodernism and Social Research
Mats Alvesson

Unobtrusive Methods in Social Research
Raymond M. Lee

Surveying the Social World
Alan Aldridge and Ken Levine

Focus Group Research
Alan Beardsworth

Social Theory and Applied Health Research
Simon Dyson

Discourse Analysis: Text, Narrative and Representation
Rosalind Gill

Social Research Methodology
Malcolm Williams

Social Research 3/e
Tim May

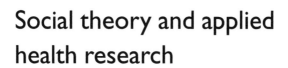

Social theory and applied health research

SIMON DYSON AND BRIAN BROWN

Open University Press

Open University Press
McGraw-Hill Education
McGraw-Hill House
Shoppenhangers Road
Maidenhead
Berkshire
England
SL6 2QL

email: enquiries@openup.co.uk
world wide web: www.openup.co.uk

and Two Penn Plaza, New York, NY 10121–2289, USA

First published 2006

A catalogue record of this book is available from the British Library

ISBN–10: 0335 21034 1 (pb) 0335 21035 X (hb)
ISBN–13: 978 0335 21034 3 (pb) 978 0335 21035 0 (hb)

Library of Congress Cataloging-in-Publication Data
CIP data applied for

Typeset by RefineCatch Limited, Bungay, Suffolk
Printed in the UK by Bell & Bain Ltd, Glasgow

Simon Dyson

For Sue, with all my love

Brian Brown

For Pat, who passed on to me her interest in nature, Greek myths and literature, little realizing what a dangerous combination it was

Contents

List of boxes, tables and figures

Boxes

Tables

Figures

Series editor's foreword

This Understanding Social Research series is designed to help students to understand how social research is carried out and to appreciate a variety of issues in social research methodology. It is designed to address the needs of students taking degree programmes in areas such as sociology, social policy, psychology, communication studies, cultural studies, human geography, political science, criminology and organization studies and who are required to take modules in social research methods. It is also designed to meet the needs of students who need to carry out a research project as part of their degree requirements. Postgraduate research students and novice researchers will find the books equally helpful.

The series is concerned to help readers to 'understand' social research methods and issues. This means developing an appreciation of the pleasures and frustrations of social research, an understanding of how to implement certain techniques, and an awareness of key areas of debate. The relative emphasis on these different features varies from book to book, but in each one the aim is to see the method or issue from the position of a practising researcher and not simply to present a manual of 'how to' steps. In the process, the series contains coverage of the major methods of social research and addresses a variety of issues and debates. Each book in the series is written by a practising researcher who has experience of the technique or debates that he or she is addressing. Authors are encouraged to draw on their own experiences and inside knowledge.

This book by Simon Dyson and Brian Brown presents a very original approach to the discussion of methodological issues. The authors are concerned to bring out the epistemological and ontological bases and assumptions on which matters of collecting and analysing research data are founded. For Dyson and Brown, an awareness of the wider philosophical context in which decisions about social research methods are located is crucial to the research enterprise. The effect of their exposition is to make the reader think about the grounds upon which knowledge claims are and can be founded. Many of the areas covered will be familiar to some readers. Examples include issues like survey research, ethnography, grounded theory, meta-analysis, conversation analysis, and randomized controlled trials. In addition, a host of theoretical and philosophical positions and traditions are explored, such as positivism, realism, phenomenology, critical theory, postmodernism, and actor-network theory. The book makes a major contribution by marrying the two levels of discourse – on the one hand, the essentially technical issues surrounding the collection and analysis of data; on the other hand, the world of philosophy and thereby the assumptions of the research process.

As the book's title signals, Dyson and Brown locate their discussions in applied health research. This a burgeoning field that raises many issues (and allows many interesting issues to be raised) concerning the nature of the research process. Social science students will also find that the health context is a highly fertile area for the discussion of important research principles and for examples of the complexities of research. Their approach is to be very critical of many of the taken-for-granted assumptions that guide much research. Students will find their constantly questioning approach, coupled with their penchant for unusual examples of key points, original and striking.

At a time when many students and researchers generally are being encouraged on the one hand to be aware of epistemological issues and principles and on the other hand to engage in policy-relevant research, this book provides a timely opportunity to bring the two together.

Alan Bryman

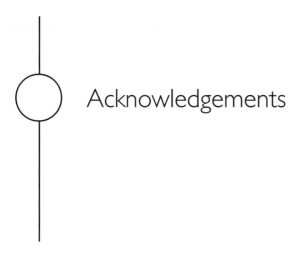

Acknowledgements

We would like to thank all our academic colleagues, especially Dave Hiles, Scott Yates and Martyn Denscombe for their help in inspiring the book and in helping to clarify some of our thoughts in discussions over the years. Thank you also to our series editor Alan Bryman and the two reviewers who gave us the chance to write this book, and to the two anonymous reviewers of the first draft. As is usual in these cases, we will take the credit for any good in the book, and vehemently deny all responsibility for the rest of it.

1 Introduction: in a field of possibilities

A feature of the growth of contemporary health services research is that in the rush to secure health care practice based on 'evidence', few have stopped to ask fundamental questions such as what is to count as evidence (Brown *et al.* 2003). But research in the social world necessitates making what Gouldner (1970) has called 'background assumptions'. By this phrase is meant that all researchers, whether they are conscious of it or not, make certain assumptions in undertaking research. These assumptions are about what we are actually studying when we conduct social research and how we can justify our claims to have created knowledge. This book is about those background assumptions.

The book aims to provide a resource for the increasing number of students, including students from professional backgrounds, who wish to undertake social research at an advanced level, but who are dissatisfied with the assumptions of traditional research on the one hand and the inaccessibility of complex philosophies of research on the other. This book aims to provide an accessible assessment of dilemmas facing social researchers in trying to make sense of the world. It further tries to link theory and method, neither by rejecting wholesale particular forms of research, nor by accepting the possibility of triangulation at a philosophical level, but by presenting an account of how reflection on a field of possibilities can help amend, complement and strengthen a practical research strategy.

Levels of research

We need to start by saying something of how we conceive different levels of the research process, how these levels are linked, and in particular how theory may be connected to method. Denscombe (2003) usefully distinguishes between the levels of what he calls research strategies and the level of research methods. Research strategies are the broader organizing features of the research design. Major research strategies include experiments, surveys, case studies, action research, ethnography and grounded theory. The methods are the techniques that will be used to collect data, and include questionnaires, interviews, observations and documents. The distinction is useful because it reminds us of possibilities that applied researchers have often closed down. A survey strategy does not necessarily entail a questionnaire, as surveys could equally be undertaken using observation or documents. Grounded theory is not reducible to conducting semi-structured interviews (Silverman 1998).

However, the choice a researcher makes about strategies and methods is always a contextual choice. Sometimes the chosen research problem is better addressed using one strategy rather than another, and sometimes by adopting one method of data collection over another. Strategies and methods are neither inherently better nor worse than one another. Note, too, that there are other levels of the research process to consider. At a higher level of abstraction than the research strategy, there are the different philosophical traditions that underpin different approaches to research, such as positivism, subjectivism, critical realism and postmodernism. There are a variety of means to analyse and present data, including the use of inferential statistics, descriptive statistics, content analysis, thematic analysis, discourse analysis and interpretive phenomenological analysis. The levels of the research process may be represented as in Table 1.1.

However, what is the researcher engaged in applied research to make of the relationship between these different conceptual levels of research? There are a number of possible views on this that we would reject.

One possible approach we do not wish to endorse is the 'ignorance is bliss' approach to research. In this approach applied researchers are disdainful of philosophy, because, in true *X-Files* style, the 'truth is out there'. In this scenario, researchers are indeed making assumptions at the philosophical level (about what the social world is made up of and how we can make claims to knowledge about the social world) but are not aware that they are implicitly making these assumptions in the research choices they make. The researchers may indeed be unaware of alternative conceptions of thinking about claims to knowledge and remain unreflective of their own position as researchers in the field of possibilities. This seems to us to be reflected in the 'evidence-based medicine' movement, which does not reflect on its own social location (Harrison 1998).

Table 1.1 Different conceptual levels of the research process

---

Research philosophies
(positivism, subjectivism, critical realism, postmodernism)
Methodological criteria
(internal validity, external validity, reliability)
Research strategies
(experiments, surveys, action research, case studies, ethnography, grounded theory)
Research methods
(questionnaires, interviews, observation, documents)
Methods of analysis
(inferential statistics, descriptive statistics, content analysis, thematic analysis, discourse analysis and interpretive phenomenological analysis)

A second possible approach to the relationship between conceptual levels in the research process is to start at the level of philosophy and explicitly, from the outset of the research, make a hard and fast decision about key philosophical debates. In this approach, researchers effectively subscribe to a static philosophical position, one that forever after informs their approach to research. In this approach, researchers incorporate into their very identity a belief in the correctness of a philosophical stance, which then determines their approach to research. For example, the term phenomenology has been used to describe approaches to research at the level of philosophy (Porter 1998); strategy (Denscombe 2003); methods (Moustakas 1994) and analysis (Smith *et al.* 1999). The advantage of an approach to research that starts from a clear paradigm that then drives decisions at the level of strategy, method and analysis is that at least logical consistency is imposed onto the research problem. The disadvantage, it seems to us, is that, whatever paradigm one adopts as one's own, one has to disavow a number of other possible philosophical assumptions. These alternative assumptions are those adopted by many other researchers much more clever than oneself. Unless you can lay claim to being able simultaneously to out-think Popper, Heidegger, Wittgenstein, de Beauvoir, Oakley, Habermas, Archer, Hall, Sivanandan, Foucault and Derrida (in which case this book is not for you), then it seems to us that modesty compels us to admit that there is 'something' in each of those other philosophical assumptions that would not be our first choice. Adopting a paradigm as a cloak in which we then go out into the world and conduct research has the attraction of consistency. But it has the considerable disadvantage of institutionalizing into the research then conducted all the criticisms offered collectively of that position by other philosophers of research. The research is thereby based on a questionable assertion that one has found the 'correct' philosophical position. This is therefore not an approach we support in this book.

As we shall see over the course of the book, a number of the debates can be presented as philosophical opposites. The habit of thinking in opposites or dualities has been much criticized (Oakley 1992). However, the alternative to dualities is to develop concepts that claim to transcend dualities, though in this process we run the risk of blurring issues so as to render them less amenable to analysis. For example, a coin has two sides, heads and tails, though of course they are both integral to the whole. One does not have to deny the existence of the tails side in order to examine the heads, but one does (short of the use of mirrors) temporarily have to hide one side from view in order to examine closely the other side. Our analysis of the coin is not helped by conflating the two sides into a new concept such as 'hails' or 'teads'. We therefore do not subscribe to approaches that seek to dissolve the philosophical debates that underpin decisions about research.

Instead, if we treat the background philosophical dilemmas as 'analytical dualisms' (Archer 2000), then we may make links to other levels of research, particularly the levels of research strategies and research methods. We may also make links to data analysis in that it may be the status accorded to data and the differential manner in which the researcher may work with materials that defines different approaches.

It is our contention that an applied social researcher appropriately starts the research process by making decisions at the level of *research strategy*, and to a lesser extent at the level of which research methods are most suited to the research problem at hand. However, by making practical decisions at the level of strategy, the researcher is implicitly drawing upon assumptions about how social research works. The philosophies of research are *implied* in which strategies are selected, which methods are employed, and which methodological standards are adopted. The usefulness of theory to the applied researcher is twofold. First, it lies in an appreciation of the implicit decisions made. Second, it also lies in the ability to *compensate*, that is to see what other data might be produced, what it might be like if other assumptions were made.

In summary, we argue that researchers start with strategies sensitive to the contextual features of the research problem, but our sensitivity and awareness as researchers (and the ability to be critical and analytical with our data) can arguably be improved by reflecting upon where the contingent choices in the research process leave us in a field of analytical possibilities. The awareness of our own position as researchers in a field of possibilities confers a number of possible benefits to the research. First, it permits appropriate caveats and cautions to be included in a discussion. Second, it allows researchers to situate themselves in the research process and at least makes possible reflection upon the effects of their activities on the creation of the data. Third, it enables researchers to anticipate criticisms of the respective scientific community, and to address those concerns within the overall strategy.

It is for these reasons that an understanding of research philosophies has, we feel, the potential to help researchers make sense of the research process and the data they generate.

The structure of the book

The first part of the book outlines three key analytical dualisms. The dualisms are about how researchers construct three key background assumptions. Chapter 2 considers issues concerning the subject matter of social research. To what extent should we focus on the material world, external to us as human beings? Or to what extent should we be studying the internal thought processes inside ourselves as humans through which we make sense of the world? We term this analytical dualism materialism/idealism.

Chapter 3 considers another of these dualisms, which we term nominalism/scientific realism. This concerns a debate about where one can draw the line in terms of how we can legitimately gain knowledge about the social world. The issue at stake here is whether we should restrict what we allow as legitimate knowledge to the type of knowledge that can be obtained from individual people (external actions and behaviour or internal thoughts and motivations). The alternative is to permit as legitimate knowledge those claims about reality that refer to unobservable collectivities ('market forces', 'institutional racism' or 'community spirit'). These unobservable collectivities, it will be apparent, are not immediately verifiable by reference to individuals.

Chapter 4 considers a third dualism, one that we term essentialism/anti-essentialism. This dualism is prompted by the work of Michel Foucault. The range of approaches discussed in Chapters 2 and 3 are essentialist in the sense that, in their different ways, each approach claims to be getting to the 'heart of the matter', to the fundamentals of knowledge, to providing the principal insight underlying how to research. The anti-essentialist approach conceives both the subject matter of research and the production of knowledge as consisting merely of possibilities, possibilities that never quite succeed in excluding other ways of seeing and ways of knowing.

In Chapter 5, we review the respective approaches discussed in earlier chapters and outline the corresponding value positions for the researcher. The unreflective researcher may presume that it is 'obvious' that social research should strive to be objective and researchers to minimize the influence of their moral and political values on the research process. However, as we discuss, there are several challenges to this position, including positions that advocate giving a voice to the less powerful, or that involve the researcher recognizing that social change can itself be conceived as a test of the legitimacy of knowledge. Different approaches are also considered with respect to the place of the researcher in the research process, and to what extent the researcher can stand outside the research process.

Chapter 6 takes as its theme the consequences of the social researcher being part of a wider community of researchers who support and hinder, praise and criticize, and who, collectively, are points of reference for the social researcher. The direct and indirect effects of researchers conducting their research within scientific communities are outlined in considering what counts as social scientific research.

The latter part of the book considers these dilemmas and encourages researchers to situate themselves reflexively in the field of possibilities offered, and we begin to apply this perspective to some of the well-known issues in research. In Chapter 7, we appraise the ideas of reliability and validity. We show how they originated in fields such as history and state-craft; how difficult it is to apply them adequately to health services research; and why the ability to think beyond them is important. In particular, it is worth being aware of how they entered the health care disciplines, and that there is nothing natural or inevitable about their presence in our knowledge. They exist for historical and political reasons, as well as for reasons that are epistemological – that is, to do with the nature of knowledge.

In Chapter 8 we consider how decisions about strategy and method imply choices in the field of possibilities. Strategies in research in the social sciences are often complicated by the fact that research participants are often just as self-aware, inquiring and questioning as researchers themselves. Research strategies may also merely replicate assumptions, values and beliefs from the society within which the researcher lives, whilst some widely advocated strategies such as triangulation may well not be as desirable as some uncritical thinkers have proposed. We will explain how critical reflection on one's position as a researcher in this field can help modify strategy and method to offset the implicit philosophical weaknesses of the initial choice. An awareness of analytical dilemmas, and the implications of choices they presuppose, may also inform the analysis and presentation of data, and this forms the subject of Chapter 9. The agency of the researcher or writer is often concealed in academic writing but the frame of reference the analyst adopts can make a big difference to whether the phenomena appear intelligible or incomprehensible. Culturally significant practices that look abusive or brutal to observers in the West may make a lot more sense to the people directly involved.

Chapter 10 revisits the notions of validity and reliability and shows how some researchers and theorists have tried to go beyond these notions. Depending on how the researchers locate themselves in terms of the series of implicit choices in conducting research they can generate different types of claims to the quality and trustworthiness of the data they are generating. In a sense, most researchers are trying to get the reader to believe something and there are a whole variety of tricks that can be used to make one's own story more credible than that of other people.

The wide range of approaches covered in the book is not intended as an advocacy of 'anything goes' but represents an argument to acknowledge the inevitable limitations consequent upon any research decisions. It is suggested that field decisions in research should be driven by contextual considerations of appropriate strategy and method. However, reflection upon where this leaves a researcher in 'a field of possibilities' is not merely a caveat to knowledge, but can be a resource to extend, enhance or complement an overall design. Furthermore, such reflection may also be used to open up other 'ways of seeing' the data constructed through the research process.

2 The world out there and the world in here: positivism and subjectivism

Introduction

In this chapter we discuss the first key analytical dualism. To what extent do we conduct research in the implicit belief that the social world exists independently of what we as people or researchers think of it? Or to what extent do we take the view that as social actors we actively create our world through our perceptions, meanings and motives?

This chapter will outline the origins of empiricism, a belief in a material world 'out there' (Johnson *et al*. 1984: 30) as a reaction to medieval theological thought. It will then provide an outline of the positivist response to the acknowledged problems of naïve empiricism, and link these to features of contemporary social research, including the aspiration to standardize approaches. These approaches will be contrasted to assumptions that privilege the internal constructs of social actors and that emphasize variability in meanings; the constructed nature of meanings; correspondence problems (Cicourel 1964) in relation to language, culture and domain; and the problems of assessing the contribution of the imposition of the researcher's frame to the results of research.

Empiricism and positivism

Imagine that medieval scholars are disputing what angels look like. We would probably despair that such people are not in touch with the 'real world', that their debate is not grounded in experience, that the whole dispute lacks reference to 'hard evidence'. We would be displaying a type of scepticism about claims to knowledge that is characteristic of empiricism. In particular we are implicitly holding to the view that there is a 'truth' that we as researchers can know, there is a real world of evidence that we can observe.

There is, however, a problem. If we take a simple diagram (Figure 2.1) and appeal to our senses for evidence, it is ambiguous. It is a corner, certainly, but are we outside, looking at a corner protruding towards us, or are we inside a room, looking at the corner where walls and ceiling meet? A direct appeal to the senses is problematic because observation always presupposes theory. There is no looking without a pre-existing theoretical framework that tells us what to look for, what to expect to see. If we respond that it is possible for the enquirer to see *either* the corner of a room or the corner of a building, then the problem changes. If the enquirer can choose either, then what is to prevent them insisting on the choice that best suits themselves for their own practical, moral or political purposes?

This is where the orientation to research that is termed positivism comes into play. Positivism is a view in which, first, social research is scientific to the extent that it adopts the methods and approaches of natural sciences and couches explanations in terms of laws, laws which may then enable us to predict and control the world. Second, positivism also requires that knowledge should be observable, thus disallowing theoretical concepts as knowledge. Third, the test of whether knowledge is scientific is whether 'competent observers' can agree upon what is there, an agreement most likely when empirical data can be expressed in quantifiable forms (Keat

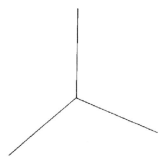

Figure 2.1 Observation presupposes theory

1979). However, although there is a truth 'out there' which in principle can be known, we cannot rely directly on our senses to distinguish between competing truth claims. The researcher is frustrated in this endeavour by two forms of selective perception.

One is unconscious selective perception. We are always selective in our perceptions of the world. Indeed, were our brains to try to process all external stimuli, then they would be overloaded and unable to make sense of anything at all. (The phrase 'making sense' is an interesting one since it hints at our role as humans in *creating* rather than reflecting reality, and is an idea that we shall return to in later chapters.) If we unconsciously register certain aspects of reality but not others, then the human grasp of empirical evidence is fallible, and something needs to be done to make good this fallibility.

The other form of selective perception is more deliberate. This might be called political or moral bias. This refers to situations where the researcher registers certain evidence but chooses not to report it. Or, perhaps to be more subtle, researchers may amplify aspects of reality that fit with their preferences or tastes and may play down those aspects that run counter to their wishes. Indeed, in the most extreme cases, how are we to know that researchers have not made up parts or the whole of data sets (Brown *et al.* 2003)?

The answer that a positivist attitude provides for these problems of unintentional and intentional selectivity is the notion of a standardized research instrument. Take, for example, a survey. If the respondents are asked exactly the same questions in exactly the same order, by either the same interviewer or by interviewers trained to behave in much the same manner, and if respondents are guided to choose between pre-set answers, then the scope for the agency of the human enquirer in contributing to variation in responses is thought to be minimized. Whether such human variation is *actually* minimized is another matter. But the idea is that the standard instrument filters out the selective biases of particular fallible human researchers and leaves us with a close approximation to a material world that is 'out there' irrespective of what we as humans or researchers think of it.

Furthermore, the notion of a research instrument implies an artefact that can be applied in a variety of contexts. It therefore follows that it is in principle available for inspection by other researchers not directly involved in the data collection. These researchers, acting as a scientific community (see Chapter 6), can check such instruments for technical faults, but also for any biases of a political or moral nature.

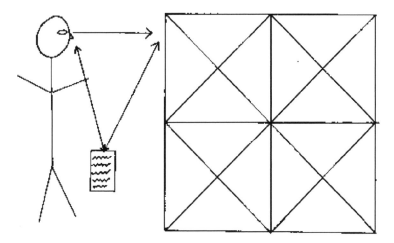

Figure 2.2   Positivist researcher, the 'world out there', and structured research instrument

Subjectivism

On the other hand, what if we cease to assume there is a social world independent of what the social researcher may make of it? Let us take as an example a rather clichéd piece of melodrama. Imagine that a soldier lies wounded and dying in a field hospital. He is delirious with fever, and does not recognize the female nurse who cares for him. In his state of delirium, he mistakes her for his wife back home. He addresses her as if she is his wife, and she, wishing to offer what comfort she can, replies as if she were actually his wife. Presently, the solider dies, comforted. We know that the nurse is not the soldier's wife, but he believed her to be so and this belief had real effects, namely that he felt comforted. This, we believe, is the spirit of the phrase that 'If men (sic) define situations as real they are real in their consequences' (Thomas and Thomas 1928: 572).

What the example illustrates is an approach to the nature of the social world that regards it as impossible to know except through concepts internal to our mind, through perceptions, meanings, feelings, emotions and motives. If we have no direct access to the reality of the social world, then social research must study the internal meanings with which human beings make sense of the world. Social reality thus consists of the intersection of a series of meanings of individual social actors, who create and recreate their reality in relation to this ongoing symbolic interchange.

It follows from this subjectivist view of the nature of the social world that there is not a single unitary reality that can be appealed to outside

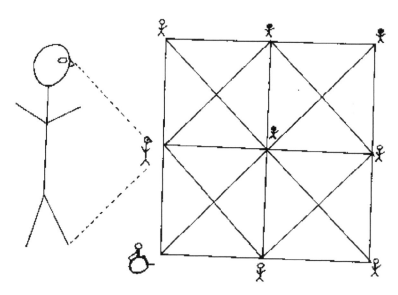

Figure 2.3 Reality as a product of intersecting perspectives, the researcher included

human perception. Instead we have to come to terms with 'multiple realities'.

We are using 'subjectivism' as an umbrella term to cover a variety of approaches to thinking about social research, each of which emphasizes different aspects of the assumption that human experience is always a product of our interpretation. There are several aspects that may be associated with such a conception of social reality. These include the notion that meaning is variable; that meaning is constructed; that meaning is negotiated; that meaning is generated in the process of social interaction; that meaning involves the exchange of human symbols. The sections that follow examine each of these aspects of subjectivism in more detail.

The variability of meaning

Cicourel (1964) provides a useful framework for thinking about variability in meaning, a framework that comes in three parts. First, there is variability in the meaning of words. Consider, for example, a survey question on health education. The question reads: 'How often do you eat red meat?' and the answer written onto the questionnaire is 'Never. I always make sure it is properly cooked first.' Here is a simple example of respondents understanding something different at the level of the individual word from the intention of the interviewer. The problem in a survey, where quantification of results may be deemed important to inform policy, is that the respondent may have ticked a box from a list of pre-determined choices and the *difference in understanding may never emerge*.

Second, there is the possibility of variation in meaning at the level of culture. People may understand the same thing by a word, but the connotation of that concept may be entirely different between cultures. Currer (1986) notes how for women of Pathan descent in the UK, a question on mental health translated into Pashto did not resonate with their cultural experience. The question asked whether they felt they would be better off in someone else's shoes. Although through an interpreter the actual words could be made clear, and more importantly the meaning of the idiom could be made clear by using different words, the meaning could not be conveyed at any deep cultural level because the whole idea was incommensurate with what was considered possible by the Pathan women. Since one's place on earth was given by Allah, it made no sense to conceive of any other possibility.

Third, there is the possibility that for any given topic or context, there may be fundamental differences between enquirers and respondents as to the domain of that topic that is important. For example, Hey (1999) interviews an elderly woman. The researcher is trying to ascertain the woman's views on her need for care services. The woman responds in terms that, from an ageist perspective, one might attribute to the confused ramblings of a person who cannot concentrate for long on the topic in hand. However, the agenda of the encounter for the elderly woman is not a needs assessment interview, but a resistance to the imparting of any information that might conceivably be used against her to reallocate her from her own home into a care home. For Hey, the domain of the encounter that was important was research; from the perspective of the elder, the domain constituted was one of resistance to service provision.

A second example of the domain type of variation in meaning concerns the smoking of cigarettes by pregnant women. Graham (1976, 1984) shows how concerns about well-being on the part of health care professionals do not address the domains of concern of the women. The concern of the professionals is the health of the unborn baby, and as a secondary consideration the health of the mother. However, for women who are single parents of children under 5, who are living on low levels of income such as welfare benefits, the place of smoking in their lives rests in entirely different domains from those of concern to health workers.

First, health usually ranks below family, employment and housing as the important areas of concern in people's lives (Calnan 1987). Second, in a situation of scarce monetary resource, smoking depresses appetite and enables the mother to prioritize the giving of food (and hence love) to her children. Third, in a lifestyle almost totally denuded of all luxuries, smoking is the one thing that the women do 'just for themselves', the one luxury that allows them to cope with the other deprivations in their lives. Fourth, in a situation of pressured and unrelenting childcare, in which the social worlds of the mother and her children may be coterminous for 24 hours a day, the woman can put some symbolic space around her with a cigarette break. Fifth, although smoking may be harmful to the mother's health, it is arguably beneficial for family health as a whole to the extent that it is said by them to help them avoid smacking the children. For such mothers to be asked if they smoke cigarettes, there may be an 'answer', indeed an answer that correlates at statistically significant levels with low birthweight of babies, but it *completely* misses the point in all the ways noted above. This is potentially the most damning criticism of knowledge based on positivism: that it simply misses the point of social situations.

The social construction of meaning

Meaning is not 'naturally' present in social events, situations and artefacts. If it were, we might be able to assume that a child's rag doll always represented innocence, fun, comfort, play and so on. But meaning is constructed. It is created by humans. Let us take an example from the Disney film *Mulan*. A key moment in the film is the second time we see the 'baddie' Shan Yu, the leader of the Huns who are invading China. Shan Yu produces a rag doll on which his army scouts detect pine needles, sulphur from gunpowder and the white hair of a stallion. From this Shan Yu's scouts have established that the Emperor's army is waiting for the Huns. Shan Yu announces that the doll came from a small village in a mountain pass. He says that a little girl must be missing her doll, and that they should return it to her. Suddenly the doll no longer represents innocence. Instead, by a process of draining away the usual meaning from an everyday object (Radley 1999), and imbuing it with other sinister connotations, we have an object that represents horrifying events to come, namely the razing to the ground of a village and its people, possibly even with the death of the little girl herself (see Box 2.1).

For the next example, we are indebted to our colleague Dave Hiles. What is the object in Figure 2.4? What does it mean? Try to answer *without* actually naming the object in any commonsense way.

Some possible answers, all also actual answers given by our students, include:

a love token;
gardens;
a political symbol;
summer shows;

Box 2.1 The social construction of meaning

Shan Yu cuts the top off a tree. The hawk flies overhead and drops a small doll. Shan Yu jumps down from the tree and throws the doll to one of the Huns.

Shan Yu:

What do you see?

Hun #1:

Black pine . . . from the high mountains!

Hun #2:

White horse hair . . . Imperial stallions.

Hun #3:

Sulphur . . . from cannons.

Shan Yu:

This doll came from a village in the Tung Show Pass, where the Imperial Army is waiting.

Hun Archer:

We can avoid them easily.

Shan Yu:

No. The quickest way to the emperor is through that pass. Besides, the little girl will be missing her doll. We should return it to her.

Source: Ketchem (2004)

---

flamenco dancing;
ice skating.

If such rich social meanings are capable of being constructed around such a simple object, then what social meanings may be constructed of a white coat in a hospital, a bell in a school, or a set of keys in a prison?

The point about the social construction of meaning is that one cannot therefore 'read off' the significance of social events from their external material appearances. One has to suspend one's own presumptions about what a social situation or object 'means' in order to discover what it means to the person concerned. This emphasis derives from the philosophical tradition of phenomenology.

Figure 2.4 An everyday object imbued with rich social meanings

Phenomenology

Phenomenology involves an attempt to describe the 'life-world' of others, to understand, almost at a deep emotional level, what the 'lived experience' of people is like. To do this requires researchers to 'bracket off' their own assumptions or 'typifications' of what an experience may be like (Giorgi 1970).

The metaphor that we use to think about phenomenology is the encounter between Elliott and *ET* in the film *Extra Terrestrial*. When the child hero of the film, Elliott, and *ET* are really connecting, the essence-like redness within *ET* glows like an inner soul. Indeed, in the film the boy and *ET* almost become one, so closely do they come to empathize with one another. The aim of phenomenology might then be expressed as the researcher attempting to understand the people studied in a deep way, such that the researcher and, through the researcher, the wider audience of readers of the research feel they have grasped the very inner essence of that experience.

For example, take a young person with asthma. We might presume we know what it must be like to feel breathless, to use or mislay an inhaler, to attend the hospital in an emergency. But we must put our own 'typifications' (our rough-and-ready generalizations about what we think other people's experiences are like) aside and really listen to the words of a sufferer. Clarke (1990) describes moving beyond her assumptions about what the experience of asthma must be like for her teenage daughter, to a deeper understanding. Although she has grown up with her daughter's asthma, it is only when her daughter writes a composition about her experiences that the mother moves to this deeper empathy. Before reading her child's composition, the mother did not understand that for the child asthma is experienced as ambiguity, running out of time, concealment, a threat to coming freedom (see Box 2.2).

Thus phenomenology draws our attention to the extreme difficulty of really understanding one another, of the meanings we give to experience really being the same as the meanings others have. The implication for health research is that we cannot assume we people understand things in the same way, even in situations where a professional and client may come together around ostensibly the 'same' issue such as asthma.

Box 2.2 Example of phenomenological research

Ambiguity – asthma is not a sickness, nor can it be ignored, so the child dwells in limbo between the worlds of well-being and illness, an ambiguous world for which there are no rules, increasing the uncertainty for the child.

Running out of time – running out of air is running out of time, and each time must be experienced as a unique crisis. Exhortations to remember that last time it was all right are not helpful.

Tears as comfort – having a good cry as a source of comfort is not an option in an asthma attack, as it is likely to swell and further restrict the throat.

Concealment – young people with asthma learn to conceal their condition from those around them.

Freedom – for the child on the verge of becoming an adult, the drive to be independent is experienced as frustrated and held back by the asthma.

Source: Adapted from Clarke (1990)

Meaning is negotiated

Meaning is also negotiated. Both students and teachers are very familiar with the negotiated character of meaning. According to the formal college timetable a lesson lasts from 10 until 11 o'clock. However, if at five to eleven the lecturer is not summarizing, anticipating the content of the next session or in some other way signalling that the end of the lecture is close at hand, the students will. They will close books, cease taking notes, shuffle papers, place their bags on the table in front of them, and generally 'negotiate' the end of the lesson.

In a similar way, Allen (1997) demonstrates how the boundaries between doctor and nurse are not fixed according to prescribed roles and respective statuses, but are fluid, and the outcome of a series of formal and informal negotiations. The idea of reality constituting a 'negotiated order' first came from Strauss *et al.* (1963) in their work on the hospital organization. In the UK, junior doctors work long hours in which they may be on duty for long periods over several nights and days (Beecham 1998). In order to be able to function at all they try to sleep at night, whilst being available or 'on call' to deal with any issues that arise. Officially, before a patient can be administered a painkiller, the drug must be prescribed or 'written up' by the doctor in the patient's notes. According to the rules, the nurse should phone the doctor, waking her from her sleep. However, the nurse may use discretion, administer the painkilling drug anyway, and ask the doctor to write up the drug retrospectively when she next visits the ward. The doctor may well implicitly sanction this behaviour since she is thereby more likely to enjoy a period of uninterrupted sleep. The nurse may wish to do this because the patient obtains the relief faster. The patient may be happier because he obtains the drug more quickly. However, notice too that the 'negotiation' is not necessarily (or even usually) conducted by a formal exchange of opinions between two sides of an argument (often attempts between employers and unions to agree a pay dispute). Most negotiations take place in less overt and more subtle ways. In our nurse–doctor interaction the nurse may ask the doctor if she will write up drugs retrospectively. However, the nurse has several other possible strategies open to her. She could simply take the action and present the doctor with a *fait accompli*, and, if challenged, point out the contribution to the patient's well-being that her actions have made. She could play on the novice status of the junior doctor and tell her that this is how it is usually done. If the doctor is arrogant, she may resent the implied slur to the accepted relationship in which she is the higher status professional. If she is an anxious person, she may worry about what she sees as breaking the rules. But if she is attuned to the social climate of the hospital, she will see that the consequence of not accepting the order the nurse is trying to negotiate is that she will be woken up and called to the ward several times a night, not only to write prescriptions but also for other trivial issues that the nurse could (mis)represent as requiring the attention of a doctor. Accepting the informal division of labour will certainly seem to the doctor as the path of least resistance.

From this we can take the lessons that the order of society is not 'given' in any simple sense, but negotiated and continually renegotiated. These negotiations are not necessarily adversarial, public, and reliant on a formal exchange of words. People can negotiate their world around them in many ways – by not saying or doing anything as well as by speech and action. In this sense, inaction is as much a form of social action, as much a contribution to the social order as taking an action. The problem is, whilst we are taking or avoiding actions in the social world, speaking or declining speech opportunities, others are doing the same. Thus the outcomes of multiple negotiations may not be what we wish, nor what we expect. The newness, originality or unanticipated consequences of our negotiations in the world compel us to adjust, and in the process new meanings may be created. Whilst the structure of social reality may be taken for granted and might seem obvious to the participants who navigate it as part of their everyday lives, the implications for research are important. From this perspective, it is vital to be aware of how 'realities' are created by the people involved in them. Everyday concepts like pain, stress, depression, or even the symptoms of physical conditions like diabetes and asthma (Williams 1999) are meticulously brought into being by social actors working together.

Meaning is generated in the process of social interaction

We have seen by now that social meaning is not automatically located within an object or a situation. It is created by human beings. Moreover, it is created by human beings in their interactions with one another. A key approach here is that of symbolic interactionism. For symbolic interactionists, language is what permits us to become self-conscious beings. This self-consciousness permits us to look at ourselves as if from the outside. Social context is important in terms of giving experience form and establishing its shared meaning. Meanings derive from the exchange of mutually intelligible symbols, combined with clues about how to interpret what one's fellow interactors intend.

Symbolic interactionism may be thought of as analysing social encounters according to the format of Figure 2.5. When we take part in a social encounter, we present not our inner identities, our inner selves (if indeed we have such things), but our 'selves-in-the-world'. These 'selves-in-the-world' are in a sense the version of ourselves that we wish others to see. This is represented in the figure by the convention of a mask. In colloquial terms we might talk of a 'real self' behind the mask, which is somehow authentic or is 'who we really are'. Even this metaphor can be seen as saturated with layers of enculturated meaning (Gergen 2000) and is given form with concepts invented by psychology and diffused into popular discourse (Rose 1989). At the very least, we are capable of presenting a number of possible selves-in-the-world that we are choosing not to foreground for the purposes of the current social encounter.

In applying this type of analysis to going to see the doctor, Stimson and Webb (1975) point out that patients, despite the gap in power between themselves and the doctor, still have the capacity to withhold information from the exchange that is within their power to divulge should they wish. They could tell the doctor that they never obtained the prescription that was written for them. They could say they continued to drink alcohol whilst taking antibiotics despite the advice not to. They could say that they shared

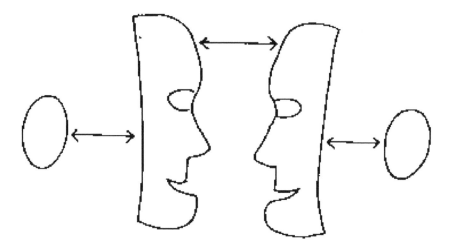

Figure 2.5 Symbolic interactionism diagram of selves and selves-in-the-world

their drugs with a friend who had the same symptoms. But they choose not to. This is what Goffman (1959) refers to when he writes about the presentation of self in everyday life. The self-in-the-world is what social actors put forward of themselves in any encounter, which may be a version of their inner self, their sense of themselves. The (inner) self is best thought of as a resource that can be drawn upon to construct the series of 'selves-in-the-world', the suite of different presentations people give of themselves in everyday life.

However, this is not merely a question of a false public face and a true private one. For an actor the purpose of a mask is not to conceal, but to transform (Rushdie 1985). The self is not an inner essence, static and unchanging. It is itself continually under construction, modified sometimes dramatically in the process of encountering other selves-in-the-world. Our sense of ourselves changes in the process of interaction, and thus the resources out of which to construct our self-in-the-world are also constantly in flux.

Meaning involves the exchange of human symbols

Since meaning is constructed, negotiated and very often variable, events, places and objects do not have a given quality, but are symbols that potentially index a wide possibility of meanings. Take for example a cup of coffee. On one level it is a liquid in a physical container. But it is also a symbol. When at the end of a date between a heterosexual couple, a woman may ask a man if he wishes to come back to her flat for coffee, 'coffee' potentially takes on the status of a symbol, albeit a symbol whose meaning is unclear and changeable.

If coffee can take on a series of complex meanings, marking the mutual assessment of the likelihood and desirability of taking a relationship to the next stage, then so can other apparently 'obvious' human activities. For example, Lupton *et al.* (1995) describe the symbolic meanings of having an HIV-antibody test. It may seem straightforward and obvious that a rational person has such a test in order to find out if they are HIV antibody positive. However, Lupton *et al.* (1995) show that the test has many contextual meanings, linked to the particular social context of the person's life. Some heterosexual men reported having the test at the insistence of their female partners in order to be permitted to have sex without a condom. Some women said they had the test because they regarded it as a statement about their own degree of responsibility and sensibleness. Others conceived the issue in terms of contagion, and wanted to demonstrate they were clean, especially in terms of starting a new relationship with a 'clean slate'. Still others conceptualized the test as providing peace of mind, or even as constituting a preventive measure, as if somehow, magically, having a test will protect one from such exposure in the future. Some regarded a negative result as symbolically marking a springboard from which they would in the future feel more confident in asserting their adherence to safer sex guidelines.

From this it follows that we need to be aware of the exchange of symbols in special kinds of social interactions, the kind we call research interviews. Other possible constructions of the research interview by the respondent are summarized in Table 2.1.

Ethnography

When ethnography was first developed it was as a completely new paradigm. However, it has become apparent that as an approach to research, it is amenable to several philosophical views of the world. In this way, ethnography has slipped down a level, from being a distinct paradigm to being a strategy potentially usable within a number of different paradigms. Ethnography has roots in that anthropological tradition which says, rather than assuming we know what is going on in so-called less developed societies, let us go out and empirically observe such communities, living with them for long periods of time to try to understand their culture.

Ethnography is a strategy associated with a multi-method approach including participant observation, interviews and fieldwork diaries. The ethnographer does not just observe, but rather asks, collects artefacts and tries to relate everything together by cross-checking the meaning of information. It comprises a detailed qualitative observation that is trying to

Table 2.1 The social construction of meanings of the research interview

The 'meaning' of the interview to those being researched	Reference
The interviewees appreciate the social contact that the research interviews offer them, reducing their social isolation.	Finch (1984)
The interviewees use the interviews to resist what they perceive as officialdom, subtly avoiding the line of questioning and asserting their wish to remain in their own home, not moved into care.	Hey (1999)
Patients use the interview to relate 'stories' of the atrocious behaviour of doctors. These stories are an attempt by patients to redress the imbalance of power between themselves and the doctor, an imbalance which prevents patients airing complaints directly to the doctor.	Stimson and Webb (1975)
Parents of disabled children feel that they are being inspected by officialdom when interviewed. They wish to demonstrate that they are bringing up their child 'properly'. The parents ask the child to perform rhymes and counting games to show the interviewer they are 'morally worthy' parents.	Dyson (1987)
Pregnant women answer questions about their experience and develop a relationship with the interviewer over the course of several interviews. Some ask extremely naïve questions ('which hole does the baby come out of?') and the interviewer feels morally obliged to answer these questions honestly.	Oakley (1981)

grasp the culture of the group studied. Ethnography is sometimes referred to as 'small world research' because by its very nature you cannot research many instances of the phenomenon at the same time. One way to capture the sense of ethnography is to examine the word itself: 'ethnos', meaning an ethnic group that shares a distinctive culture, and 'graphic' – think about the phrase 'in graphic detail'. Hence what you are trying to do is describe a culture in graphic detail.

Now, when we refer to a culture, this could be culture in a number of different senses. Originally, the reference was to the culture of a whole society. But it might equally refer to a sub-culture in the sense that a culture, perhaps counter to the values of the broader society in which it is situated, arises and is practised by an identifiable grouping. For example, Whyte (1984) and Patrick (1973) have studied criminal gangs, Fielding (1981) studied fascist groups and Wallis (1976) studied the cult of scientologists. In health research ethnography has been used to look at occupational groups, including nurses (Porter 1993; Allen 1997), midwives (Bowler 1993) and kitchen maids (Paterson 1981). Researchers have also used ethnographic strategies to examine the sub-culture of doctors. Howard Becker *et al.*'s (1961) work was called *Boys in White* which captures the flavour of the study, where doctors tended to be white and male, white coated and surprisingly disdainful of their clients, quite contrary to the outsider's view (at least at that time) of the doctors as heroic and caring advocates for their clients. In educational settings a sub-culture may consist of deliberately subverting the values of the mainstream culture and asserting a value system that delights in the antithesis of the dominant values of the wider society (Willis 1977; Burgess 1984).

A key question in research using an ethnographic strategy is whether it is the researcher's role actively to change as well as record what is going on. This idea lies behind the development of so-called 'critical ethnography'. Critical ethnography aims not only to understand the culture from the inside, but also to challenge it. One might examine the sub-culture of the British Army in the North of Ireland, and understand the world through the eyes of a British soldier (Hockey 1986). However, you could move beyond description and, as Porter (1993) argues, identify the ideology that merely describing the culture reinforces. Porter therefore choses not to implicitly endorse the dominant ideology by failing to draw attention to it, but instead challenge it and assert that it should not be so. So there are very different ways of working with the data you derive from ethnographic approaches. Since it is amenable to use within different philosophical positions, it seems sensible to regard ethnography not as a distinct philosophy but as a strategy (Denscombe 2003).

Grounded theory

The founders of grounded theory, Glaser and Strauss (1967), arguably developed grounded theory out of the paradigm of symbolic interactionism. But as an approach it has, like ethnography, slipped down a level. When it was first developed, it was very much as if this was a different philosophy of research, yet over the years it has become apparent that one can use some of the general strategies and approaches of grounded theory (thematic analysis; analytic memos; constant comparative method) without necessarily subscribing to the same philosophical underlying beliefs as the original authors.

Grounded theory was originally reacting against the kind of social research which built up very grand abstract generalizations about roles, social rules and social structures governing behaviour. Glaser and Strauss developed a much more down to earth theory which was closer to the reality 'on the ground' – what they called substantive theory. This theory prioritized the concepts, categories and, in some instances, the very words used by the participants in the research themselves.

For example, Skidmore (1995) undertook research with young men engaged in sharing needles for intravenous drug use and/or unprotected sex, both activities being examples of behaviour likely to increase the risk of

HIV. Both groups were knowledgeable about possible transmission. However, both used the concept of 'knowing' a fellow participant in the activity, either a drug-using partner with whom syringes are shared or else a sexual partner. 'Knowing' someone amounted to perceiving them as a friend, and a friend was someone like oneself.

'Knowing' therefore amounted to seeing yourself in the person with whom you had sex or shared needles, and because the young men conceived of themselves as 'clean' (from infection via either sex or drugs) it followed that someone like them, someone they 'knew', could not be unclean. Unprotected sex or sharing needles was then not conceptualized as risky behaviour because they 'knew' the person concerned. Knowing did not depend on a long timescale, and the young men could 'know' someone after as little as two days. Even when they had knowledge of the other person having been infected with hepatitis or with a sexually transmitted infection, this merely extended the timescale from a few days to a few weeks, by which time 'knowing' the person meant they could revert to unprotected penetrative sex or to sharing injecting equipment.

So rather than building up theory based on concepts that are generated by the researcher, grounded theory, such as the Skidmore study, attempts to build up theory based on the concepts and internal constructs of subjects of the research. It is inductivist – in other words, it builds knowledge from the ground up. Thus you try and listen to the words and the concepts of people themselves and say, well, this idea seems to go with this concept and these two concepts form a slightly bigger building block. In this way the researcher builds from the ground up towards the broader theories that are being generated. In this case the theory generated comprises a view of 'knowing' as an analytic concept that links how friendships are formed by recognizing ourselves in others, the image of ourselves we carry, and how we might conceive of risk in the types of behaviour we are prepared to engage in with other people.

Box 2.3 Knowing the score

'I know all the girls I go with.'
'I only sleep with girls I know are safe.'
'You just know (shared works are clean) . . . you can tell when you share a squat with someone.'
'When you do things together you get to know if you can trust them.'

Source: Skidmore (1995: 19)

Ethnomethodology and conversation analysis

The final variant of subjectivism we wish to introduce is 'ethnomethod-ology'. This has arguably left a legacy of detailed ways of analysing taped conversations, which has endured beyond the demise of the general approach. Once again we can break down the word to understand its meaning. Ethnos: about human culture. Methodology: how do we know we know? Ethnomethodology asks how we come to know the rules of our own culture. Ethnomethodologists start from the point of asking, if reality is not given but created and is continually recreated, how do people accomplish this? Accomplish is a very key word for ethnomethodologists. They refer to reality being *accomplished*. In other words, reality is not there as a pre-given entity. It is rather like taking the fluidity and negotiated element of symbolic interactionism, but pushing it to a logical extreme.

However, ethnomethodologists would argue that people are not puppets in a theatre of life who simply carry out the rules of our culture in a straightforward mechanistic way. Rather, the rules of the game for living, the principles, values, rules that govern our behaviour, are rules that people use contingently. In other words, people do not use the rules in an unchanging way, they use them flexibly and differently according to different circumstances. This is reflected in the way people use language contingently. Contingent use of language is what usually happens, and it is not a sign of immorality, psychosis or anything necessarily negative. If patients give logically contradictory accounts, the traditional health professional view would be to say that the person is unreliable. But, from looking at thousands of transcripts of the way people deploy mundane language, ethnomethodologists argue that this variability or 'contingency' – applying different rules in different situations – is par for the course, and is a feature of the discourse of every group of people who have been studied.

Garfinkel (1967) developed the concept of *natural experiments* in which, for example, he invited his students to go home in vacation time and behave to their parents as if they were lodgers in their own house, putting money on the table for rent and expecting meals in return for the payment. The aim of these natural experiments was, by deliberately breaking the expected rules, to thereby reveal what those taken-for-granted rules are. So the way in which you make people uncomfortable and not able to know what to do or how to respond is the means by which you make people conscious of those rules and bring them to the surface. Another very simple example is to phone someone up and say 'Hello, who is it?' So, rather than waiting for them to say it, you are disturbing the usual conventions of who says what in which order, and this completely throws the person answering the phone. By completely disrupting the prevailing notion of initiating conversations and taking turns, we reveal what those rules of everyday behaviour and speech are. Ethnomethodology was very closely linked to a detailed form of analysis of taped interview transcript called conversation analysis in which researchers, using newly developing technologies of the time like the audio-cassette recorder, began to analyse the details of conversational exchanges. Conversation analysis is one strand that has fed into the later approach of discourse analysis. We can illustrate this approach with a classic example and a more rough-and-ready example from some of our own work.

By examining many examples of everyday, 'normative' conversation, and establishing what the rules of normal conversation are, you can then learn a lot by looking either at deviant conversation which breaks those rules or at institutional conversation, that is conversation that takes place in very spe-cialized settings, such as an encounter in a hospital clinic, between a doctor and a patient. The first example (see Box 2.4) is from two leading conversa-tion analysts and comprises a conversation between a child and his mother.

The child is playing with some scissors and cutting up paper, and the child says 'Have to cut these Mummy.' Notice the two dots in the middle of the transcribed word 'these'. Attempting to read pure conversation analyst transcripts of taped interviews can be daunting, because many transcription conventions are employed to try to capture the minutiae of conversation. These two dots indicate an elongated vowel sound, with the word being said in a more 'spread out' way than usual. The figures 1.3 and 1.5 refer to the number of seconds between utterances, timings recorded using a stopwatch. Usual conversational practices do not feature pauses of such lengths, so the appearance of the gaps becomes a noteworthy feature of the conversation. So the child is saying, as he plays with scissors and paper, 'Have to cut these Mummy.' Now in normative conversation, a question demands an answer. So you would expect the mother to say yes or no or to reply in some way, but the mother hasn't given a reply. The child then says 'Won't we Mummy?' – and there follows another even longer gap, before finally, 'Won't we?' Con-versation analysis argues that the child who is saying 'Have to cut these Mummy' is waiting for the reply. However, it is not a question of the mother

---

Box 2.4 Conversation analysis

Child: Have to cut the:se Mummy

(1.3)

Child: Won't we Mummy?

(1.5)

Child: Won't we?

(Atkinson and Drew 1979: 52)

not having heard the child. The way the child signals that he thinks the mother has heard, but is not replying, is *not* to repeat the whole question. Rather it is to abbreviate the question. So by saying 'Won't we Mummy?' the child is effectively communicating the idea, hang on a minute, I know you have just heard what I've said, but you have not responded and you should have responded, so now I'm going to express myself in this particular way that conveys a sense that I want a response. So the child continues 'Won't we Mummy?' There follows another long pause in the conversation and no reply is forthcoming, so the child ups the stakes even more and says – I know you have heard me twice now and you have not replied so I'm going to chop the sentence down still further 'Won't we?', and by this rule of conversation (though I don't even know what a rule is yet) I am going to convey to you that my question demands a reply. Eventually in the exchange the mother says something like 'Yes dear.' So by looking at how conversation usually runs you can begin to see how people are, in the jargon of ethnomethodologists, *accomplishing* reality by the kind of structure of conversation, the kind of ways in which they are breaking and making rules of conversation. Our own view of this is that you perhaps don't have to go down the full road of conversational analysis in order to take a detailed look at conversation.

The example in Box 2.5 is from a paediatrician's clinic for a mother and her child who has Down's Syndrome. Children with Down's Syndrome sometimes have heart murmurs. At this particular paediatric appointment, the junior doctor, rather than the consultant, was present. This particular child did not have a heart murmur. However, at a previous clinic, this doctor had claimed to have found the heart murmur, partly, our reading of it was, because he thought he ought to find it, because it ought to be there in such a child. What interests us about this particular exchange is how the doctor does not attend to the problems that the mother actually wants to introduce. He has his agenda, 'OK, any problems?', and the mother has a

---

Box 2.5 Analysis of conversation

Doctor: OK. Any problems?

Mother: Not really, she/

Doctor: Particularly heart problems first thing.

Mother: No. Not at the moment, she/

Doctor: OK. Absolutely OK. Right.

(Dyson 1987:51)

particular issue that she wants to raise, 'Not really, she/.' The mother is cut off by the doctor interrupting with 'Particularly heart problems, first thing.' The mother replies, and the doctor cuts her off again. Indeed, the doctor's use of three separate utterances (1) OK, (2) Absolutely OK and (3) Right, seems to us to close down the possibility of the mother coming back again with her agenda. It seems to us that in order to demonstrate that, for example, on occasions doctors don't listen to mothers in clinic, you don't need to go down the full road of the conversation analysis, and we offer this example as a more applied version, what might be termed analysis of conversation.

What's in a name?

Let us return briefly to the subject of names of philosophies. The variety of names and the various ideas to which they refer in one sense confirms the legitimacy of the subjectivist view, since authors refer to what we are naming materialism (Dandeker and Scott 1979) in a number of different ways. The approach to social research, that assumes there exists a unitary reality independent of what we as researchers actually think of it, is referred to in a variety of ways. Some call it realism (Radley 1999), though this risks confusion with the quite distinctive scientific and critical realisms we shall look at in Chapter 3. Others have referred to it as naïve realism (Porter 1998) precisely in order to draw this distinction. However, both forms of terminology assume that the way we study the world can be logically deduced from the assumptions we make about what the social world consists of, and this is not necessarily the case. Materialism seems to us the most appropriate, though this depends upon whether one can be sufficiently astute to recognize that materialism potentially contains several ideas in one, namely the physicality of things, the topography of the landscape in which those things are situated, and economic materialism. An appreciation of the distinction of these aspects of materialism can provide us with some means of enhancing our practical researching in the social world.

Conclusion

In this chapter, we have considered the analytical dualism between materialism and idealism. Materialism is a view of what knowledge of the social world consists of if we accept that there is a real social world irrespective of what we think of it and that research can obtain objective knowledge of that world. To achieve this, positivism identifies the problem of naïve empiricism, namely that observation is vulnerable to distortion by the twin biases of unintended selective perception and intended moral/political preferences. To counter this, data must be gathered in a manner which is less susceptible to bias, through the use of standardized research instruments. To the extent that researchers are themselves research instruments, their human variability must be minimized by adherence to standardized procedures, training and cross-checks. The variability of human responses must be controlled by the imposition of structure onto the respondent. By contrast, idealism refers to the notion that we can study the internal constructs of social actors, and demonstrate that shared meanings of words, cultures and domains of experience cannot be assumed. Further, meanings are not immanent in social situations, but constructed by interactions as humans undergo lived experiences, negotiate their worlds by use of language and other symbols, construct variable meanings, and accomplish the rules of everyday life by their words. This dualism concerns a debate about what the substance of our research can and should be, and we attempt to summarize the key features of both positivism and subjectivism in Table 2.2. But there is another debate, concerning how we can in principle gain knowledge about the social world we wish to research. This debate is the subject of the next chapter.

Table 2.2 A comparison of the characteristics of positivism and subjectivism

	POSITIVISM	SUBJECTIVISM
What? (Ontology) **How do we get to know?** (Epistemology)	Observable relationships. Observe objective causal relationships between phenomena.	Meanings, motives, actions, feelings. Understand reality as an ongoing product of meaningful social interaction between people.
How do we know we know? (Methodology) Internal validity*	Phrase concepts in terms that can be observed and measured in order to hypothesize about causal relationships between variables.	Accept terms used by social actors to account for their actions. Descriptions of how social life is 'achieved' that would be understood or have meaning for the social actors studied.
Reliability*	Imposing structure/control onto the social world to reduce the researcher effect and reduce variability between researchers and variability over time.	Understanding production of knowledge by being reflexive about the effect of the researcher and by use of qualitative evidence.
Generalizability*	Sampling of population to enable claims of statistical generalization to be made.	Small world research that does not seek to generalize. Research as generating rather than testing theory. Analytic generalizations. Research process auditable so that other researchers can judge transferability.
What practical methods or techniques are used? (Methods)	Comparison, statistics, questionnaires, structured interviews, structured observations.	Naturalistic observation, participant observation, case studies, unstructured/depth interviews.

* These terms are themselves usually introduced in the context of positivist science. As such one would expect them to sit more comfortably within positivism than within any of the other traditions. Nevertheless, interpreted more broadly than within a positivist framework, they arguably represent domains of the research experience that all researchers can, and perhaps should, be able to reflect upon.

Further reading

For introductory accounts of positivism, see:
Keat, R. (1979) Positivism and statistics in social science. In J. Irvine, I. Miles and
J. Evans (eds) *Demystifying Social Statistics*. London: Pluto Press, 75–86.
Kolakowski, L. (1972) An overall view of positivism. In M. Hammersley (ed.) (1993)
Social Research: Philosophy, Politics and Practice. London: Sage Publications;
Buckingham: Open University Press, 1–8.

For examples of the limitations of positivism, see:

Pawson, R. (1989) *A Measure for Measures*. London: Routledge.
Taylor, S. (1992) Measuring child abuse, *Sociology Review*, 1 (3): 23–7.

For examples of the various strands of subjectivism, see:

Atkinson, P., Coffey, A., Delamont, S., Lofland, J. and Lofland, L. (2001) *Handbook
of Ethnography*. London: Sage Publications. (Contains chapters on the
ethnography of health and medicine, and ethics and ethnography.)
Drew, P. and Heritage, J. (eds) (1992) *Talk at Work*. Cambridge: Cambridge
University Press. (An application of conversational analysis to the delivery and
reception of diagnosis in the general practice consultation; the use of discretion
in psychiatry, and the delivery and reception of advice in interactions between
health visitors and first-time mothers.)
Glaser, B. G. and Strauss, A. L. (1967) *The Discovery of Grounded Theory: Strategies
for Qualitative Research*. Chicago, IL: Aldine.
Goffman, E. (1968) *Asylums: Essays on the Social Situation of Mental Patients and
Other Inmates*. Harmondsworth: Penguin.
Goffman, E. (1968) *Stigma: Notes on the Management of Spoiled Identity*.
Harmondsworth: Penguin.
Moustakas, C. (1994) *Phenomenological Research Methods*. London: Sage Publica-
tions. (Contains examples of phenomenological analysis applied to psycho-
therapists' concept of presence, and to the experience of adults abused as
children.)

3 Taking at face value and knowing better: scientific realism

Introduction

In the previous chapter we looked at a first key analytical dualism, namely a debate about what the social world is made up of. This debate concerns the issue of whether the assumptions we make as researchers privilege the external world 'out there' over the internal world 'in here', or vice versa. A second key analytical dualism relates to ways of knowing the social world. This new question hinges on where, in principle, one should draw the limits of acceptable strategies for gaining knowledge about the social world.

We have already seen that the British tradition of empiricism was in part constituted as a reaction to claims to knowledge based on fanciful speculation from an armchair. Factors that really counted for empiricism included direct observation, direct hearing of accounts from individuals, or documentary evidence. But note that these are also the factors that count for subjectivist traditions, albeit with a different focus. It is still individuals who are listened to or observed in the subjectivist traditions. It is still individual consciousness that is the focus for obtaining knowledge. The approaches of empiricism and positivism and the varieties of subjectivism draw the line at the level of the individual as a legitimate source of knowledge about the social world.

However, there is another possibility for the production of knowledge, and that is knowledge of collective entities (examples of collective entities might be social class, patriarchy or racism). To the extent that empiricism or subjectivism would accept these terms as a legitimate part of social scientific knowledge at all, they would regard them as collections of individual actions and thoughts. But there is an approach to knowledge that argues that such collectivities are real, even though we cannot immediately see or touch such entities, and are real in the sense that they cannot be reduced to the sum of the actions and thoughts of individuals. This approach has been termed scientific realism.

Scientific realism as an epistemology

In the previous chapter, we have looked at positivism and at several strands of subjectivism. What we have done so far is look at different approaches to social research that entail a fundamental disagreement in terms of *what* is being studied. You will see from the headings in Table 3.1 that we have summarized that disagreement as a debate between *materialism*: is there a world 'out there' (empiricism or positivism), and *idealism*: is what we can research only the world 'in here', the world of internal constructs that are inside the head of social actors, and which involves looking at the meanings, motivations, understandings and perceptions that people work with, in making sense of their everyday worlds (subjectivism)? By idealism is meant not idealism in the sense of Utopia or the best of all possible worlds, but idealism in the sense of being in the realm of ideas and concepts.

However, you will see from the table that that is only one dimension in terms of which social researchers implicitly disagree about what is important to emphasize in social research. The more complex way of expressing what is to be studied is *ontology* – what is the stuff made of that we are studying? So in a sense the materialism/idealism dualism is a debate in terms of ontology, in that it is concerned with the question of what it is that we are studying. However, despite their disagreements in terms of what is to be studied, note that we have grouped empiricism and subjectivism *together* in another dimension – that of epistemology.

As you can see from Table 3.1 there is another tension that needs examining and that is a continuum in terms of *epistemology*. Epistemology refers to the debate about the terms of how, in principle, we can come to know the social reality that we are trying to study. Nominalism/scientific realism represents a tension between different principles that may guide us in terms of the epistemological decisions (how they are going to get knowledge) that a social researcher needs to make.

Now, another way of trying to explain how nominalism gets its name is to start with the conception of something called methodological individualism (Lukes, cited in Oliver 1992). Methodological individualism concerns the boundaries of what is allowable as knowledge. In methodological

Table 3.1 A review of two analytical dualisms[1]

How do we obtain knowledge of reality? [Epistemology]	What is the nature of reality? [Ontology]	
	Material	Ideal
Nominalism	Empiricism	Subjectivism
Scientific realism	Critical realism	Structuralism[2]

[1] Derived and adapted from Johnson *et al.* (1984: 17, 19, 23) and Dandeker and Scott (1979). Note that the analytical dualisms represent tensions in research, not static positions, and that as such actual researchers may draw to a greater or lesser extent on different traditions.
[2] We do not cover this approach in this book. However, we would suggest that authors such as Durkheim and Levi-Strauss implicitly draw, at least partially, on such assumptions. For applied examples, see Helman (1978) and Chapman and Eggar (1983).

individualism you can only obtain knowledge from the individual or from individual consciousness. So in terms of empiricism you can observe individuals and record their actions. Alternatively you may ask them what they think and write their answers down onto a structured interview schedule. In terms of subjectivism you can try to understand, empathize, link up with the individual consciousnesses of the social actors. But what is not allowable in methodological individualism is the *direct* knowledge of concepts which reflect *groups* or try to capture knowledge at a level beyond the individual in terms of *collectivities*. In other words, concepts like social class for example, which are about groups not about individuals, are not allowed as knowledge by those methodological individualists who believe that you must restrict knowledge to what is either hearable, observable or otherwise apprehended from an individual. Concepts that refer to a level of organization above the individuals, such as *social class* or *the state*, are not directly allowable as knowledge. In other words, in the view of the methodological individualist, social class is not concrete in a way that would allow us to use it as a scientific reality. All social class is, according to methodological individualists, is a name (hence nominalism), a label, which we apply as a kind of shorthand for understanding what a group of individuals are doing. According to methodological individualists, all that 'the state' represents is our convenient shorthand label – our name for it – that we apply so as to conveniently sum up a group of individual activities. However, the concept has no reality beyond our convenient labelling of it in this shorthand way.

The opposing view of how we might achieve knowledge, scientific realism, is that supra-individual concepts, concepts above the level or of greater level than the individual, are allowable as expressions of knowledge. In other words, such concepts have a reality beyond being mere labels that we apply to things. So for scientific realists, concepts such as social class, racism or patriarchy are all allowable as legitimate expressions of knowledge in a way that for nominalists they are not. Nominalists would say that those kinds of concepts are merely labels that we attach to try and sum up a series of individual processes in interactions. Scientific realists would contend that unobservable, collective concepts are allowable as knowledge. However, there are different strands of scientific realism. This tension is between a view that the structures that generate appearances are material and a view that such structures are in the mind but at a group level. You might say, well how can something be in the mind but at a group level? Examples of such constructs could include 'community spirit', 'collective consciousness' or 'zeitgeist'. These concepts are certainly not methodologically individualist, but appeal to a notion of knowledge beyond any individual. But neither are they materialist, because they refer to the realm of ideas. In the remainder of this chapter, we try to explain these more methodologically collectivist approaches to knowledge.

Let us look at what might be a problem from the point of view of methodological collectivists, what might be some of the problems they have with positivist and subjectivist types of research. The following is based on an actual exchange of ideas between the authors and their students.

Suppose that we are conducting a survey of what toys boys and girls like to play with, and in particular who likes playing with Barbie dolls and who likes playing with model jet fighters. Now, if we were to undertake that survey in twenty-first-century Western societies, what do you think the results would be?

The boys would prefer the jet fighters and the girls the Barbie dolls.

So we might find that 80 per cent of the girls preferred playing with dolls and 80 per cent of boys prefer to play with the jet fighters. A fairly naïve researcher might then say, 'We infer from this objective survey that boys prefer toys related to action, and girls prefer toys related to care and nurture.' And suppose we argued that 'we are scientists and these are the facts', what else might you say about that statement? In order to answer, presume that you are satisfied with the technical aspects of the data collection in undertaking the survey: if we are saying that we have undertaken this survey, it was a representative sample, we achieved a 100 per cent response rate, we employed fully trained interviewers who had a good rapport with all the children and we obtained these 'facts'. These are the facts – boys will be boys and girls will be girls. What might you say in response to that?

But it's also a reflection of parts of our culture.

OK, so the first thing that you are beginning to say is not just I'm going to accept these results, but I'm going to ask you *how come* this appears to be the case. So it reflects culture, what precisely about our culture that might have generated those results?

Parents.

Yes, anything else?

Nursery schools and pre-school play groups. Other children. Friends, families and neighbours. Television and the media.

Yes. So in a sense we are beginning to move to a situation in which we are not just saying, this is the case. Rather we're moving to a situation where we are saying to ourselves, *why* is this the case? As soon as we ask the why question, we open up the possibility of thinking, could the situation be different? Could there be a situation in which there was an equal preference for different types of toys? Or to put it another way, what would have to be different in order for the results to be different? You said it was about culture, media/parents. What if we could change the culture? What if we could get primary schools to stop offering sex-specific toys to boys and girls and either offer them something regarded as more neutral as playthings, or perhaps to make sure that boys play with dolls and girls play with the model jets – would that make a difference to the answers?

Probably not.

Why not?

Because you are just changing one element. There are other things going on, so you have still got the media, you have still got a strong ideology; just trying to change one thing might have some effect but the kids would still be going home and watching TV.

So, in order to change it, what would you need to do?

Change everything.

OK, so a lot depends on what kind of broader social arrangements are in place in terms of what kind of results you might get. Now, the scientific realist tradition does not simply stop at a statement to the effect that this is the way things are. Scientific realism acknowledges that this is the way things appear at the moment. But it is also saying that it doesn't have to be this way. It starts by asking, could things be different? And the second stage is to ask, well if we changed this and this and this, *would* things be different? *Could* things be different if we changed these broader societal parameters? Furthermore, *would* they be different in the manner that we anticipate they would be? More controversially, and this is where *critical realism* comes in, there are some (Dandeker 1983) that argue that you can almost logically begin to deduce what *should* be different. So there are at least three stages of questioning, although not necessarily all scientific realists would wish to support all of those types of challenges, but certainly *could* things be different if we changed them, *would* they be different, and, in moral/political terms, *should* they be different?

There are two key authors who illustrate something of the scientific realist approach to knowledge, namely Bhaskar (1979) and Lukes (1974). Bhaskar (1979) makes the distinction between realms of knowledge that he calls the observable, the actual and the real. Now, these realms of knowledge can be illustrated if we start again with our matchstick observer who is looking at the social world (Figure 3.1).

The realm of the *observable* is fairly straightforward: it's what you can see or hear through the senses, corresponding to a naïve sense of what's 'actually happening'. Suppose we come and put a brick wall there and soundproof the wall as well. Now there's something happening here, it is obviously actually going on, it's the realm of the *actual*, even though, if you like, it is hidden from our researcher in an immediate sense. In principle, our researcher could get to this but she doesn't necessarily know it's going on and she cannot get to it in any immediate sense, so it's a different kind of domain of knowledge; it's not observable but it is actual.

Below the line (which marks the boundary of what is even potentially observable) we have the realm of what Bhaskar calls the real. This is where scientific realism as an epistemology makes its radical distinction from positivism and subjectivism. The realm of the real comprises structures – whether they are material or ideas – that generate appearances on the surface. It is like the root system of a plant that generates the flower. Suppose that we could not dig up the soil and actually look at the root system. What we see as an effect, as the 'facts' if you like, on the surface are in fact generated by underlying structures of some kind. Scientific realism allows as

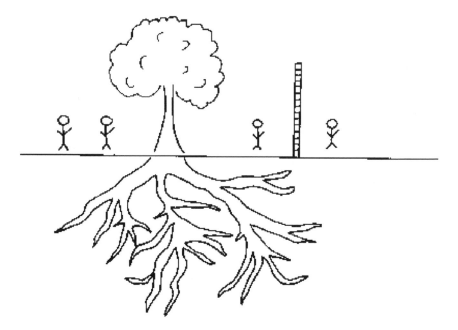

Figure 3.1 The domains of the observable, the actual and the real

knowledge, structures which, even in principle, you could never observe or test empirically. Concepts such as patriarchy, ablism, institutional racism, each of which may generate patterns of observable discrimination, are analytically useful, and allow us to think about the world in epistemologically and politically productive ways, yet one can never directly observe them.

What is interesting is that this conception – allowing as knowledge things that you cannot ever see – is something that some natural scientists would abhor. They would say this is in the realm of 'ideology', the realm of people making things up, playing politics with science. However, what is interesting, if you look at the forefront of natural sciences, is that it is this scientific realist approach that prevails. If you look at quantum physics and advanced astronomy, this approach of allowing sometimes highly speculative constructs to have a place in science is well established. Collins (2004) catalogues the efforts of physicists to detect 'gravity waves' to explain the phenomenon of gravity. These have proved elusive and have required the creation of ever larger and more expensive pieces of equipment called 'interferometers' to identify them. Despite the highly specific and contrived circumstances in which even mere trace evidence for the phenomenon can be detected, increasingly large proportions of the scientific community are convinced of their existence. Thus, creating scientific knowledge which is full of things that you can't ever grasp directly is precisely what the advanced physicists are doing. Our machine might detect the gravitational perturbations accompanying a star collapse or nebula exploding. We can't see any connection but we know that there is some kind of unobservable process that is generating both of those things and that they are connected in some way.

To return to our previous example of gender and toy preferences, another way of thinking about this is to reconsider our positivist survey of girls' preference for Barbie dolls and boys' for model jet fighters. The expressed preference was in a sense factual, but we also concluded that those circumstances did not necessarily have to be as they were. What we are beginning to do is think counter-factually, to think counter to the apparent facts, to think things don't have to be like this. This is precisely what people like Galileo and Copernicus, who argued that the earth revolves round the sun rather than the other way round, had to do. They had to think counter to the 'facts', because of course you get up in the morning, you observe the sun and during the course of the day the sun moves around the earth. These thinkers therefore had to think counter to assumptions derived from their observations. In terms of the laws of physics, you could never have empirically proven that the earth revolves around the sun unless you had gone into space in a rocket and observed it. But the possibility of being able to observe it is predicated on understanding that things aren't the way they seem. Unless the whole space programme understood that the earth went around the sun, and not vice versa, they wouldn't have been able to go and observe the fact that it did so.

Let us consider another version of this distinction between the observable, the actual and the real. Lukes (1974) examined the processes of local democracy and identified what he termed three dimensions of power. These three dimensions of power mirror Bhaskar's distinction between observable, actual and real. Lukes conceived of the first dimension of power in terms of the publicly observable processes of local government democracy. The first dimension of power is equivalent to a public committee that discusses issues and arrives at a decision, for example one of the committee meetings in local councils that are, in principle, open to the public. In other words, there is a public agenda, things are discussed and voted on, decisions are made, and everything is apparently open and above board.

However, as Lukes and we all know, there is more to it than this, because the second dimension of power is that even before that committee meets, other manoeuvrings take place. These take place in closed rooms, where deals are struck behind closed doors, not directly observable by the public. There are negotiations undertaken beforehand, items are kept off the agenda, and some are not even voted on. The agenda is pre-set, and to some extent public debate is pre-empted, if not totally directed, by events behind closed doors. This is what Lukes calls the second dimension of power, and parallels Bhaskar's realm of the actual.

The third dimension of power has very strong parallels with Bhaskar's domain of the real. For Lukes, the third dimension of power is to think counter-factually and say, not what is it that people actually express as their views and opinions (the first dimension). It is not even to say, well what if the public could actually have knowledge of all the things that have been left off the agenda and discussed in back rooms; what would they want then? (That's the second dimension of power.)

There is something beyond both of those dimensions, the third dimension of power, which is how people's desires are shaped: what would people want if wider social arrangements were different? If we could change the parameters of society, the way society is organized, what would people want then? Let us apply this to the issue of health. The health debate would not then centre on greater or fewer health professionals and hospitals, but what kind of way we wish to organize our society to care for our health. This might, if there were different arrangements, not involve doctors and nurses at all – who knows? Lukes argues that people's choices are partially determined and closed down by what they are aware of as possibilities. What people want is determined by the current structure of society because they have become accustomed to seeing things in particular ways, and limited to seeing certain possibilities. The realm of the real (in Bhaskar's terms) or the third dimension of power (in Lukes's terms) is for people to think counter-factually and say what if things could be different, even what if things could be different in quite dramatic broad ways? What would people's real interests be then? What would they want, not given current ways of thinking, but if those parameters were shattered and people could have a vision of what things might be like in other circumstances.

The structures that researchers seem to assign as to this unobservable realm of the real are what we have come to recognize as dimensions of social oppression. We suggest that these ideas have been heavily influenced, first of all, by Marxism, which proposes, rather than, 'Do you want a little more money?' asks instead 'What if the workers had control over the factories rather than bosses, what could be different and what different things would flow from that then?' Early scientific realist thinking was arguably heavily tied up with Marxism. It is also tied up with feminism because part of what feminism also suggests is that things need not be the way they are; they could be different. What if women in 1950s Britain did not stay at home, could take paid public employment and/or have the work of home-making and childcare valued economically? What if they did not have to ask for money from the husband, but had their own money and control over their lives? What if, instead of worrying what would happen when he dies because they know little about finances, we lived in a society where all were routinely taught about finances? From the vantage point of the twenty-first century we can appreciate that things can indeed be different, albeit not as different as one might wish. But note that a scientific realist approach entails asking: what if things were different, wouldn't you think differently, and wouldn't you want different things?

It's an approach that seems to us to have informed the disability rights movements (Oliver 1992). It seems to us to be almost at the heart of the UK's Disability Discrimination Act 1995, which asserts that things don't have to be the way they are – what if all public buildings were made wheelchair-accessible with wide enough doors and ramps and what if the social arrangements were changed, wouldn't that make things different?

You can see in relation to the work of Bhaskar and Lukes that part of the emphasis of this epistemological realism or methodological collectivism is that the unit of analysis that is allowable as knowledge can be the whole of society or the whole of the culture and not just the parts. Realism offers a critique of positivism for being atomistic, viewing society as a series of discrete individual parts and never being holistic. Positivism thereby fails to identify connections between different areas of social life, and fails to account for false ways of looking at the world (ideologies) that hide or deny these connections, and that thus give people the false sense that wider social arrangements are 'natural' or otherwise not changeable.

By contrast, the sense of everything being connected characterizes realist approaches. Even when realists are studying quite small areas of social life they are continually trying to make links to broader society and structures like racism. Porter (1993) is only looking at one ward on a hospital setting, but he is trying to think how it is that wider structures (which, as a scientific realist, he thinks are really out there and making a difference to how things are) contribute to what is actually happening on that single ward. He is asking, what are the connections, what are the ways in which the broader structure of racism is working its way through in this particular context? And because of those two concerns, with both broader structures and with particular contexts, realists would see themselves as dealing with two very different elements of social research which are usually quite difficult to hold together. These two elements are, first, agency, which is about the intentions and actions of people at an individual level; it is the microcosm view – what's going on at the level of fine detail in terms of personal interaction, in terms of the intentionality of people. And second, structure, which is a more macrocosm view – how are people's actions formed by wider influences, how are their experiences created, limited and structured by wider constraints? Now, some forms of research have overemphasized structure and treated people almost as if they were puppets on a string, and have not conceived of people as having an active part to play in their own lives. For example, an explanation that did not take sufficient account of agency might involve saying, well, all women learn to stay at home and cook, do the ironing and washing; they are socialized into that role and grow up thinking like that and they socialize their own daughters into that role and so it goes on. This example is deliberately crude for the purpose of illustration, but what that kind of explanation doesn't take account of is the activeness, the humanness, the creativeness of people. They don't just take on roles, as if wearing a coat; they are creative and active in performing the roles of, say, a man or a woman (Butler 1990).

Now, realism tries to reconcile the two elements of social scientific explanation. First, agency, which involves people being active and intentional in what they are doing and second, the structure that provides the parameters within which the social actors work. These parameters are sometimes seen as restrictive, yet they also provide a framework which can be interpreted creatively or even playfully by the actors. So, once again it's not just that someone can suddenly get up and kick against the system and be immediately able to do all the things that they are not supposed to do according to their social role in, say, a heterosexist and patriarchal society. People are constrained as well. So again, to give an example in Medieval Europe, a woman who it was thought might be able to cure people with herbs and spices and laying on of hands and healing was in a problematic position. In a religious context this might result in her being revered as a saint, yet in secular contexts she would risk being burnt as a witch (Roper 1994). This would indeed constitute a very serious restriction to the degree to which you had the freedom to be active.

Scientific realism, in this sense, then involves trying to come up with a form of social explanation that can relate what is going on at the microcosmic level, in terms of what individual actors are thinking or doing, to the broader societal level, to the broader structures of society, whether they are structures of class, gender, 'race', disability and so on. It is also allowing as knowledge factors which are beyond individual control and awareness. In other words, there is no one person who can control the direction of racism, patriarchy, disability discrimination or whatever generative concept is being applied.

Furthermore, in some cases people may not be aware of those broader structures that are influencing their lives. People frequently come to see their way of viewing the world as natural and anything else as alien or antisocial. Hence one of the controversial implications of scientific realists' approach is their claim that there are underlying unobservable structures generating the reality that people experience, *whether they realize it or not*. It is effectively a claim to know better than people actually experiencing this situation. It is arguably the origin of the Marxist concept of false consciousness, a concept that describes how the 'motive forces' which propel individuals are often unknown to them (Eagleton 1991: 89).

Similarly, some feminists might accuse other women of false consciousness. In other words, if some women say, no, I like things the way that they are, I like not being in control, I like having flowers and chocolates instead of a wage and a bank account, certain types of feminists would say, yes, but that's because you don't know any better, that's because you don't know the wider situation, you don't have access to the debates, you have not had the parameters expanded so you could see that things could be different if certain other broader things were different. According to the feminist writer Wolf (1991: 39), 'our media-led culture conspires to keep women permanently insecure and anxious because they do not measure up to some abstract and unattainable standard of beauty'. Concern with looks, she warns, 'literally kills women, frequently through anorexia, sometimes through breast implants'. On the other hand Fox-Genovese (1996: 56) found amongst the women she interviewed a good deal of enjoyment of the 'complexities of costuming'. Indeed, 'whatever the frustration and pain, most women clearly value the distinctly female core of their identities'. Now one might say that this sense that beauty and fashion are 'core' to one's identity is an aspect of false consciousness. But the often heated nature of such debates highlights how dangerous it is to claim to 'know better'.

Indeed, a simple way of summing up this opposition between nominalism and scientific realism, is to take the phrases 'taking at face value' and 'knowing better'. It seems to us that what nominalists do is to take things at face value. They only accept as knowledge what they can see or observe or derive from individuals. The strength of this view is that, at least in principle, you are guided towards listening to people, grounding research in individual experience, and validating individual people by taking their views seriously. The disadvantage is that this could be relatively naïve, because you are only looking at the surface, not at what is generating the way that things are. If, for example, a phenomenological study were conducted we would expect it to describe people's experiences, and to take these deep emotional experiences very seriously. A phenomenological study of domestic violence could produce a very heartrending account of a woman's experience of domestic violence and her resilience in the face of it (for example, Davis 2002). But isn't the point to change it, not just to describe it? That is where an element of Marx's famous quotation (1845) in *Theses on Feuerbach* becomes relevant: 'The philosophers have only interpreted the world in various ways; the point, however, is to change it.' So taking at face value, taking people's views seriously, also risks being superficial, and inadvertently supporting the status quo.

However, if we look at scientific realism, and the phrase 'knowing better', then its advantage is that it is potentially insightful. It can include an examination and analysis of several layers of reality and is able to probe what is ultimately generating the way things are. It doesn't stop short; it asks why things are happening. Could they be different if we changed the wider parameters? Would they be different? And, perhaps most interestingly, should they be different?

Despite these advantages of a critical realist perspective, it is difficult to resolve the issue of 'false consciousness'. That is, one opens up the possibility of critical researchers saying, 'You only think that because you don't know any better. And because we are critical researchers, because we know about these underlying generative structures that cause society to be the way it is, then we know better than you.' Critical realism thus privileges the kind of knowledge the researcher achieves, over and above that of the person who is experiencing the phenomenon. So, there are risks and advantages in both nominalist and critical realist conceptions of knowledge and approaches to research. The two phrases – 'taking at face value' and 'knowing better' – with their respective strengths and weaknesses, might usefully be marshalled to think through this tension.

In one applied version of the wider scientific realist approach to knowledge, Pawson and Tilley (1997) employ a three-part notion of the research endeavour. They refer to the researcher appreciating the respective importance and connectedness of three factors: of context, mechanism and outcome. Moreover, they reject what they call a secessionist notion of causality. This involves the idea that one thing leads directly on to another. In the secessionist version of causality you have a mechanism at work and you have an outcome. Instead, Pawson and Tilley try to develop a more sophisticated notion, which they call generative causality. They have undertaken evaluation work in health, education and crime. In conducting evaluation research, they are trying to get away from the simplistic secessionist notion of causality. For example, if you have a neighbourhood watch scheme (mechanism) the result could be the reduction of levels of crime (outcome). The problem with that is that one of the things that neighbourhood watch schemes do is displace crime into a different neighbourhood. You may reduce crime in the area where there is a neighbourhood watch scheme but you just displace it to a neighbouring area, for example.

Pawson and Tilley have a nice metaphorical example to demonstrate the limitations of a secessionist version of causality. They point out that if you strike a match next to gunpowder you get an explosion. But of course, you don't always achieve an explosion, because if the gunpowder is wet you don't get an explosion; if the match doesn't touch the gunpowder for more than the critical number of seconds you don't get an explosion. If the gunpowder isn't correctly compacted you don't get an explosion. So it's a lot more sophisticated, and you have to know what is happening to a range of contextual factors too. Perhaps early attempts at developing realist theories in the social sciences yielded rather mechanistic accounts of human phenomena. That is, great explanatory value was attached to constructs like class struggle, racism or patriarchy or some single pre-eminent causal construct. However, once we accept that events may be most effectively explained by positing some underlying construct, it may be elaborated and made more sophisticated with the recognition that it might work differently according to a whole range of different contextual features. Pawson and Tilley's (1997) scheme, considering context, mechanism and outcome, can thus yield a more complex and multi-factorial causal picture.

A key problem with the term scientific realism is the potential for confusion between realism as an ontological claim (what is the stuff we are studying made of?) and an epistemological claim (how in principle may we come to know what we are studying?). Some (for example, Porter 1998) have attempted to address this by distinguishing between naïve realism (a straightforward belief in a world 'out there' independent of what we think of it, or what we have termed materialism) and scientific realism, in which an underlying generative reality produces appearances. We would prefer to argue that (naïve) realism is a claim about ontology, but that social scientific realism is a claim about epistemology, about *how* we may know, not about *what* we may know. Scientific realism is an epistemology because it concerns the view that as researchers we do not have direct access to 'what matters'. 'What matters' is not specified and leaves open the ontological question of whether 'what matters' is material (critical realism) or ideal (structuralism, which we do not cover in this book).

Scientific realism insists we cannot have direct access to 'what matters'. However, this leaves open not only what 'what matters' is made of, but some (methodological) issues about how indirect access is negotiated.

There are several aspects that may be associated with such ways of accessing 'what matters'. In this respect we are using the term scientific realism as an umbrella term to cover a variety of approaches to thinking about social research, each of which emphasizes different aspects of the assumption that reference beyond the empirical facts is a legitimate way of knowing. These aspects include:

- the notion that one may think counter to the apparent facts;
- that there are essential structures underlying social phenomena that generate surface appearances;
- that the researchers, having helped to lay bare what is generating the reality we experience, will also be 'people of goodwill' who will see that an *ought* follows from a particular *is*, and will jointly take action;
- that the researcher constructs data to test theoretical constructs, since (because data is always theory-dependent there can be no theory-free facts) one cannot test theory by 'facts', only by other theory; and
- that theoretical concepts are historically grounded in the mental labours of successive generations.

The sections that follow examine each of these aspects of scientific realism in more detail.

One technique is described by Lukes (1974), who suggests counterfactual reflection. Thinking counter to the facts (empirical evidence) involves suppositions about what things might be like if other contextual features of the situation were changed. This has three interesting connotations. First it alerts us to the power of what is sometimes disparagingly called the lay perspective. One of Graham's (1976) respondents refers to smoking cessation advice as based on 'only facts'. This hints at the sophistication of lay perspectives in contrast to the professional characterization of recidivist smokers as weak-willed, ignorant or feckless. Second, it prompts reflection on the need for a democratization of social science, in which the agenda, terms of reference, orientation, problem definition are the product of investigation, not the topic of investigation. Third, it hints that there is a relationship between what is the case (empirical), what could be the case (counterfactual) and what ought to be the case (moral–political). That is, in relation to some of the research examples we have given, it might involve asking, 'What if it made sense?' where apparently hazardous activities such as smoking, intravenous drug use and unprotected sex were concerned. This leads us to a more sensitive and nuanced understanding of how apparently incomprehensible events not only take place, but are orderly and meaningful.

Critical realism: racism in health settings

Porter (1993) is one author who has adopted a critical realist approach to social research, and particularly the manner in which the (unobservable) entity of racism can be used meaningfully to connect the surface appearances of relationships on a hospital ward. Porter is especially interested in racism in such a setting because the professionalism of health care workers should, in theory, mean that neither doctors nor nurses are implicated in racist behaviour and attitudes. Indeed, when Porter observes the relation between nurses and internationally recruited 'overseas' doctors from the Middle East in the public spaces of the hospital ward, he does not witness any direct expressions of racism. In the realm of the observable, then, at the first dimension of power, no racist attitudes are to be seen or heard.

However, Porter introduces the notion of racisms occurring 'backstage' when the mask of professional relations is let slip, when nurses are on breaks or in other informal circumstances. In the sluice room off the main ward, the nurses are heard to make derogatory comments about the overseas doctors. This is an illustration of the second dimension of power, or the realm of the actual. The racism is actually being expressed, but not in a public manner.

For an illustration of the third dimension of power, an example of Bhaskar's realm of the real, we want to turn to some of our own work. Culley *et al.* (2001) examined the experiences of Caribbean-born nurses who came to work in Britain in the 1950s and 1960s, and who then gave over thirty years of their working lives to the NHS. The important point about racisms for a realist epistemology is that those racisms must be considered as structuring experiences of the Caribbean nurses *even when those racisms are not observable in any immediate interactions.* Porter (1993) was able to access and observe the racisms of the nurses in his study, but the overseas doctors were not. Similarly, in the Culley *et al.* (2001) study, the Caribbean nurses do not themselves necessarily have access to these 'backstage racisms'. Thus they may be faced with situations where they are conscious of racism as actually or potentially informing encounters, but where they are unsure of its precise role in a given situation.

> Because when I qualified, when I got my general (nursing training), I recall going to see the chief male nurse. I told him, I want to discuss the future, what my situation would be like if I stayed on, and he said, 'You come to ask me for advice, I will say to you get out', he said, 'there's nothing here for you'. Well I didn't run off and say his views are racist. I just took his advice and I decided, well, I'm going and try elsewhere.
>
> (Male Caribbean nurse, cited in Culley *et al.* 2001: 244)

This Caribbean nurse is faced with a dilemma. By definition, he does not have access to any backstage racisms, and it is not clear whether he is experiencing racism in promotion (there's nothing for you here because I, the chief nurse, am a racist) or whether the advice is a recognition that the wider society is racist (there's nothing for you here because other people here are racist). It could also be the case that the apparent acknowledgement of a racist society by the chief nurse is actually a self-protecting racism in operation (I'm using other people's racism as an excuse to encourage you to leave but really I want you to leave as well).

When faced with living in a society where some overt racism is experienced, and where backstage racisms may be suspected, the Caribbean nurses may structure their own experiences to take account of previous or anticipated racisms.

> I worked in highly intensive areas [smiles] because the patients don't argue with you. They're too ill to argue with you [laughing]. So maybe I don't get the full brunt of what patients on big wards, or any wards for that matter, who are not so well (. . .) to, to, to, erm criticize you too much. The majority of my senior time has been in specialized care. And probably that's why I think, they are more or less, the relatives are so appreciative, of what you can, of what you do to them, that I don't get time, I don't have the experience of *pettiness* [pettiness said with contempt] you know. (. . .) I don't know if you understand what I'm saying.
>
> (Female Caribbean nurse, cited in Culley *et al.* 2001: 244)

The implication is that the racism of both the patients and relatives is moderated in an intensive care situation – patients because they are too ill and dependent and relatives because racism is temporarily suspended in extreme situations where their relative may die. This is presented as an experience which is unlike the more overt racism she felt she had experienced elsewhere. Moreover, it was a motivating factor for her to enter and remain within the speciality of intensive care. She continues to work in intensive care rather than return to work on general medical wards, where she suspects (on the basis of other experiences reported to her by other Caribbean nurses) that she would again experience the 'usual' racism. The racism that a realist would argue is operating here is in the realm of the real. There are no *observable* racist comments on the ward. There is not even any sign of *actual* backstage racisms. However, in the absence of observable or actual racism, racism is still *real* in structuring the experiences of the Caribbean nurse.

A measure for measures

One problem that the insights of subjectivism pose for the applied researcher is how any research can be based on quantifiable data if meanings are so variable at the levels of words, cultures and domains. If researchers cannot be certain they are putting the same concepts together, cannot be certain that they are counting like with like, how can we ever trust statistical data? To understand the arguments of social scientific realists, we need to trace the history of the debate.

The debate begins with the French sociologist Emile Durkheim ([1897] 1970) who by comparing official statistics on suicide between and across European societies developed theories to explain the variations in suicide rate. One aspect of this was to suggest that the rate of suicides went down the more closely knit a community was. However, subjectivist researchers such as Atkinson (1978) and Douglas (1967) criticize such use of official statistics.

Such subjectivists argue that observers use 'background assumptions and expectations' to make sense of observed events. Thus one coroner's decision as to whether or not to classify a sudden unexplained death as suicide may be based on whether or not a suicide note is found with the body. The problem for official statistics, argue the subjectivists, is that these background assumptions vary from culture to culture, from community to community, and even from one person to another person. Thus in the Christian tradition, suicide is associated with a sense of shame. In the Japanese tradition it may be an honourable death, or one that preserves family honour. For certain Pacific Islanders attempted suicide may be an accepted sanction in marital disputes (think of Princess Diana's reported attempted suicide as a sanction against her husband's infidelity).

The problem with official statistics is that it involves putting together the reports of many different researchers or observers. It cannot therefore be assumed that the resulting statistic (in other words, what we are counting up) represents the same phenomenon. Thus, in assigning a sudden death to the category of a suicide, for example, the coroner may or may not take into account different contextual factors such as the existence or otherwise of a suicide note, entries into the deceased's personal diaries, what is read into the mode of death or the location of death or the deceased's mental state, the extent of the thoroughness of questioning relatives are subjected to, the extent and nature of any deputations requesting or disclaiming a verdict of suicide on the part of relatives or friends. In short we do not know, argue the subjectivists, that we are counting like with like. We may be counting different phenomena as the same, or the same phenomena as different.

However, Hindess (1973) makes three criticisms of these claims of the subjectivist. First, he points out that researchers have their own background assumptions and expectations. Therefore the researcher's accounts and explanations of what is going on are subject to the same limitations as all other accounts. Second, Hindess points out that no knowledge is possible except that which has been through the subjective distortions of the researcher's accounts. Third, it is logically impossible to know what the distorting mechanisms of the background assumptions are because they can only be known through those same distorting assumptions (effectively a critique of the logical impossibility of phenomenological 'bracketing'). In practice in official statistics, argues Hindess, the compilation of many observers' accounts are categorized by bureaucrats – and disagreements are resolved by head bureaucrats imposing their decision (see Roth 1966).

Furthermore, according to Hindess, subjectivist researchers do not seem concerned to try to find out *how often* these types of disagreement of classification and meaning occur either amongst researchers or amongst bureaucrats. Nor does it appear to be any concern of the subjectivist researcher to establish which categories are problematic, and to try to assess the impact of these on the data created.

Here we turn to the work of Pawson (1989) and of Taylor (1992). Pawson poses a similar problem to Hindess in terms of asking what criteria we could apply as researchers to judge whether a concept or category is appropriate to use in those styles of research, such as questionnaire-surveys, that seek to quantify data. The theoretical tool that Pawson proposes to deal with this issue is to distinguish external constructs and internal constructs. Internal constructs are those concepts that are dependent upon what different people mean by them. Take for example child abuse (Taylor 1992).

Several hundred years ago in Europe a man could marry a 12-year-old girl, but in contemporary Europe it would be seen as child abuse. In other words, different people have, at different historical points of time and in different cultural settings, regarded different activities as child abuse. There is no universal standard we can appeal to across time and across history. It is not dependent on some objective external reality. Rather it is dependent on what people think about the construct 'child abuse'. Furthermore, even if we take the concept at one historical point in time within one society, then there are variations in what different individual people might count as child abuse. Take the following actions:

Shouting at a child
Smacking your own child
Smacking someone else's child
Sending a child to bed with no supper
Sending a child away to boarding school
Showing a child an adult-rated film

It is likely, argues Taylor, that different people will count none, some or all of these activities as child abuse. What Taylor and Pawson are therefore saying is that as soon as you have got a concept which is vulnerable to individual differences in meaning, then that is a concept that ought not to be asked about in questionnaires with any degree of claims to be scientific because you can't be certain, other than by simply taking a leap of faith, that everyone is understanding the same thing by it. In other words, when a concept is an internal construct (vulnerable to differences in meaning to different individuals) it is a concept that should not be used within questionnaire-style research that is based on quantifying such categories, because we cannot be clear that we are counting like with like.

Subjectivists argue that this means we can't ever conduct that type of questionnaire research; we must abandon all attempts to quantify and to add up categories because how do we ever know that people mean the same thing by the same concepts? By contrast, authors such as Pawson and Taylor do not abandon attempts to quantify, but rather attempt to assess how far that variation in meaning goes. They have this notion that it is legitimate to undertake this more quantitative questionnaire-type research if you restrict yourself to external constructs. External constructs are ideas or concepts or words on which we can be relatively certain people do agree. To illustrate this we again turn to an exchange with our students:

> Can you think of a straightforward example that could be answered on a questionnaire that wouldn't be vulnerable to that same difference of meaning as child abuse?
> *Age, sex, ethnicity*
> Yes, now, in other words, most people would understand the same thing by the question, like if we asked them, what's your age? Note that this is not to deny, there are people who will give different ages in different contexts, perhaps when applying for a job, or in presenting themselves for a date. Let's also look at sex, because most people will understand very clearly what we mean by male or female, but will everyone? Can you think of anyone, however rare, of someone who might find a problem with that?
> *People who were born of indeterminate gender*
> Yes, so whilst most people would have no problem in answering that, there are a

small minority who would a) find it very difficult and b) become angry and offended by the assumption that everyone is unambiguously male or female. Ethnicity: we are perhaps moving here into a concept which is even more vulnerable to situations. Sociologists sometimes talk about situational ethnicity (Okamura 1981); in other words, people will conceive of their ethnic identity slightly differently in different contexts or for different purposes. So, whilst Taylor and Pawson would, generally speaking, count constructs such as age, gender or ethnicity as external, even those relatively hard factual things are vulnerable to some differences. However, how many people are going to find it difficult to call themselves male and female?

Not many

Yes, relatively few. But as soon as we show that the concept which you are trying to measure is vulnerable to any variation, however rare, does that mean that we have to abandon all attempts to quantify and measure how many men and women there are in society? If so, you would never be able to measure or quantify anything. Pawson has perhaps slightly overstated the case for an absolute distinction terms of external constructs and internal constructs, because it seems to us that it is more like a continuum and nothing is entirely ever an external construct. Because even in things like age and gender and ethnicity, you will find there is some variation, if not misunderstanding, and perhaps some deliberate misreporting of what is the case. But having said that, it's going to be happening relatively few times, there are other contextual issues that you can draw upon to be relatively confident that most people, most of the time, will understand and tune into what you are asking about. On the other hand there are other concepts, and child abuse might be one of them, which are relatively much more internal constructs, much more vulnerable to significant variations in what people think and thereby much less attractive as concepts to work with in questionnaire/survey type of studies.

Conclusion

The respective problems of nominalism and realism may be clearer if we take the phrases 'taking at face value' and 'knowing better'. Nominalism takes at face value in the sense that evidence must be immediately apprehensible by observation or through language communicated to the researcher. For example, bearing witness to suffering expressed by a respondent takes at face value, but ignores the possibility that the suffering may not be necessary. If all we do is bear witness to current suffering then we forgo the opportunity to campaign for changes in social arrangements which may have felt beneficial effects.

On the other hand, if we claim to 'know better' in the sense that we think we can apprehend how different social arrangements may dissolve pain, we risk neither acknowledging nor ameliorating the lived experience of pain within current social arrangements. But the counterfactual reflection of realism may be posited as entailing claims by the researcher to 'know better' than the respondent. As such these claims contain the potential for, in terms of Frank (1991), appropriation and domination, for respondents to be framed within an intellectual discourse.

Realism, then, represents a very different epistemological approach to either positivism or subjectivism. Once more, we conclude the chapter by trying to draw together, in tabular form, the major features of the scientific realist approach to research (see Table 3.2). Nevertheless, in the latter half of the twentieth century, a further analytic dualism came to the fore, one that raised significant problems for all the research traditions discussed so far, and this further analytic dualism is the subject of our next chapter.

Table 3.2 Characteristics of critical realism

	CRITICAL REALISM
What? (Ontology)	Underlying material structures.
How do we get to know? (Epistemology)	Distinguish individual consciousness and underlying material relations (of production, patriarchy, racism, disability discrimination).
How do we know we know? (Methodology)	
Internal validity*	Concepts for research are built upon the (mental) labour of previous generations in developing theory. There is no observation that does not pre-suppose theory, therefore empirical data cannot test theory.
Reliability*	Counterfactual reflection. The researcher constructs data to test theories.
Generalizability*	Social change. Praxis: does it work? Are the social actions transferable to other contexts? 'Philosophers have interpreted the world. The point, however, is to change it' (Karl Marx).
What practical methods or techniques are used? (Methods)	Action research, participatory action research, critical social research, critical ethnography.

* These terms are themselves usually introduced in the context of positivist science. As such one would expect them to sit more comfortably within positivism than within any of the other traditions. Nevertheless, interpreted more broadly than within a positivist framework, they arguably represent domains of the research experience that all researchers can, and perhaps should, be able to reflect upon.

Further reading

For other examples of authors drawing upon the ideas of critical realism, see:

Carter, B. (2000) *Realism and Racism: Concepts of Race in Sociological Research*. London: Routledge.
Carter, B. and New, C. (2004) *Making Realism Work: Realist Social Theory and Empirical Research*. London: Routledge.

Note that authors do not have to explicitly cast themselves as critical realists to implicitly draw upon scientific realist ideas.

Culley, L., Dyson, S.M., Ham-Ying, S. and Young, W. (2001) Caribbean nurses and racism in the NHS. In L. Culley and S. M. Dyson (eds) *Ethnicity and Nursing Practice*. Basingstoke: Palgrave, 231–49.

For examples of scientific realist approaches tending to emphasize that the underlying structures comprise collective ideas, see:

Leach, E. (1970) *Levi-Strauss*. London: Fontana.
Taylor, S. and Ashworth, C. (1987) Durkheim and social realism: an approach to health and illness. In G. Scambler (1987) *Sociological Theory and Medical Sociology*. London: Tavistock.

4 Projecting the field: postmodernism

Introduction

In Chapter 2 we examined a key analytical dualism, namely whether the social world is an external world 'out there' or an internal world 'in here'. A second key debate concerns the acceptability of different ways of knowing the social world, and was discussed in Chapter 3. In this chapter, we look at a third analytical tension between essentialist and anti-essentialist conceptions of the social world and of research knowledge. In order to analyse the essentialism/anti-essentialism dualism we consider two related traditions that between them challenge all the approaches to knowledge outlined thus far in the book. One is the work of Michel Foucault (1971, 1973, 1978, 1979) and those he has influenced (sometimes collectively termed post-structuralists or Foucauldians). The other is a broader tradition, within which Foucauldian work is sometimes subsumed, and that is postmodernism.

Foucault and the post-structuralists draw our attention to the manner in which the reality we think we know is not essentially 'there' but is merely one of several possibilities that 'could be there'. What is seen to be there is actually the product of particular sets of power relationships. The implication is that in other sets of power relationships a very different reality could be produced.

The postmodernists reject claims that all-embracing underlying structures generate the social world. Instead they focus on the manner in which research knowledge is communicated by language. They highlight how the human activities of the researcher create, rather than reflect, the social world. Social research is not considered a superior form of knowledge but a series of rhetorical devices by which researchers try to stake claims to persuade others to their view of the world.

The influence of Michel Foucault

The work of Foucault is extensive and complex, and we have divided it here into three main areas: those concerned respectively with truth, knowledge and ethics.

Truth

One way of thinking about what we claim to know is to think about the fact that any notion of what we regard as established truth is to some extent the history of the winners. In other words, knowledge is a reflection of which social groups have emerged as 'winners' in the historical past. Another way of referring to the winners is to talk about a dominant discourse. The term discourse is used to capture a set of ideas of concepts and a way of thinking about things, but it is also a set of material social arrangements, including architectural and economic arrangements, in terms of reflecting a particular order of things.

Foucault is interested not only in the dominant discourse, but in the other discourses that are implied by the dominant one, discourses that may have been partially or wholly suppressed. For, in order for these discourses to be dominant, other alternative discourses have to have been lost, or to have been suppressed. One of Foucault's approaches is thus to undertake what he calls an archaeology of knowledge.

Imagine we are archaeologists digging up the ruins of a Norman church from eleventh-century Britain, only to find that beneath these ruins, comprising Norman arches and pillars, we come across earlier foundation stones upon which a previously existing Saxon church was built. In other words, here is an archaeological illustration of how a Norman church (with the Norman victory under William the Conqueror: the winners if you like) was built on the foundation of the losers, the church that had been destroyed, the Anglo-Saxon church. Note, too, how language changes as well as material structures, not least that in English history we are now more familiar with 'William the Conqueror' rather than the name he was known by before he won (and presumably would have been to this day had he lost), namely 'William the Bastard'. A dominant discourse is the prevailing system of thought, but if we examine this dominant thought system carefully we will see the traces of other alternative discourses, other ways of seeing the world, that have been nearly lost from sight.

One way that we think about his idea, this idea that there are numerous discourses, one of which emerges as dominant, is to think about colours, which comprise various refractions of white light. If you take the colour yellow, this represents one of many potential colours within white light. What we know as all the colours of the rainbow potentially contained in white light are refracted, say through a prism, and one of the colours we then see is yellow. In Foucauldian terms there is nothing *essential* about the colour yellow cast onto the wall, since a slight turn of the prism and that same spot would be blue or red. The spot is potentially any colour, it just happens to be yellow, and all the colours that it is not, because they are the wavelength that is refracted differently, are the equivalent to the suppressed discourses. So in other words the colour on the wall is not essentially yellow; it could be many things. This is a metaphor we try and use to understand Foucault's emphasis on anti-essentialism. Anti-essentialism is thus a very radical departure from the kind of ideas that we looked at in phenomenology, with its ideas of an inner essence, something very deep and permanent and identifiable. Foucault's ideas lend themselves to very different conceptions of being because they are anti-essentialist. Things are not essentially so; they are one of many possibilities, others of which have been suppressed, perhaps temporarily.

Foucault terms one aspect of his approach genealogical. Genealogy is the study of lineage or one's family tree. In tracing one's family tree one can see junctures where the line comes to an end, where someone dies before reproductive age, or else never has children of their own whether by choice or circumstance. These broken lines can result in part of the family becoming unknown to others, becoming long-lost relatives. Foucault contrasts his genealogical approach with historical study. History is in one sense the accounts of the 'winners', those whose discourses have become dominant. Genealogy focuses on the 'runners-up', the 'also-rans' and the 'losers', and how their discourses came to be lost, suppressed or downgraded. But of course, the very fact they have been lost means that, like archaeologists, we may only have fragments with which to reconstruct them.

What this means in terms of contemporary social research is that the researcher may have to search for clues about suppressed discourses within the current dominant discourses. This may involve revealing contradictions within the discourse, for example how passive language ('a questionnaire was distributed . . .') obscures the activity of the researcher. It may involve pointedly asking what is not there, as well as what is there. What views are suppressed? Whose view is presented? Whose view is absent? To whom is the text addressed? What could have been said that is not said?

Power/knowledge

Now in looking at what constitutes the truth or the dominant discourse and other potential discourses which have been suppressed, this leads Foucault on to the second of this three key elements of his approach, which is power/knowledge. The phrase is deliberately written in this way because, in working out how things come to be regarded as truth, Foucault concluded that truth has to do with the exercise of power, and that power and knowledge are two sides of the same coin. As he argues:

> . . . we must cease once and for all to describe the effects of power in negative terms; in fact power produces, it produces reality, it produces domains of objects and rituals of truth. The individual and the knowledge that may be gained of him (sic) belong to this production.
>
> (Foucault 1979: 194)

Thus when we talk about the relationship between knowledge and power, we usually talk about power in negative terms. We say that power conceals knowledge, the powerful keep knowledge to themselves, knowledge is power. Thus we usually argue that power is a negative force that is used to hide knowledge away from people. But for Foucault, power has a positive effect. Power is actually the condition of certain types of knowledge. Knowledge is the effect or consequence of certain types of power.

It is almost as if you walked into a dark room with several different types of lighting. You would see different things if the power were based on standard light, infra-red light, ultra-violet light or thermal imaging. Each of those sets of lighting is a different type of power. It is quite useful, we think, to consider power not in terms of physical power and social power but in terms of being akin to electricity. Electricity is not in itself good or bad. It is potentially dangerous, not least because we can electrocute ourselves. For Foucault that sums up his approach to power, which is that it is not inherently good or bad; it produces things, it produces different types of things, depending on the type of power that it is. However, power is always potentially dangerous. But whether or not it is oppressive depends upon evaluating the exercise of power in each individual situation.

For Foucault, certain types of knowledge emerge out of certain discourses, certain types of power relationships. The knowledge of psychiatry emerges from the power of the asylum, clinical medicine emerges from the development of the clinic and criminology emerges from the development of the prison both as a discourse and as a set of an architectural forms. These forms of relationships and institutions, the asylum, the clinic, the prison, are not only dealing with madness, illness and crime, they are actually creating those domains of social life. In this view, the power of these institutions is to create certain kinds of people such as the 'patient' or the 'criminal'. In the conventional view, clinics might exist to cure the patient and prisons might rehabilitate the criminal, but in this view we might equally say that the institutions and their associated discourses project pathological identities – 'patient', 'invalid', 'criminal' – onto socially marginalized people.

For example, before the development of the medical clinic knowledge of health was based around the individual patient. This type of health knowledge, one we would now call holistic, was based on ancient Greek ideas of the balance of the four humours – blood, phlegm, yellow bile and black bile. The humours, or liquids of the body, were considered as out of balance and could be brought into alignment via bleeding, purging or vomiting. These then were the kinds of knowledge systems which were involved in pre-clinical medicine. However, with the development of institutions like fever hospitals, leprosaria and, later, madhouses, you have a situation in which for the first time the class of problematic persons is brought together into a centralized place. By studying this variety of people, what you then have is the possibility of tracing the course of a disease independent of its manifestation in any one individual. You no longer have person A whose humours are out of balance, you have got person A in the bed next to person B in the bed next to person C. The power involved in putting people together in a centralized place permits the emergence of clinical medical knowledge. Knowledge is based on what all these people have in common – the signs and symptoms – and that begins to make possible the description of a disease independent of its manifestation in any one individual. A Foucauldian argument involves saying, not that doctors have medical knowledge and therefore have the social power to compel people to come in to fever hospitals to be treated, rather that they have the power to require people to come into centralized hospitals and as a consequence of that power are able to develop certain types of clinical knowledge.

Similarly, before asylums were built people who we now might call mentally ill may well have been integrated into everyday village life (perhaps the origin of the notion of the village idiot). In some cases at least, that person had a place in the medieval village. It is only the development of industrial capitalism and the requirement for people to be much more disciplined in workshops and factories that creates a social system which makes it very difficult for those types of institutions to accommodate people with 'mental illnesses'. Once again, it is not that psychiatrists had a body of knowledge about how mental illness works, but rather that by the exclusion of these groups from communal society and their placement in asylums for the first time psychiatrists have the possibility to view the cause of mental illness independent of their manifestation in any one individual because they can now see the range and the commonalities across cases.

In analysing criminal justice systems, Foucault (1979) asks how we move away from a situation in which punishment is physical and centred on the body, in which, for example, the person who commits murder of a king is hung, drawn and quartered. How do we move from this to a situation where, in later times, somebody who commits murder would be imprisoned for life? How is it that we have moved between two very radically different types of meting out social punishment? The answer is that it is to do with other changes that are going on in society. In early accounts of public executions, the soldiers guarding the accused would be facing inwards toward the execution scaffold so as to stop the prisoner escaping. But later, and increasingly, those soldiers were facing outwards to stop the crowd rescuing the condemned person. This was to do with the kinds of crimes that came to characterize early industrial capitalism, crimes in which the poor were stealing from the rich. The mob surrounding the condemned person might actually be feeling a good deal of empathy with the accused who had stolen from the rich man. Public executions then became untenable because of the potential to make popular heroes out of the condemned people, and to provoke public unrest.

The whole notion of the prison is no longer focused on punishing the body but on punishing the soul. Prison revolves around surveillance and reform, and indeed the architecture of prisons is based on this notion of reforming criminals, so that they no longer want to commit crime. One of the ways in which that is achieved is by constant surveillance. Observation holes into prisoners' cells ensure they can never fully be private, that they are always under constant watch. The architecture of prisons, in which the internal courtyard of landings within the prison offers a good all round view of what is going on at any one time, ensures that prisoners can never escape the watchful gaze of the warders and are always under surveillance, in the hope that they will repent and reform (Foucault 1979).

Now, from the point of view of the relationship of power and knowledge being the flip sides of the same coin, something interesting is happening here. One of the effects of the constant surveillance of prisoners, combined with the intimation that the causes somehow reside inside their heads, is that the intellectuals of the day began to build up a body of knowledge of what they thought criminals were like. In other words, the body of knowledge called criminology was brought into being. One of the things that emerges from this conception of the relationship between power and knowledge is a key Foucauldian concept, that of 'subject positions'. The concept of subject position represents a completely different way of thinking about individuals, and represents an alternative to any of the approaches we have covered in Chapters 2 and 3.

Positivists, subjectivists and critical realists are accused by Foucauldian scholars of having an essentialist conception of the individual as a human subject, as having a rather uncritical acceptance of the idea of the individual as a unitary whole. Instead of thinking of the individual human subject as being a pre-given starting point, we can look at the individual subject as being something that emerges from a set of conditions. If you think of a hologram, the hologram isn't anything in essence; it is only a particular intersection of beams of light based on power. So that it's only this particular constellation formed by the beams of light and of power that give a formation of something that comes to appear as the individual human subject. But it's not an essential pre-given human subject. It only emerges in particular ways, as a result of particular discourses. Imagine these beams of light making up a hologram, not as beams of light but as discourses. In other words, that the clinical human subject isn't something that is out there waiting to be discovered, it only comes into being as a result of the discourse made possible by clinics. The criminal is only there in the form that we know it because of the discourse of prisons. The person who is mentally ill is only there because of a particular discourse of psychiatry emerging after the historical development of asylums. So in Foucauldian terms we have what is referred to as anti-essentialist notions of the subject and from that anti-essentialist notion of the subject we have the development of something called subject positions, which are positions, or types of identity, available to a particular person that they can take up in any given situation.

Imagine that we have a circle of people. They throw a ball of string across the circle to one another until they make a network between them. Imagine that the string represents a series of discourses and all the individual subject is, is the node where the strings intersect. Within that particular discourse, individual people only have a limited number of possibilities. They cannot be in the gaps between the string, because there is no foothold; if they situated themselves there they would simply fall through. The particular subject positions that are available to them are the nodes of the intersection of this string as they cross one another.

There are only certain subject positions available to the person to take up within that particular discourse. For example, in the MacPherson Report (1999), consider the position of the overtly racist white youths who were required by law to attend the inquiry into the murder in 1993 of the black teenager Stephen Lawrence. They were questioned about several instruments of violence found in their homes. This was against a backdrop of records of their conversations in which they were documented as stating their willingness to commit extreme violence against minoritized ethnic peoples. When a barrister suggested to one that the only plausible reason for the domestic possession of a claw hammer was to inflict violence against others, the youth had two possible subject positions, each equally implausible. Either there is an alternative (with the implication that any subsequent suggestion will sound ridiculous) or there is no alternative (with the implied suggestion that they own weapons of violence in a context of their expressed willingness to inflict violence against Black British and British Asians). The reply given, 'I don't know', was the only one that would not further implicate the group in the murder of Stephen Lawrence. In fact it is

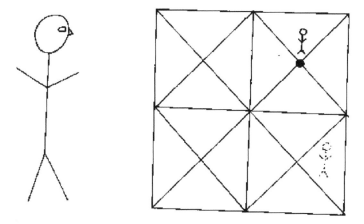

Figure 4.1 A representation of the Foucauldian concept of subject positions

an example of what Potter (1997) has called 'stake innoculation'. Making any statement entails staking a claim. But staking a claim means that you can be held to account for the logical consequences of that claim. 'I don't know' is a way of insulating yourself from counter accusations, because you evade making any specific claim in the first place. The youth happens upon the one course of action that does not further incriminate him.

Now this notion of the anti-essentialist subject and the subject positions is very crucial to the analysis that takes place in Foucauldian type of research. If we go back to our essentialist subject who has a particular identity and a particular set of ideas we can apply this to a professional–client encounter. If a client says different things to that professional on different occasions, then the essentialist analysis of that variation is to say this person is either lying, being inconsistent, being an unreliable observer, or else they are somebody whose testimony cannot be trusted. In other words, in traditional professional thinking, there is an assumption that somewhere there is a single true person with a consistent joined-up, rational, unitary set of beliefs. This has sometimes been called the 'honest soul' theory of persons, as if they were characters in a TV adaptation of a Charles Dickens novel (Potter and Wetherell 1987). Furthermore, to the extent that that person doesn't present an internally consistent account, an essentialist view of humanity is that this inconsistency represents irrational or even bad behaviour. On the other hand, if you take an anti-essentialist's view of the human subject, this moves us to a situation in which variation in a person's presentation of beliefs and views is almost inevitable. Here people are expected to take up different subject positions available to them contingently, depending on their particular circumstances and situations.

Traditional analysis of taped interview data could be called an essential-ist view of the subject. In other words, there is an assumption that what people say in their speech to people being interviewed is somehow a repre-sentation of (1) some inner held belief, inner held stable unitary identity at the core of their essential self, or (2) an external event. On the other hand, with the anti-essentialist's conception of the subject we expect as the norm for there to be variation, we expect people to take up different subject positions contingently based on their particular situation and on what subject positions are available to them.

Anti-essentialist research: accounting for oneself in a diabetic clinic

As an illustration of how an anti-essentialist conception of the human subject can not only aid our understanding of the social world, but may have applications to professional practice, we are going to examine a study of outpatient diabetic clinics. In the extracts that follow, the mother (M) is attending the clinic with the doctor (D) on behalf of her daughter who has diabetes. The two extracts are from different parts of the same encounter.

Silverman (1993) argues that the doctor makes an implicit charge against the mother's parenting and the mother rejects the charge. The mother suggests that her daughter is not conforming to her diet unless she is pushed. The doctor, argues Silverman, *topicalizes* the word 'pushing'. Topicalizes means to draw atten-tion to it in a manner that implicitly suggests the mother is the one taking responsibility for her daughter's behaviour, when perhaps it should be the daugh-ter. The implicit 'accusation' the mother hears is that she is not developing in her daughter an appropriate sense of independent responsibility for her behaviour. The mother then backtracks and almost contradicts herself by suggesting she now respects her daughter's autonomy and leaves her to be independent. The second extract is almost a mirror image of the first.

In this extract the mother suggests her daughter is not sticking to her diet. The doctor produces what Silverman calls a 'hearable charge' against the mother, this

---

Box 4.1a Accounting for oneself in a diabetic clinic (1)

M: She's going through a very languid stage ( ) she won't do anything unless you push her

D: so you find you're having to push her quite a lot?

M: mm no well I don't (. . .) I just leave her now

(Silverman 1993: 121)

Box 4.1b Accounting for oneself in a diabetic clinic (2)

M: I don't think she's really sticking to her diet (. . .) I don't know the effects this will have on her (. . .) it's bound to alter her sugar if she's not got the right insulin isn't it? I mean I know what she eats at home but   [outside

D: [so there's no real consistency to her diet? It's sort [of

M: [no well I keep it as consistent as I can at home

(Silverman 1993: 122)

---

time that she is not taking enough responsibility for monitoring and controlling her diabetic child's diet. This time the mother adjusts her account to state she *does* take responsibility for monitoring at home – her specific domain – but cannot be blamed for what happens outside her control outside home.

An essentialist analysis of these two extracts would focus on the manner in which the mother is apparently contradicting herself and might regard her as unreliable. However, an anti-essentialist approach recognizes that the mother is merely responding contingently to two opposite charges against her, that she is not promoting independence (extract 1) and that she is not monitoring tightly enough (extract 2). Silverman (1993) argues that this has very real practical applications: talking through the extracts with doctors shows them how their line of questioning places the mother in an impossible position. Doing the same with the mothers helps clarify how our society puts carers in the double bind of being responsible for monitoring child behaviour on the one hand, whilst being responsible for nurturing them to be independent. This dilemma is deep at the heart of our culture and not necessarily a failing of the individual parent.

Ethics

Now, for the final part of Foucault's trilogy let us go back to our earlier diagram that we used for symbolic interactionism in which we said, here are two masks, two selves in the world which are related to each other but there's an inner self and this symbolic interaction of selves in the world is also transforming our ideas of what we ourselves are.

The ethics part of Foucault's tripartite theory concerns the relationship between our subject positions in the world and our own conception of who we are. Our own conception of who we are doesn't have to be an essentialist one, either; it can also be one based on different subject positions that we could take up. What Foucault is talking about in terms of ethics is our

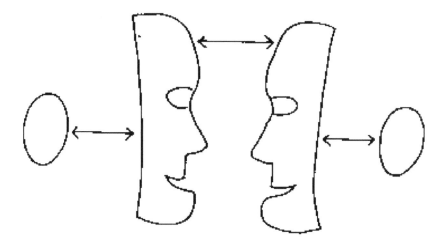

Figure 4.2 Technologies of the self

relationship to ourselves, what he terms 'technologies of the self'. What we have said so far about subject positions can also be applied to our sense of who we think we are. Now, one of the things that derives from the externally orientated subject positions is the concept of risk. The idea of risk becomes quite central to social life because, if there are several potential subject positions each with their advantages and disadvantages, which could be taken up at different points in time, then social interaction is about making decisions with regard to risk because when you take up one subject position, you gain some advantages but you risk losing others. If you apply that to the relationship between ourselves and our internal subject positions of who we could be, then within each of us we find not one stable unitary identity, but the potential to have many identities with many facets. Indeed, sometimes it is difficult to know which subject position to take up in particular situations, and this challenge can be associated with a chronic uncertainty and uncertain identities.

This realm of ethics which Foucault identifies concerning ways of relating to ourselves has generated concepts like 'governmentality' and 'governance'. The Foucauldian phrase governmentality means 'having the mentality to be governed'. In other words, one way of running society is through the kind of social power exemplified by the absolute state, where power is enforced by physical terror and extreme physical punishment meted out directly on the body. By contrast, a different and arguably much more successful way to rule is to persuade people to govern themselves. Rather than having to rely on extreme violence against the body of anyone who has committed stealing, one persuades people to accept that it is wrong to steal and to recognize that not to do so is for the public good. It involves getting people to willingly submit themselves to certain restrictions. Clinical governance in the NHS involves getting health care professionals to willingly submit themselves to restrictions, for example over their choice of treatments. But as well as their practice, this kind of initiative has implications for how they come to see themselves. There is, in a sense, a 'clinical governance of the soul' (Brown and Crawford 2003). This involves their taking on new roles and responsibilities and remodelling themselves through programmes of professional development and training, acquiring research literacy and spending time digging out evidence about treatment effectiveness. There is, in other words, a new mindset which these kinds of policy initiatives seek to promote.

Let us consider some of the implications of this for research. One kind of influence on the research process can be seen if we go back to the notion that Foucauldian scholars are interested in discourses. This might involve attempting to discern the dominant discourse, but also identifying which other potential discourses have been suppressed. Thus we can begin to see how they might regard a traditional positivist research report. In other words, if we take a statement like 'a questionnaire was distributed and 86 per cent of respondents agreed that they were satisfied with the treatment at the outpatient clinic', a Foucaldian approach would not only involve being interested in the dominant discourse, but would begin to try and pick out or look for clues about discourses that have been suppressed. They might be interested in examining questions such as what we mean by phrases like 'a questionnaire was distributed'. In other words, did someone give it out with a smile to people face-to-face at the clinic or did they do it before, during or after the end of that person's treatment process? These are lots of other possibilities. In other words, they would explore the unsaid in the research report. They would be interested in the way in which traditional positivist research reports try to tie everything up in a neat bundle and report a particular viewpoint. They accuse positivists of hiding away some of the processes which have constructed the data.

To illustrate this, Cuff *et al.* (1990) refer to the Pompidou Centre in Paris. One of its famous characteristics is that, in contrast to a traditional building, its architect acknowledges how the building is produced as a building, as a functioning building. A building is produced by a combination of light, heat, power and so on. In a traditional building, the electric wiring that powers the light is hidden away behind the walls either behind panels or plasterboard. The pipes that lead into the radiators are hidden, perhaps tucked under floorboards or in ceiling areas of the room. In other words, the processes upon which the production of the room depend are hidden away at the end of that process. So the room is 'produced' without acknowledging explicitly the conditions of its production because we hide away certain features of that construction. By contrast, the Pompidou Centre makes an architectural feature of many of these types of elements that go into the construction of the building so that the electrical wiring is carried around in brightly coloured red steel tubing and the gas supply in yellow tubing and the water supply in blue tubing and those tubes run around the exterior and the interior of the building making very clear, making explicit, bringing to the fore, the conditions under which that building has come to be produced as a building.

The Foucauldian notion of the production of research is to accuse traditional positivist research of doing exactly what a traditional room has done, which is to hide away the conditions under which the research was produced and not make a feature of the research report, the conditions of that report's production. Foucauldian scholars want to know why certain aspects of the research process are chosen to be hidden away and others chosen to be brought to the fore; what it is that the positivist authors are trying to achieve by choosing to hide some things and choosing to amplify other aspects of the process of research production.

Researching power and subjectivity in care homes

To illustrate the ethics part of Foucault's research, we turn to the work of Scott Yates (2002), and a Foucauldian discourse analysis of the experiences of people with learning difficulties in community care homes. Yates examines how people position themselves in terms of being in care homes, how they talk about their own subject positions they need to adopt when being looked after by care staff.

When the resident in the care home is talking about herself in a relatively

---

Box 4.2 Ethical stances to oneself in a care home

'When there's a staff shortage in the kitchen I love to go in the kitchen, but you *cannot* do that

[. . .]

'I want to go and buy them something but you *cannot* do that; it's not your place, it's the staff's place to go out and buy things

[. . .]

You see you *cannot, cannot* (1.0) you *cannot* throw out what's good without the staff's permission'

(Yates 2002: 186)

powerful position, or in a position in which she is anticipating a degree of autonomy, she uses the first person pronoun, 'I'. Hence *I* would love to go into the kitchen when it's somebody's birthday (in order to make them a cake); *I* want to go and buy them something (a birthday present). But when she talks about restrictions, she switches and she uses the pronoun 'You'. But she doesn't mean 'You' as in the interviewer, because he is self-evidently not a resident in the care home. By 'You' she effectively means the old-fashioned pronoun 'one'. The pronoun one can be used in the sense of: one mustn't do that, one mustn't do something without permission. But of course that's a fairly archaic way of speaking and in everyday language we use the word 'You', as in, You have got to go to your lectures whether you like it or not – it means one has to go to one's lectures whether people like them or not.

And so the care resident switches pronouns. In doing so, she is effectively referring to a subject position, which is that when 'one' is a disabled person in a care home, 'one' is not allowed to do that, anyone in that position is not allowed to do that. Referring to this subject position (this is the way things are in care homes and anyone has to conform to that restriction) implies other, different subject positions, positions that might not be found as discomforting.

In a sense what this person is doing is governing herself in terms of ethical relations to herself. She has learned the rules of the game, learned to restrict what she does even though she does not like it. It is a good illustration of Foucault's contention that power creates particular subject positions and that power itself is not necessarily bad but that it is always dangerous. But because it is always potentially dangerous it is always necessary to question it and, in this instance, one might want to examine it and say that is an unnecessary restriction. Note, however, that in terms of actually generating the data there is not very much that has been done differently than if someone were perhaps conducting a grounded theory type of interview; it's tape recorded, it's qualitative, it's as open-ended as possible but then the analysis is executed in a very different way. The philosophical positions these differences in analysis imply are summarized in Table 4.1, page 77.

Researching the community

When he was writing about prisons Foucault referred to a particular architectural design called the Panoptican which enables the warders to keep inmates under constant surveillance. For Foucault, what is interesting is that if you look at the architecture of asylums, of prisons, of public schools and of barracks, they show those same characteristics; they are all about keeping the inhabitants under surveillance.

Armstrong (1983) extends this notion of surveillance, or to use the

Foucauldian phrase, 'the gaze'. Foucault uses the phrase 'the clinical gaze' to describe the way that when live bodies are brought into the clinic as people they are made amenable to the clinical gaze. Armstrong refers to something he calls the Dispensary which describes how this medical gaze is extended out into the community, rather than the pure clinical subject who is brought into being in the health clinic. This extended gaze in terms of community health focuses not on bodies, but on relationships between bodies. In other words, community health focuses not just on the individual body but on its relationship to other entities, family members for example, or to the environment. We can see this concern in issues such as STD (sexually transmitted diseases) contact tracing, or environmental pollution and asthma. So it is now not only a gaze that is focused on the individual clinical body, it is focused on the social body, bodies in their social context. And thus we see the emergence in medicine of epidemiological and survey methods. Having brought the body into the clinic and established a clinical version of what diseases are, we are now moving back out into the community, looking at the relationships between bodies and extending the gaze to look at relationships, to look at people and their environment, and using epidemiology and social survey strategies.

The ultimate in the extension of this surveillance is, ironically, the in-depth interview. The limitation of the epidemiological survey is that you extend this surveillance, this gaze, to look at people in the community, but you do so within the researcher's own frame of reference. In imposing their framework onto the people in the community the researchers may only get round answers to their square questions, as it were. A subjectivist researcher might conceive of the in-depth interview as not imposing a framework on subjects, but rather letting them express themselves in their own terms of reference. But for Foucauldian analysis, the depth interview is the ultimate of the extension of surveillance because it's getting people to do the work for you. It's getting people to survey themselves, to chart for researchers their innermost thoughts, feelings and relationships. It is, in a sense, confessional, with the domination coming from the one who listens and says nothing (Foucault 1978: 61–2). The research participant, then, maps themselves out in a particular way at the behest of the implicitly more powerful interrogator.

During the eighteenth century the unruly 'mob' was an urban grouping, made up variously of people we would now call criminals, people who were illiterate, people who were unemployed, disabled people or people we would now call mentally ill. What might seem extraordinary to us nowadays was that to policy makers of the time they were undifferentiated, they were just 'the mob'. In his various texts Foucault draws our attention to the way in which we move from an undifferentiated mob of population to a situation where that mob is brought into various institutions. The nineteenth century saw the progressive drawing in of such peoples to institutions which themselves were at first undifferentiated, often in the form of workhouses. But eventually out of those early institutions come developments that begin to sort that mob out into different groupings like those severely learning disabled, for whom we now have residential care homes; people with mental illnesses for whom there were asylums; people who were criminals for whom there were prisons; people who were illiterate for whom there were schools. Thus, policy makers, philanthropists and charities were undertaking a programme of creating large institutions. Many of these institutions share similar characteristics: asylums, prisons, certain types of schools, certain types of army barracks. By contrast, in the latter half of the twentieth century with the movement away from large institutions, surveillance has been extended out into the community. So in parallel with the closure of long-stay mental hospital beds, we see the development of hospital at home initiatives, care in the community and assertive outreach. Equally, criminological initiatives like tagging and antisocial behaviour orders attempt to regulate the conduct of people who have been identified as problematic once they are back out on to the streets and away from institutions of the judicial system.

A further parallel in terms of crime and health is the way in which we have moved from a focus on those who are ill, or who are committing crimes, to those who potentially do so. So in the field of health the emphasis is increasingly not on those who are ill but those who might become ill if we do not implement preventive medicine, if our programmes of immunization fall short, if we fail to undertake health education, if we don't examine patterns of illness in relation to epidemiological patterns of where sick people are in the community.

A significant new field into which this has been extended in the health domain is the notion of genetic risk, involving the study of people who are not ill themselves but where they or their children potentially could become so. It is possible to see parallels to this in the field of crime, because not only do current initiatives address people who have committed crimes but there is surveillance of everyone through CCTV (closed circuit television), ostensibly to try and get at those who might commit crime. In addition, we have criminal profiling and risk assessment in order to try to establish which people might commit crimes, and community profiling in order to try to establish people who might become ill.

Our final example from the field of post-structuralism is the work of Donzelot (1979). Donzelot provides a very useful theoretical tool for anyone involved in community health or community criminal justice. One approach that the Foucauldian idea of anti-essentialism makes easier is that, rather than taking social institutions as a fixed starting point, you look at how such institutions result from, or arise out of, other trajectories of power relations and discourses. In other words, a conventional approach might involve taking 'the family' and then move on to look in terms of social policy or family therapy at how we are going to work with 'the family'. Usually the way that it happens is to assume that the family is a married heterosexual couple, living in the same household with their biological children. Then, having taken that for granted as the starting point, we might look at how other situations, families and households vary from that supposed essence of a family. By contrast, what Donzelot says is rather than start with a family as a taken-for-granted starting point, let us look instead at the relationship between the state and individual.

For example, a Victorian family might typically have the patriarch, the male head of the household through whom the power of the state is transmitted down to the women and the children of the household, dominating the family, not only economically, but if necessary by violence. The state backed that patriarchal position up with the force of law. The power of the state impacts directly onto women and children via the patriarchal head of the household. Donzelot argues that women escaped this oppression of patricharchy in the early twentieth century by being themselves co-opted into public surveillance roles in new state inventions in health and education arenas. Middle-class women were able to escape from the patriarchal family by taking on roles in primary education, health visiting and community health in which they were acting as the eyes and ears of the state in making sure that young children, when they went to primary school, knew how to toilet and feed themselves as well as learn to read and write and become socialized citizens. Health visitors went out into working-class communities in the 1900s and lent scrubbing brushes and cleaning materials to working-class women to try to ensure that they brought their children up in a clean environment, and made sure that they got milk supplements at the emerging infant and mother welfare clinics (Smith 1979). One factor that terrified the British state was their inability to obtain healthy recruits for the Boer War and later the First World War. Many recruits were not physically fit because of the general living conditions of the working classes. So it was out of a desire to have a fit military fighting force that the young male working class of the country were much better fed and brought up. And it was largely middle-class women who filled those roles in primary education and community health. Their escape from the patriarchal family was to have their own waged income, but only by being co-opted by the state to be their eyes and ears in terms of the surveillance of the health and education of the community. This kind of role is, arguably, still a major part of the profession of health visiting (Peckover 2002).

Thus, rather than seeing families as a starting point, Donzelot sees the family as a particular network emerging from power relations between the state and individuals. This is a powerful approach that could be used to analyse contemporary family arrangements because it does not rely on assuming a norm and documenting departures from that norm. We can look at how relationships between men and women have changed due to the availability of housing, new employment patterns, Marie Stopes's clinics, and access to contraception and divorce. Financial arrangements such as child benefit and other welfare payments have also created new relationships between the state, the individual and the family. All these factors lead to different social patterns and power relationships. If the child benefit is paid to the mother she is perhaps in a relatively more powerful position to leave a violent man than if she was entirely dependent on any income coming through that violent man. Thus, Donzelot's perspective provides some fresh insights into the nexus of relationships which exist between the individual, the family, other larger scale institutions and the state itself. In this way we are able to reconfigure insightfully what we mean by the family in relation to social analysis.

Policing the family: health visiting and the public surveillance of private behaviour

In order to appreciate more thoroughly Donzelot's insights into the family, let us explore further the role of health visiting in 'policing the family'. These ideas were applied in a study of the role of the British health visitor in the twentieth century by Dingwall and Robinson (1993). The health visitor for most of that century visited homes with a particular agenda concerning the health of infants and children under 5. As well as basic cleanliness and nutrition this agenda included vaccinations and surveillance for possible child abuse. Health visitors have certain rights of entry to an individual's home to ensure this role is fulfilled. This contrasts with the situation in the USA where the individual home has more legal protections against surveillance from public officials. Dingwall and Robinson note an important consequence of this contextual difference in the place of public health nurses between the two societies. The power of the British health visitor to secure access to homes for surveillance is certainly a form of Foucauldian power, and as such is 'dangerous' from the point of view of the family members. One need only think of children 'wrongly' taken away from parents who are under suspicion of child abuse. Power produces that particular reality. The health visitor gaze throws light on squalor, disease and poverty and brings it into public consciousness, so that it cannot be ignored. Thus such power, although *potentially* 'dangerous' to families can produce important knowledge, namely that in industrial capitalist societies some households live in such poverty that it compromises the well-being of children. Without such power the health visitor cannot survey, and the relative squalor and degradation is more likely to continue, as in the USA. The dangerous power of the health visitor produces positive knowledge about social conditions. The relative power of the US householder permits the persistence of squalor by rendering it private, hidden away from the searchlight of health visitor power.

The British context changed in the late twentieth century when a system of 'community profiling', in which health visitors were encouraged to adopt demographic measures to establish which types or groups of families were likely to be at risk of poverty and disease, came to the fore at the expense of the home visit. This illustrates a further Foucauldian principle, and that is that change is not progress, but merely the exercise of a different type of power. What is lost in the move to profiling is the emphasis on bearing direct witness to appalling social conditions, and, as such, profiling permits the return of squalor behind closed doors, and the decline of the health visit reduces the exercise of the very power that shed direct light on the household-level consequences of deprivation. This questioning of the automatic assumption that society is making 'progress' is a characteristic of the tradition to which we turn our attention next, namely postmodernism.

Postmodernism

Postmodernism may be understood as a reaction again modernism, or at least the characterization of modernism by postmodern thinkers. The rather caricatured version of modernism they criticize consists of those naïve versions of critical realist theories which talk about how things could be different and how there are underlying structures generating society, but which do so in a very crude, mechanistic and all-encompassing way. For some Marxists it might appear that everything in society can be explained in terms of the relations and forces of production. For some feminists, everything that goes on in society can be explained by the gendered order of society in which all men are all-powerful at all times. These kinds of viewpoints could be multiplied across a variety of interest groups and concerns.

Such all-encompassing theories postmodernists call *meta-narratives*. Meta-narratives are grand overarching theories that try to explain everything. They tie everything up together with no acknowledgement of any counter-trajectories in the argument. Postmodernists refer to these as *totalizing fallacies*, trying to explain everything without any recognition of counter-currents.

However, in terms of how postmodernists actually conduct research, you would not find very much different in the actual techniques used. They would tend to favour ethnographic strategies in which they undertook detailed qualitative fieldwork (including tapes of how people stake claims in conversations with each other, as well as how they do so in open-ended interviews with the researcher) and examined the text of documents, including what one might call low-status documents. In traditional documentary research the focus has been upon what one might call high-status documents, such as policy documents, medical/nursing records, or historical accounts that are written by the powerful, like politicians. Bannister *et al.* (1994) look at an example of low status documents, namely the instructions on a tube of toothpaste, for what those instructions tell us about the relationships between health professionals, parents and children. Postmodernists would frequently use discourse analysis in analysing taped conversations, depth interviews or documents, and would examine how and why people take up particular subject positions.

To the extent that postmodernists would characterize what they do as 'research' at all, many would emphasize the importance of reflexivity, articulating how you yourself construct the data. There is a value in putting your agency, your human activity as a researcher back into the research process. Thus it is no longer a case of 'a questionnaire was distributed', but it becomes 'I chose to do this in this way, here are others ways I could have done it but this is the particular way that I did it and I think that it had this particular impact on the kind of data that was created.' Because positivistic research reports suppress or silence these elements, postmodernists are also interested in what they call 'interrogating the silences' in existing research reports, by asking 'what could they have said that they didn't say?' The philosophical positions that this emphasis on language implies are outlined in Table 4.1 (page 77). A useful way of looking at more traditional research is to examine why the authors have left certain things out, why it is in their vested interest not to open up a particular element of reflexivity in their work. This process of asking what could have been said and wasn't, or why it was said in one way at the expense of another, is part of the process of what postmodernists call deconstruction, to which we shall return in Chapter 10.

For the moment, however, let us note that deconstruction is the means by which postmodernists try to analyse dominant discourses, and try to discover what the rhetorical linguistic tricks are that are used to legitimate claims of privileged insight or authority to speak on certain matters. To illustrate this process of deconstruction let us consider the work of Fox (1991) on the evaluation of health care.

Postmodernism, rationality and the evaluation of health care

When confronted with a 'text', whether this be written or spoken, postmodernists are interested first of all in identifying the subject position, then working out what its logical opposite is; again what could have been said but wasn't. Then the analysis proceeds to the 'negation of the negation': nothing is ever completely untrue, a dilemma is never 100 per cent black and white; there are always slight counter-currents going against the major trends identified. So the analyst might then be interested in how it is that the subject position denies its opposite. How does it explain away, cover up, or deny any relevance of those counter-currents? How does it negate the opposite of what it wants to argue? If you can expose a convincing case of why it is that the particular discourse, the particular subject position is denying its opposite, or is suppressing its alternative discourses, you have effected a deconstruction or an explanation of what is going on.

Fox (1991) uses the postmodernist technique of *deconstruction* in examining the relationship between clinicians and managers in running operating theatres. He starts by explaining the difference between formal rationality and substantive rationality. Another expression that you can substitute for formal rationality is calculability – being able to be calculated. For example, if you look at the emergence of the possibility of capitalism as a world order, this phenomenon depends upon a certain degree of predictability or calculability – that if you do one thing certain other things are going to happen. Thus you can only expand trade if you have got a pacified territory. In other words, you can't set off as a market trader from one end of the country with your cart filled up with goods unless you can be relatively certain that you are going to get to the other end of the country without having had all your goods stolen by bandits. In the age of steam trains, you can only successfully conclude business between London and Bristol if you know that you are going to be working to the same time. So, gradually, free market trade was facilitated by an increase in formal calculability or formal rationality. We could be relatively more certain that if we go and see a doctor they will give us the treatment that we need. Formal rationality is the predictability of a relationship between the means and ends: if I go and see a doctor I'll get treatment. It is that kind of predictability or being able to rely on something happening in the future.

Substantive rationality on the other hand is a form of relationship between means and ends which depends on having a particular type of goal. Substantive rationality is a more localized rationality which depends on a particular immediate vested interest, on having a particular goal. A group of people regard something as desirable because they have an aim, a desire that is particular to that group. Doing something then becomes rational in the restricted terms of meeting the needs of that very localized goal. Striving to achieve this localized goal may result in a great deal of wider unpredictability, particularly if we are unaware of what the goals of that local group, and of other localized groups, are.

Fox (1991) is interested in how the process of managing operating lists in a hospital, which ought to be predictable, actually comes to be very unpredictable. The reasons for this, Fox argues, are the local rationalities that the clinical surgeons work with on the one hand, and the very different local rationalities that others such as nurses and managers work with on the other hand. Fox analyses the different discourses of the two groups by means of a deconstruction. This consists of the following stages:

Position: By examining what they say when being observed or interviewed, the researcher identifies the position or viewpoint being advocated by the group.

Negation: However, no position or claim is ever totally black and white. So the researcher asks what is the opposite claim to the one being implicitly supported by the group, because the opposite must always have something going for it.

Negation of negation: Because the group recognizes the negation but wishes to assert their position, they have to come up with ways of neutralizing the power of the opposite argument to their position. In other words they find a way of negating the negation.

Deconstruction: By working through these steps, the researcher reveals what the local rationality is that the local group are trying to advance. They are trying to get their own way, but what does their own way consist of?

Fox (1991) applied this approach of deconstruction to the tensions between surgeons and managers in an operating theatre of a hospital. The tension revolves around who should be the legitimate arbiter of how long operations should take. The doctors argue that they should decide since each patient is unique and only they are qualified to make clinical judgements. However, and in contradiction to this position, the reality is also that different patients requiring the same operation have many similarities. The doctors try to deal with this counter-claim by arguing that the only patient who matters is the one they are currently operating upon. Fox concludes that the situation they are trying to maintain is one where their claims about professional responsibility are used to help them keep control of the organization of their work.

By contrast, the managers argue that having set routines enables better planning in the operating theatre, so operations do not run late and are not cancelled. This sounds fine, but the reality is also that people have real anatomical differences that mean some operations do take considerably longer than others. The managers try to deal with this counter-claim by insisting that it could be resolved by planning ahead. Fox concludes that the managers are trying to maintain a situation where they control the flow and pace of work, by claims that their way benefits the whole team including the nurses and operating assistants (see Box 4.3).

Any resolution, claims Fox (1991), can only be forthcoming if the claims of each opposing discourse are laid bare and made explicit to the other.

Conclusion

In this chapter we have tried to illustrate a third analytical dualism, between essentialist and anti-essentialist views of the human subject. Rather than seeing the human subject as a single, rational, unitary and consistent whole, anti-essentialist approaches (such as Foucauldian and postmodern approaches) emphasize that humans may be different things to different people in different circumstances. Different discourses help create and make different subject positions potentially available.

Box 4.3 An example of deconstruction

The local rationalities of clinicians in the operating theatre (OT)

Position: Uniqueness of patient requiring clinical assessment.

Negation: Patient is not unique but one of many.

Negation of negation: No patient other than the one in the OT is important.

Deconstruction: Clinicians use professional responsibility as a means of organizing their work to their advantage, and to legitimate disruption.

The local rationalities of managers and others in the operating theatre (OT)

Position: Surgical routines enable the smooth running of OT.

Negation: Surgery involves uncertainty because cases are different.

Negation of negation: Planning ahead can ensure surgical routines are not disrupted.

Deconstruction: Surgical routines contribute to job satisfaction and create a discourse of teamwork which benefits lower levels of a hierarchy.

(Adapted from Fox 1991:736)

Indeed, the analysis that we have given in Chapters 2 and 3 can itself be thought of as a particular type of academic discourse, in which a particular, one could say modernist, viewpoint is advanced. The postmodernist could argue that the dilemmas of ontology and epistemology represented by empiricism, subjectivism and scientific realism in the 'field of possibilities' (Table 3.1, page 34) is itself a discourse, brought into view as if projected onto a cinema screen. As such it is potentially dangerous and requires interrogation to see what possibilities have also been closed down.

Table 4.1 A comparison of the characteristics of postmodernism and Foucauldian approaches

	FOUCAULDIAN	POSTMODERNISM
What? (Ontology)	Discourses	Researcher-as-creator
How do we get to know? (Epistemology)	Power/knowledge	Only from historically and culturally specific vantage point
How do we know we know? (Methodology)		
Internal validity*	Archaeology of knowledge. There is a truth not *the* truth.	Language produces meaning in ways writer/speaker cannot control.
Reliability*	The researcher is an instrument of power creating a particular disciplinary discourse. Power is always dangerous, and should be interrogated. The researcher should not speak over and for the research participants.	Researchers writes self into the research process and accounts for their own role in the construction of knowledge.
Generalizability*	External validity is a topic of enquiry, not an external reference point. Generalizability is a feature of modernity in that the surveillance of populations, the identification of norms makes possible delineation of the norm and therefore the domain of social becomes amenable to study in that the similarities and differences between the social individual and the individual population can be mapped.	There is no universal truth – all knowledge is relative and local.
What practical methods or techniques are used? (Methods)	Analysis of discourse (Parker and Burman). Genealogical enquiry.	Analysis of texts, deconstruction, discourse analysis (Potter and Wetherall).

* These terms are themselves usually introduced in the context of positivist science. As such one would expect them to sit more comfortably within positivism than within any of the other traditions. Nevertheless, interpreted more broadly than within a positivist framework, they arguably represent domains of the research experience that all researchers can, and perhaps should, be able to reflect upon.

Further reading

For examples of applied research drawing on Foucauldian insights, see:

Bloor, M. and McIntosh, J. (1990) Surveillance and concealment: a comparison of techniques of client resistance in therapeutic communities and health visiting. In S. Cunningham-Burley and N. McKeganey (eds) (1990) *Readings in Medical Sociology*. London: Routledge, 159–81.
Brown, B. and Crawford, P. (2003) The clinical governance of the soul: 'deep management' and the self-regulating subject in integrated community mental health teams, *Social Science and Medicine*, 56(1): 67–81.
Heaton, J. (1999) The gaze and visibility of the carer: a Foucauldian analysis of the discourse of informal care, *Sociology of Health and Illness*, 21(6): 759–77.

For a postmodern approach to research see:

Fox, N. (1993) *Postmodernism, Sociology and Health*. Buckingham: Open University Press.

5　The values of thinking and doing

Introduction

At this stage, we are going to revisit all the different approaches that we have considered so far, and re-examine them in the light of a key issue in social research. This issue is objectivity. To what extent can and should social science research be objective? The answer may seem obvious. It should be completely objective. However, the concept of objectivity contains two distinct but related ideas. First, what is the relationship between the research process and the degree to which the researcher is detached from the subject matter of social research? Second, what is the connection between the research and moral and political values? As we will see, the different working resolutions to debates about materialism and idealism; nominalism and scientific realism; and essential and anti-essential views of the human subject result in different approaches to the issue of objectivity, and with it the place of the researcher and their values in the research process.

The value positions of positivism

We can start our review of values and research by returning to positivism. Positivism has two key problems that it is trying to address in terms of not distorting what it perceives to be the relationship between the researcher and reality. The first of these conceptions is mind independence. Mind independence is that aspect of positivism that proposes that the world is 'out there' irrespective of what we think of it. Independent of the internal constructs of the social actors, there is a real material world that the researcher can observe and discover.

The second factor that positivists subscribe to is the notion of value freedom, of attempts to be value-free in research. In other words, the researcher ought to be interested in the scientific truth that can be revealed to them through well-conducted research, and not in advancing their own preferences, their own moral and political interests in terms of their own social values. You can see that notion of value freedom in the work of the psychologists Hans Eysenck and Arthur Jensen. Both advanced claims that intelligence is largely inherited, and that significant differences in levels of intelligence, as allegedly measured by IQ tests, could be distinguished across different 'races'. They stood by their claim when fascists used such arguments in court in an attempt to justify their racist behaviour (Billig 1979). Although they expressed regret that their science might be used by people to justify social disadvantage, they maintained that what they were doing was reporting the objective truth, and that what people made of that information was not their concern as scientists. It might be their concern *as citizens*, but it wasn't their concern *as scientists*. This is perhaps the most infamous example of positivist science attempting to distance itself from any social consequences of its claims to knowledge.

However, there are other ways of thinking about the relationship between science, truth and politics. In this chapter we are going to examine some of the objections that there have been to two key tenets of positivist thinking, mind independence and value neutrality.

Objectivity: mind independence and value neutrality

Mind independence is the idea that the world exists out there irrespective of our internal constructs. The way that this influences research is, first, that for positivists evidence can only count, things can only exist, to the extent that that they can be apprehended by the senses. For example, we can observe a situation, or we can hear an account, or we can read what somebody has reported in a questionnaire: in each of these examples, we have the evidence of our senses to rely on. In other words, positivists do not allow as legitimate research concepts things that cannot be grasped in some way by the senses. The extreme version of this view is called 'operationalism'.

Operationalism is the view that indirect measures not only give a rough approximation to the concept being measured, but that the operations that comprise the measurement actually constitute that phenomenon (Brown *et al.* 2003). Positivists disagree with pure operationalism because, first, concepts cannot be completely reduced to what measures them, and second, understanding this lack of fit between scientific concepts and attempts to measure them is itself the stuff that scientific endeavours are made of (Brown *et al.* 2003). Nevertheless, positivists make use of a less extreme notion, operationalization, based on the belief that there is a reality independent of the (fallible) indicators we use to measure it.

Positivists argue that in everyday language we use a number of terms, some of which are too loose to be accorded scientific status. What we need to do is to tighten them up, to express them only in terms of indirect indicators that we use to measure the phenomenon.

For example, if one were to take a positivist approach to looking at the relationship between health and class, both health and social class would need to be operationalized because neither is an immediately observable, apprehensible concept. We cannot directly measure 'health', so we would need to turn it into something that could be measured such as premature death rates, number of visits per year to the GP, or number of sickness days off work. These three operational definitions, premature death rates, sickness absence returns, or GP visits are measurable in a direct way that the concept 'health' is not.

Similarly, social class as a concept is not directly measurable. To operationalize that term, we might look at factors such as level of income, or scale of ownership of certain types of amenities (such as an indoor toilet, or access to a refrigerator or a bathroom that doesn't have to be shared with other families). In such ways positivists would try to turn more theoretical concepts into factors that can be directly measured. They would also try to emphasize inter-observer reliability – in other words, can different observers or researchers undertake the same piece of research and obtain similar results? These are some of the practical aspects of positivist research that flow from their notion of mind independence. In assessing the extent to which there is agreement in observing the real world, positivists sometimes refer to so-called 'competent observers'. This seems to us to represent a circular argument in which 'competence' is reserved for those who agree with the judgements of positivist scientists!

Let us now turn and consider the other strand of this objectivity, and that is the concern of the positivist scientist to conduct value-free research. This second strand to objectivity, value freedom, is to insist that science can explain what is the case, but not what should or ought to happen. To illustrate this, we can refer back to our example of the alleged relationship between intelligence and different ethnic communities. The example of intelligence and 'race' seems to us to involve a chain of argument that goes something like this: science has discovered a factual relationship, but because it is politically inconvenient or controversial does not make it any less scientific. Nor does it tell us how we should respond to this (alleged) scientific fact, for that is in the realm of politics. Science provides you with the objective truth, warts and all, and what's done with this scientific information is another matter.

More sophisticated versions of value freedom in research have also been produced. Hammersley and Gomm (1997) have argued that recognizing that the production of research is dependent upon the social position of the researcher does not require that the researcher give up the aim of objectivity. They also propose that a research community is likely to be relatively more sceptical in examining truth claims if the primary objective of research remains avoiding presenting as true that which is false, in other words value neutrality in research. Hammersley (1995) has further indicated a belief that such terms of reference for a research community help to keep it relatively autonomous from the state and other political interests.

Romm (1997) has countered that Hammersley and Gomm do not consider views on knowledge construction which try to form relationships that do not privilege particular ways of accounting at the expense of others. Lather (1991) contends that research processes can make a difference to the lives of others by changing their conceptions of possibilities for seeing and acting. Romm (1997) therefore charges researchers with a responsibility to provide others with maximum opportunities to develop constructions and choices.

However, if we examine more closely what claims for value freedom entail, we can see that positivism has smuggled into its rhetoric some hidden political values of its own. Value freedom implies making a sharp distinction between the political aims, the ultimate ends or goals of what we are trying to do, how we are trying to run society. As a scientist, the positivist absolutely cannot comment on these political aims and goals. Positivist science cannot comment on the legitimacy of political or moral goals, only on the means, on what, if we want to achieve these goals, is the best way to accomplish this? If, for example, we want to look at boosting the IQ of children in low-income areas, what is the best input to achieve those ends? So positivists argue that they can always comment on the best technical way to get to a particular goal (science) but not whether that goal is the goal that we should be striving for (values and politics).

What's wrong with mind independence?

Let us turn to some of the objections to the positivist notion of objectivity. In this section, we examine counter-arguments to that strand of objectivity that we have termed mind independence. Now Karl Popper, who is sometimes misidentified as a positivist, actually spent a good deal of his work criticizing positivism. If we were to try and characterize his own stance, we might describe him as a sophisticated empiricist in the sense that he is aware of the problems of naïve empiricism, he's aware of the problems of positivism but he is still ultimately working with notions of objective science. His way of dealing with more theoretical concepts is to say that of course we use these in everyday work, and even in everyday science. Let us try to illustrate our understanding of this position. For example, if we are talking about concepts such as 'health', 'class' and 'the state', then what we are actually doing is using concepts as shorthand labels for a collection of real experiences. In other words, when we talk about 'the state', there isn't really such an entity as the state, or when we talk about market forces, there is no ultimate foundation to this concept. It is not as if a market force literally creeps up on you around the corner and touches you on the shoulder and says, 'hey now you are unemployed'; there's no reality in that sense. The status attributable to those concepts – health, class, the state, market forces – is just one of labels, they are merely names, hence the term nominalism. They are merely names or labels by which we conveniently sum up more complex realities. And whilst that may be good enough for everyday talk, if you are going to produce a social *science*, then you need to do better than that, and you need to 'operationalize' these nominal terms, to turn them into something measurable.

The second broad set of objections to mind independence comes from the subjectivists, in particular the symbolic interactionists, and is encapsulated in the Thomas Maxim: 'If people define situations as real, then they are real in their consequences.' In other words, internal constructs, meanings, motives, perceptions, understandings have real consequences, and to that extent this viewpoint represents a stark challenge to the notion that it's only a world out there, a reality external to us that has consequences. In particular it draws our attention to the role of the researcher in *creating* the research setting, and in entering into human relationships in the course of research that will inevitably evoke variable emotions, reactions and responses from the research participants. Consider, for example, the social context of a research interview conducted in the home of the respondent.

> In all research, the researcher's place in this social context (including of course their role in contributing to the creation of that social context) demands to be thought about critically. Since access to research situations have usually to be negotiated in some form or other, and to the extent that research subjects are not passive 'respondents' but actively try to create the terms and conditions of their participation in research, then the *research process* is always far more extensive than the data collection itself. Take, for example, an in-depth interview. How is the interviewee 'discovered'? How is the interviewee negotiated with prior to the interview? Does the interviewee discuss the forthcoming interview with others, and if so whom? Do these discussions include anyone else who has been or is due to be interviewed as part of the same research project? Where does the interview take place? If the interview takes place in the

interviewee's home who else is present when the interviewer arrives? Do they leave the room at their own instigation, at the request of the interviewer, at the request of the interviewee, or not at all? What questions/ demands does the interviewee make of the interviewer? How is the exit from the interview negotiated? What opportunity, if any, does the interviewee have to comment on the transcript or the research report itself? How does the interviewee give their account of the interview to others?

(Dyson 1995: 11)

The positivist stance to such concerns is either, first, to intervene in ways to attempt to impose some uniformity on the processes or second, not to acknowledge these processes at all and thereby not question their taken-for-granted assumption of the integrity of the research design in their own terms. A different approach would be, first, to acknowledge these contextual factors as inevitable features of the production of research; second, document them so that they are visible to the external inspection of the reader of the research, and third, estimate the direction and the degree of the effect of these researcher–researched relations on the research knowledge produced.

Next, we turn our attention to the types of objections to mind independence made by ethnomethodology. Ethnomethodologists would take the view that rather than seeing reality, or social life, as being out there and objectively knowable, what we need to do is to understand the practicalities by which people achieve the taken-for-granted activities of their social life. In Chapter 2 we talked about natural experiments of Garfinkel in which his college students went home for the vacation and acted as if they were lodgers in their parents' house. By challenging usual assumptions, what they were able to demonstrate is the hidden rules of how we actually every day create and recreate our social lives. In other words, we don't normally think about our relationships between teenage children, parents and household activities. But you can very soon demonstrate, argues Garfinkel, that we are actively achieving and re-achieving this sense of family or household because if you do something different, it very rapidly exposes the rules that were there previously, rules that we had not consciously brought to the forefront of our minds. You could then apply that notion to researchers and ask, how do social researchers practically achieve that taken-for-granted process we call research? Or, to put it more crudely, how do researchers 'do research'? In other words, could you reveal the rules of how researchers 'achieve' research by a similar natural experiment? For example, you initiate the interview by saying to the respondent, what would you like to ask me?

In terms of mind independence, this draws our attention to the way in which researchers need to be self-conscious, because in conducting research they are constructing and reconstructing these practicalities by which we understand the process to be research. But of course if they are doing that, if that creative achievement is constantly there in the production of research, then that is very different from a notion of a researcher simply going along and apprehending objective reality.

In Chapter 4 we briefly mentioned the post-structuralist approach. We referred to the metaphor of the Pompidou Centre in Paris (Cuff *et al.* 1990). Remember that if we look at an ordinary room, all the factors which help to create the room as a living achievement and working environment are hidden away from view. In the Pompidou Centre those factors are brought to the fore; machinery is encased in see-through materials so that the workings of the building are made a feature of the design. Apply this design idea to the research process and the post-structuralists are arguing that the manner in which you create the research data needs to be part of the research design and brought to the fore. Factors such as how different stakeholder agendas contribute to the research designs, how researchers interpret their brief, how access is negotiated and denied, how 'respondents' answer back, the emotions of the researcher in conducting the research, the effects of social distance between researcher and researched in terms of relations of gender and ethnicity on the creation of data – all these are crucial to the production of knowledge. We might turn these factors back onto the positivist scientists and ask why, if objectivity consists of laying bare to external inspection the processes of research production, much applied research chooses to ignore these issues.

Finally, in the terms of scientific realism, we do need to allow for the production of knowledge concepts which are unobservable, which are never going to be directly apprehendable by the senses. Scientific realists take the view that, just because you cannot directly apprehend a concept or a process does not mean that it does not have real consequences. Furthermore, they argue that if you change that process it will have consequences for other parts of reality, parts to which we can't immediately see any direct link, but about which one can make suppositions. These suppositions are based on the belief that there is a link between different parts of reality, because if you change one thing, something else (which does not appear to be linked when merely observed), changes. So there are various different objections to the positivist conception of mind independence.

What's wrong with value neutrality?

We turn now to a series of objections to the other aspect of positivist objectivity, which is the strand of value freedom – the idea that science can and should be neutral in moral and political terms. The first two criticisms render the conception of value freedom slightly more sophisticated but are not challenging its fundamental assumption. First, Weber (1989) argues that there are values in science because we choose to research one subject rather than another. In choosing these topics, we have implicitly asserted our moral and political values. There is a sense in which we might be held to account as therefore saying that they are more interesting, more important or more valuable than other potential topics or subjects we might have researched. So Weber argues that there are inevitably values in social research, but they are about which topic you prioritize and select, and once you have made that selection and decided that that is what you are going to research, then it is possible to conduct value-free social research.

A second refinement of the initial position is suggested by Popper (1979). Once more it is not really a fundamental challenge, since Popper accepts the possibility of objectivity, but argues that it cannot be achieved at the level of the individual scientist. Rather it is only a possibility at a collective level, by virtue of being part of a scientific community. Of course, individual scientists have moral and political values, but for Popper the possibility of being objective and detached and neutral isn't solely to do with the individual integrity of the researcher. The researcher is, after all, human and fallible. Rather, the possibility for objectivity comes from the scientific community as a whole. Individual researchers may put forward their ideas in papers, in conference proceedings and in scientific seminars. In doing so, they expose their views and data to the external scrutiny of their peers in the scientific community. Precisely because data, ideas and theories are exposed in this way to others, then those other members of the scientific community can scrutinize research and identify any unintended moral and political values that have been incorporated into the research process. It is the rest of the scientific community who can guarantee scientific objectivity because they are the ones who will look out for the biases in the work of other scientists. So for Popper objectivity and, as part of that, value freedom is only a *collective* possibility of the scientific community.

The arguments of both Weber and Popper represent slightly more sophisticated versions of value freedom, but not a fundamental challenge to the possibility and desirability of value freedom in social research. We then need to move on to objections to value freedom which are a much more fundamental departure from the assumption that science can be detached and neutral. A number of these derive from the development of the ideas of Karl Marx.

Marx argues that capitalist economies are divided by class interest, the have and have-nots, and that in such unequal societies our understanding of how society works comes to be distorted, or indeed deliberately falsely represented to us, by the powerful. There is something about the material reality of economic and material inequalities that means that, first, we don't have equal access to an understanding of how things are working. And second, that, partly as a consequence of that, some groups are able deliberately to hide the workings of how society is operating away from other groups. This is where we derive the notion of what Engels called *false consciousness.* False consciousness is a situation where those who are the victims of the workings of inequalities in society don't realize that they are those victims, and falsely believe that their interests are served by the continuance of the status quo. The particular way in which Marxists would criticize positivist social science research is that it tends to fragment reality by studying it in separate compartments. This is most apparent in their rejection of collective entities, and their pursuit of measurable variables. This mindset of fragmenting reality can be seen in the use of variables in experiments, or the way in which 'indicators' are employed in questionnaire research. It can be seen in the manner in which positivists take broader complex holistic concepts like social class, the state, or health and break them down into measurable indicators that are not necessarily related to one another. Marxists develop an argument in which they point out that positivist social science tends to fragment reality by studying it in separate compartments and, in doing so, prevents people connecting local experiences to an understanding of broader social processes or the social totality of what is going on.

An example might be positivist research documenting an association between the rates of smoking of white mothers living on income support and low birthweight babies (McKnight and Merrett 1986). The research links two variables of particular group and particular type of social activity, but from a Marxist's point of view this misses the point. The women are undertaking unpaid labour in producing the workers of the future for a capitalist economy, and cigarettes are a commodity within that economy. As we saw in Chapter 2, cigarettes are a way of dealing with pressured child care, they are a way of coping when you deny yourself any other luxuries because of your economic situation. They are a way of putting up two fingers at all the nosey professionals who want to change your ways either because they don't understand the kind of conditions that you are living in, or they do, but see smoking as worsening these conditions, or because they realize advice will not compensate for material structures, but have little else in the professional repertoire to offer. The wider social relationships and the connections between them would constitute the more total social experiences that Marxist would be interested in. They would therefore argue that a study which looked at simply the relationship between the mothers' smoking and birthweight of babies is not neutral research, but very biased research indeed, because it fails to make those broader explanatory links.

Luckács (1971) further develops this idea through his concept of reification. One widespread example of reification is the manner in which commentators refer to the 'dictates of technology' (see Box 5.1).

Reification consists of the argument that technology dictates that we must use new machines or new technological processes and not, for example, use the hundred people that it took to carry out the work

---

Box 5.1 An example of reification: the (alleged) dictates of technology

Advancing technology dictates a more flexible worker, capable of adapting to rapidly changing tools and willing to acquire broader and deeper knowledge.

http://www.purdue.anderson.edu/tg.htm

For example, the logic of the technology dictates in some industries that standards be established.

http://www.ivey.uwo.ca/operations_courses/b474.htm

Our rapidly expanding technology dictates that engineering will continue to become increasingly involved in all branches of medicine.

http://www.asu.edu/provost/smis/ceas/bse/essbse.html

All accessed 18 March 2004

---

previously. However, Luckács argues that such thinking is *reification*. Reification means treating a given set of social circumstances as if they are natural and inevitable. Reification means giving a set of social arrangements a degree of concreteness, a degree of fixedness, a degree of inevitability which they don't have or don't deserve. For example, consider the case if there were an all-encompassing cleaning machine that one could set to work at one end of a hospital, and that would robotically work its way through the wards and scrub them antiseptically clean. This *could* mean you needed only that machine, and an engineer to repair it, and not the hundred cleaning staff. But is it a dictate of technology that we use that machine rather than the hundred cleaners? An example of reification would be to say, well of course one must use this machine. We must keep up with the modern world, technology is dictating the pace of change and people must simply get used to it; people must modernize or die. We have got to drag the health service into the twenty-first century. But all these kinds of assumptions, Luckács would say, are reification. There is no reason that simply because this machine exists we have to use it. We are human beings, we have choice in our social arrangements. We might decide that it is more important for patients to have the informal benefits of being able to talk with cleaners on the ward because other health workers are too busy to converse with patients and listen to them at any length. We might in any case decide that the social consequences of throwing those hundred cleaners out of work and having them unemployed in society, with the social dislocation, mental distress and physical hardship this would cause to them and their families, is a worse outcome than spending more than we might on cleaning hospitals. So to say that certain changes are fixed or inevitable is reification, and a frequent fault of positivism, argue the Marxists.

Furthermore, the language and the discourse that is used in relation to that reification amounts to ideology. In other words, to say that *of course* we must use this new all-purpose cleaning machine, and *of course* we must modernize the health service: these types of discourse would be regarded by Marxists as simply ideology. In other words, not only is it treating what could be different as inevitable but it is then wrapping it up in a particular discourse that makes any person who then challenges that discourse seem unreasonable.

Our third variation of the Marxist critique comes from Habermas (1978), who introduces the notion of what he calls *distorted speech communities*. Habermas argues that, in terms of any kind of democratic debate about how we wish to organize our social arrangements, how we wish to organize our health care, that debate between different people and different social groups is not conducted on an equal footing. Wherever there are power relationships between bosses and workers, men and women, white and black people, or indeed any axis of social differentiation where disparities of power are involved, we don't have a fair and equal debate. In situations of unequal power, we don't have a speech community in which everyone genuinely has an equal voice. Consider the case conference where a multi-disciplinary team of health and social care professionals meets with parents to discuss the needs of a disabled child. The professionals have access to technical knowledge, knowledge of processes, language of discussion or techniques of argument, resources of status and money, institutional frameworks of support in ways that most parents do not. Habermas would argue that under those circumstances you cannot have genuine democratic debate. Instead what you have is a distorted speech community, because the less powerful frequently have to think that they must take this power differential into account in what they say, and do, and think that they must not upset those upon whom they have come to depend for services. Under those circumstances, Habermas argues, you cannot have genuine dialogue and genuine science. Curiously, this brings Habermas close to another thinker with whom he has little else in common, and that is Popper (1945), who sees freedom to criticize as an integral part of both democracy and the pursuit of scientific truth.

Ill fares the land: the hidden values of technology and science

The fourth set of objections to the claims of value neutrality also derive from the work of Habermas (1978), but we will illustrate them through the work of George (1986), who works on issues concerned with world poverty and development. If we go back to the positivist position on neutrality in research, we can see that asserting the possibility and desirability of neutral research effectively draws a distinction between *ends* and *means*. In other words, science cannot tell us about the ends or goals of society but it can tell us about technically what is the best way to achieve our declared goals. Habermas (1978) takes that means/ends distinction and argues that positivist science is biased science because it hides particular political values in trying to draw that distinction between ends and means. The two hidden political values are those of technical efficiency and élitism. Let us look at each of these in turn. The means/ends distinction hides within it, argues Habermas, this value of technical efficiency. Let us turn again to our example of the hospital cleaning machine. If one could buy that machine for half the cost of the equivalent labour, one could show that it was more 'efficient'. However, this implicitly values, or even glorifies, first, technology over human beings, and second, technical efficiency. One might well ask: why isn't technical efficiency a good thing? But one has to ask, technical efficiency for whom? Is it a good thing for those hundred cleaners who are made redundant? Is it a good thing for those patients who only encounter machines, rather than the friendly cleaner who might possibly pick up a need and alert a health care assistant?

George (1986) argues that our value on concepts like technical efficiency comes from a particular historical point in time and a particular cultural setting. This setting is the United States in the nineteenth century, as wagon trains rolled across the Midwest, taking in ever increasing portions of land. Under those historical circumstances there are huge swathes of land and very few people (at least if you discount Native Americans). Under those particular, perhaps unique, social, historical and cultural circumstances you get the development of the importance of technical efficiency. With few people and much land, it makes sense to develop technology as a solution. That technological solution culminates a century later in combine harvesters that reap grain across vast expanses of wheat fields. In other words, technical efficiency works well and seems appropriate for a society where you have lots of land and few people.

By contrast, George argues, let us look at the situation in developing countries. In such societies what you have is very little land per head of population, but many people. In such societies, if you introduce technically efficient, mechanized agricultural machines, you also throw thousands of people out of work. You deny the majority of the local population access to land to grow their own crops. Thus, technical efficiency is a political value pertinent to a particular historical cultural context. When you transfer it to different historical and cultural contexts it is an imposition of a particular political value. There are several other examples that George gives. She documents how the imposition of regional steel grain silos, as opposed to clay storage pots owned by individual peasants, renders whole regions vulnerable to famine if infestation strikes the 'technically efficient' steel silo. She documents how 'technically efficient' crops, with more grain but less straw, destroyed the local peasants' source of bedding and secondary source of income, leading to mass deaths from freezing and starvation. She documents how the imposition of 'monoculture' (a single uniform strain of a crop) to enable harvesting by machine prevents 'intercropping', the peasant practices of sowing varieties of crop and complementary second crop between the main crop, leaving them vulnerable to starvation if the monoculture fails.

To return to Habermas, we can see how the argument that technical efficiency is a political value, and not necessarily a good thing, makes sense. Technical efficiency may have societal benefits in a limited range of specific circumstances, but to regard it as obviously, naturally or universally a 'good thing' is ideology.

The other value that is hidden within this means/end distinction, argues Habermas, is the value of élitism. Implicit in the idea that society must decide the goal but then scientists tell us the best way to get there is the notion that only scientists should be able to debate and influence technical decisions in medical and health research. Habermas argues that this line of thinking is élitist because it is fundamentally anti-democratic. It is akin to saying that we'll let the scientists develop scientific techniques but ordinary members of the general public never actually get to decide whether scientific money should be spent on this or that initiative. The democratic majority is excluded from debates about directions and priorities of science. So Habermas argues that the positivist's distinction between means and ends itself hides at least two moral and political values. The hidden values of positivism are technicism (glorifying technology over human relations) and élitism (privileging the views of technical experts over the democratic majority).

Whose side are we on? The hidden values of liberalism

Becker (1967) has provided what for many is the definitive case for the place of values in research working within a broadly subjectivist framework. Researchers from various subjectivist traditions have in common a tendency to listen to the voices of those who are in subordinate positions. Such researchers listen to the accounts of patients (rather than health professionals). Becker points out that by choosing to take seriously the narratives of the less powerful in any given situation, a researcher is effectively *challenging the hierarchy of credibility*, that is the prevailing assumption that it is the more powerful person (the doctor, for example) who has the overview and thus deserves to have her views taken more seriously. If we listen to the voices of the more powerful, we are less likely to be accused of bias. This is because, first, 'everyone knows' doctors are supposed to know more about health than their patients. Second, patients are generally widely dispersed, not in contact with one another, and not politically organized as are doctors. They are less likely to hear negative accounts by doctors of patient behaviour, nor are they likely to be in any position to effectively challenge such accounts if they do. In listening to the voices of doctors, we are being biased (listening to one side rather than another), but the political nature of this bias is less likely to be challenged or exposed for what it is, since the researcher is uncritically accepting the prevailing hierarchy of credibility. By contrast, in listening to the subordinate, the patient, we are implicitly upsetting the view that 'doctor knows best' and we are more likely to attract the charge of political bias in research precisely because doctors are networked, organized, and have resources to marshal their views.

The resolution that Becker (1967) proposes is that it is inevitable that researchers will implicitly be taking sides, since they cannot simultaneously study all superordinates and subordinates, as doctors may have more powerful consultants to whom they must defer, and consultants more powerful Royal Colleges above them. Whoever we study there will always be a more powerful group who complain that their view has not been taken account of. All researchers can do, suggests Becker, is study the underdog, the less powerful, state that the limitations of the research are that it sees the world through this perspective and field the complaints of political bias from the more powerful.

Hammersley (2000) has offered a reanalysis of Becker's original article. Hammersley argues that Becker's study of the production of research knowledge suggests researchers will always be accused of bias. Indeed, research that shows how the powerful lie to maintain their positions and research that may confirm the validity of the views of the subordinates will have the consequences of being politically partisan in its effects. However, argues Hammersley, that is not the same as an advocacy of the abandonment of the use of impartial methodologies and techniques to try to ascertain the scientific truth. However, Hammersley's position (Hammersley and Gomm 1997) amounts to a defence of the idea that communities of researchers are either the best or the only judges of what constitutes knowledge; as such this argument is itself vulnerable to accusations of incorporating élitism as a political value into research (see above, page 91).

Habermas (1978), too, has a problem with the values implicit in subjectivism. He argues that subjectivists who value the less powerful person's internal constructs – in other words, researchers who say, Let's listen to the underdog – are implying a value position. If we are to challenge the hierarchy of credibility, then is not one person's perception of the world just as good as the next person's? Should we then not give it equal value? The problem, Habermas would argue, is that the moral and political values implicit in subjectivism do not allow us to critique or differentiate in any way between different points of view and values. In other words, we are left without the possibility of criticizing constructs which might be associated with oppression, such as fascism or racism. This represents the ultimate problem of liberalism, which is that if you allow everyone to have freedom of speech, you end up in the position where you have to allow freedom of expression to those who would deny others freedom of expression. This situation of relativism is a problem for Habermas because such relativism is itself a moral and political value.

The science of human interests

Habermas (1978) further develops an argument in which he says not only is science itself involved in values but it can specify scientifically what *ought* to be the case. His argument is thus even more radical because he is saying that it is possible for science to develop a position in which it can specify what we ought to be doing morally and politically. More precisely, what he argues is that if we take our current distorted speech communities, we can say, well, women don't have quite the same equal voice as men because they are still only earning an average of two-thirds the wage for doing a similar job, and they are still the ones who disproportionately get left holding the baby, or who disproportionately can't walk freely through the streets at night, and therefore they still don't have quite the same equal voice, influence and power. But what science can do, Habermas argues, is to ask: what societal arrangements would we need to change to have equal economic status, equal family responsibilities, an equal freedom to walk the streets? So science can tell us, argues Habermas, what we *ought* to be doing in order to arrive at a speech community that is undistorted. Because it is only when you have an undistorted speech community that you have the democratic debate about how we want to arrange society. So the possibility of ever being able to have a genuinely democratic debate about how to arrange society is predicated on unpicking the distorted speech communities, and creating conditions in which there are undistorted speech communities. So perhaps it's not quite that science can tell us what to do, but it can tell us what we ought to be doing to create the conditions for an undistorted speech community to thrive, under which we would be able to have the democratic debate about how we want to arrange society.

The final objection to value freedom comes from Lukes (1974). If you recall from Chapter 3, Lukes argues that the first dimension of power is what we can immediately observe in, for instance, a public community meeting. The second dimension is what's going on in actuality, behind closed doors, in debates that happen in order to keep things off the agenda in the first place. The third dimension is the more difficult counterfactual thinking and asking: what would people want if they knew their own real interests? If their minds haven't been narrowed down by particular current social arrangements, if their desires had not already been shaped by existing social structures, what would people want? Without the insights of the third dimension of power, you might begin by asking what people want in terms of their health care. In response, they would probably tell you that they want the same, only they want more of it.

However, what Lukes would argue is that such science is biased science because you haven't taken account of the way in which people's perceptions of what is possible have already been constrained by current social arrangements. In other words, people are not likely to come up with the notion that what we need to do is throw the whole thing up in the air and completely re-engineer the way we think about health and caring for people. What they are more likely to think of is the current situation and what we need more of, such as more doctors, nurses and hospitals. Hence current social arrangements narrow down the range of possibilities that people are able to express, and unless we take this into account, we have produced a politically biased science of society.

Conclusion

In this chapter we have examined a variety of different approaches to two aspects of objectivity, namely mind independence and value freedom, and we have looked at the various different traditions and how they have criticized positivists for holding to this notion of objectivity.

Let us try and sum up at least four different approaches to objectivity. Remember that objectivity is made up of, first, mind independence, that is the relationship of the researcher to the researched. And second, it's made up of moral and political values, that is the relationship of the researcher's own moral and political views to the scientific truth.

For positivists, objectivity is about researchers remaining detached, objective and, in moral and political terms, remaining value neutral, not letting their own moral and political values and judgements influence the course of getting at the truth that is (allegedly) 'out there'. In contrast, for subjectivists who emphasize the role of human actors including researchers as human actor in constructing and reconstructing reality, the relationship of researchers to the researched has to be one of reflexivity, of constantly thinking about their role in the creation of this social situation. How has my position as a researcher generated the kinds of interview responses that I'm getting? The values of research are frequently about championing the less powerful in society and, in Becker's terms, challenging the hierarchy of credibility. In scientific realism, the researcher is creating data by developing theory. Here we have the notion, particularly of people like Hindess (1973), that observation is not free of theory, and if all observation is not free of theory then, logically, you can't test theory by data. This represents a radical critique of positivism and empiricism. If all data or facts are theory-laden, if there is a theoretical presupposition inherent in any observed empirical fact, then by implication you cannot assess theories by testing them against data. You can only test theories in terms of other theories. Only by developing new theories can you construct the conditions for the generation of new types of data. And the moral and political values are frequently about challenging the status quo. In Marxist terms this may be about unmasking the ideology that suggests that things have to be the way they are.

Finally the postmodernists, following Michel Foucault, emphasize the role of the researcher in creating data, of the way the researcher's research report is yet another discourse that is thrown into the melting pot, if you like. The values of postmodernism arguably can lend themselves to a form of relativism in which everybody's different discourse has to be regarded as equally valuable. Postmodernists themselves would perhaps not necessarily accept that their implicit moral and political values are about relativism, for relativism is itself a modernist concept and implies an even-handedness which is problematic in the same way as objectivity. Foucault has a notion that within any knowledge system, power is always there creating that knowledge and it's like an electricity supply – power is always dangerous, but whether it's oppressive or not is a matter which can only be resolved by looking individually in a particular context. So perhaps postmodernists would need to make contingent, in other words, localized, unique judgements depending on the circumstances. Their moral and political value stance would always be to interrogate power but not always to find against it.

A major limitation of all the conceptions of the researcher outlined in Box 5.2, and their position vis-à-vis the research participants and moral–political values, is that the researcher is referred to as an individual. But in practice, all researchers are either explicitly or implicitly linked into a broader community of researchers. In the next chapter we take up this situated nature of the researcher, and examine the consequences of belonging to scientific communities.

Box 5.2 Different approaches to the issue of objectivity in research

Positivism

Researcher: Detached

Values: Neutral

Subjectivism

Researcher: Reflexive

Values: Challenging the hierarchy of credibility

Critical realism

Researcher: Creates data by developing theory

Values: Challenging the status quo

Postmodernism

Researcher: Creates data via own discourses

Values: Interrogate power, but make value decisions dependent on context.

Further reading

Hammersley, M. (2000) *Taking Sides in Social Research: Essays in Partisanship and Bias.* London: Routledge. (A more recent and sophisticated defence of the principle of value neutrality in social research.)

Lukes, S. (2004) *Power: A Radical View*, second edition. Basingstoke: Palgrave. (In a new edition, Lukes engages with the writings of Foucault.)

A confederacy of dunces: science and scientific communities

*When a true genius appears on this world, you shall know him by this sign.
That all the dunces will be in confederacy against him.*

Jonathan Swift

Introduction

So far in the book we have examined three different tensions in making decisions about how one might conduct social research. One tension was between materialism (the world out there) and idealism (the world in here), and we have looked at positivism and subjectivism. A second tension that we have looked at is nominalism and scientific realism. Do you take things at face value, in other words do you restrict your knowledge to that which is observable, hearable, directly apprehendable by the senses either by observing or listening to people's own accounts of what they say? Or do you suppose that there are real structures generating the appearances? The third tension we examined was between essentialist and anti-essentialist conceptions of the human subject. And then we also looked at how the resolution of each of those tensions might produce different types of values in research from neutrality to challenging hierarchies of creditability right through to the realist's politically engaged values in research and the postmodernist context-dependent value judgements, listening to different standpoints and deconstructing different standpoints.

What all of our discussions so far have in common is that we have rather assumed that social research is conducted by a series of individual researchers. However, we can gain a different angle on the overall debate if we think about how research is actually conducted. Scientists, whether social or natural, work in communities, in academic or scientific groups, where people are not simply working in social vacuums. In order to approach this problem, we introduce what has come to be known as the Popper–Kuhn debate, a debate between two key thinkers in the development of philosophies of science.

What is this thing called social science?

The first question to raise is, what do we mean by social science? Can social science and social research be scientific in the same way that chemistry, biology and physics are generally considered sciences? The answer, to cut a long story short, is that it partly depends on what you mean by science.

To take us right back to the beginning of the book, you may remember that part of the tenet of positivism is that a social science can be scientific if it models itself directly on the natural sciences. In other words, if only social research could mimic the processes and methods of natural science then it would have successfully achieved the status of regarding itself as a legitimate science. However, if we think about what the general public might usually think of in terms of science, one might say that science is about white coated people in laboratories who are undertaking experimental procedures and applying methods, who are not letting their personal preferences get in the way of what is revealed to them about the natural world. We propose this as a 'common-sense' summary of how science operates.

Although there are arguments that both the natural and the social worlds comprise complex systems, and therefore have more in common than is widely assumed (Byrne 1998), our 'common-sense' summary does, we feel, carry the connotation that social sciences cannot be scientific in the same way. If we think of science in that white coated laboratory experimental way, it becomes clear that social research is not going to match up to the claimed ideal of natural sciences. The problem then becomes, how does one sort out types of knowledge which might qualify as scientific knowledge from types of knowledge which one might say are in the realms of subjective opinion and perhaps political opinion? This problem has come to be known as the *demarcation problem*.

Demarcation was a word much more used in the 1970s around industrial disputes, demarcation referring to disputes about who should do what, who should be allowed or required to carry out what job. Demarcation in this instance is a similar notion, except that it concerns how we demarcate the boundaries of legitimate science from subjective and political opinion, or if indeed such a distinction can be made at all.

Popper and the falsification principle

One of the key questions Popper (1959) addressed was what demarcates true science from pseudo-science. In other words, where can we draw the boundaries in terms of what is legitimate scientific knowledge and what is not? He starts by pointing out that there is a problem with the process of thinking known as induction. Induction is the notion of making a series of observations and gradually building them, from the ground up, to broader generalizations.

The example that Popper uses to illustrate an example of inductive thinking is to consider a series of observations about the colour of the feathers of swans. The inductivist makes a series of observations and says this swan has white feathers, so has this one, so has this one and so by building up that series of observations we come inductively to the generalization that 'all swans are white'. So inductivist notions of science would have it that science proceeds by building up generalizations from a series of observations.

But the problem with that, Popper argues, is that we can never be fully confident that we have achieved legitimate scientific knowledge, as the very next observation we make might contradict all the preceding ones. In other words, we might come across a swan with black plumage the 1079th time we made an observation. And so the problem with knowledge based on induction is that it can never fully prove anything to be true because it only takes one potential counter example in the future to undermine the argument and to say that the generalization now does not hold true. Hence, the problem with inductive thinking, according to Popper, is that it cannot leave us with genuine scientific knowledge because it can never fully prove that something is the case, but is always vulnerable to the next potential counter example.

From this problem Popper developed the principle of falsification. This can be recognized by the way in which many natural scientists have taken on this philosophical underpinning to their studies and now work with concepts like the null hypothesis in terms of conducting research. Experimental design consists not of proving that the research hypothesis is true, but in demonstrating that the null hypothesis is false. So the principle of falsification is based on the assumption that science proceeds not by proof, not by building up a series of observations in the vain hope of producing scientific generalizations. Rather it proceeds by refutation, by showing that something is not the case, by showing that certain statements are false. For, if you show that a certain proposition is false, you can assume that the opposite is true.

The falsification principle thus attempts to define the boundaries of legitimate scientific knowledge. The falsification principle states that a scientific statement is one which can in principle be shown to be false. In other words the very stark, dramatic, clear-cut claim that 'all swans are white' is a scientific statement to Popper because it is phrased in such a way that it is open to being shown to be false. It is very clear that if we come across a swan that has black plumage, as we might do in Australia, we would have shown the claim to be false. But what makes the statement scientific is not ultimately whether it is right or wrong, but rather that it is phrased in such a way that it has left open the possibility or the conditions under which it *could* be shown to be wrong.

We can try to understand the genesis of Popper's ideas if we consider the political and intellectual context within which he was developing his ideas. The characteristics of knowledge production that irritated Popper were the types of systems of thought that arose around Nazi Germany and Stalinist Russia, where scientists were right if their theories fitted the predominant political paradigm. It was this kind of thinking, where systems of knowledge developed so that they could never be wrong in principle, which heavily influenced Popper, and led him to come up with the falsification principle. For Popper, perhaps surprisingly, Karl Marx's original statement that 'there will be a revolution in advanced capitalist societies' is in fact a scientific statement. It is scientific because in the twentieth century it was shown to be false, for there was no revolution in advanced capitalist societies. The statement 'there will be a revolution in advanced capitalist societies' is scientific because within the statement itself you can anticipate what would disprove it.

However, later Marxists, argues Popper, make claims to knowledge that can never even in principle be shown to be wrong. For instance, the claim that there will be a revolution 'when conditions are right' does not contain within it any way in which you could show that statement to be wrong. As long as no revolution occurs, the Marxists just counter that, well, the conditions aren't right. 'There will be a revolution when the conditions are right' is not, according to Popper, a scientific statement because the statement contains within itself an eternal 'get-out' clause that can explain both the occurrence (the conditions are right) or non-occurrence of a revolution (the conditions are not right). So what Popper is trying to do is come up with a situation in which he can demarcate the legitimate boundaries of what constitutes scientific knowledge by establishing the falsification principle, establishing that one of the key tests of scientific status of a claim is whether *in principle* it could be shown to be false.

We can begin to see how Popper has influenced at least the rhetoric of much of contemporary health services research because the alternative to induction is what Popper calls the hypothetico-deductive method. He argues that science proceeds by a very general statement first of all, from which you logically deduce particular hypotheses or predictions about what will happen. You then test those particular predictions about what you think is going to happen in a series of specific instances. In the hypothetico-deductive method, the hypotheses are tested against specific instances, in such a way that they could, in principle, be shown to be false.

Kuhn and the structure of scientific revolutions

The major counter-argument to Popper's notion of how science works comes with the work of Kuhn (1962). This introduces us to a closer examination of how science actually works, rather than how scientists claim it works. A key concept that Kuhn uses is that of a *scientific revolution*. Kuhn (1962) claims that rather than science progressing in this small incremental, step-wise way, what happens is that things remain much the same for long periods of time and then there is something he terms a *scientific revolution*, a major shift in the way of thinking about things. This long period of continuity, where scientists all agree on the fundamental basis of their discipline, Kuhn terms a *paradigm*. The paradigm, this notion of scientists agreeing on the fundamental principles by which they operate their discipline and this long period of continuity, these flat plateaus, Kuhn refers to as *normal science*. Normal science is where all the scientists in the scientific community agree about what kind of solution ought to be found and what kinds of methods will find it. In a sense they agree about the rules of 'doing science'. However, during this plateau period, of continuities and normal science, Kuhn notes that there are ever-accumulating problems and factors that don't fit the paradigm. In other words, there are strange things that don't seem to be explainable within the ways of thinking with which the scientists are operating.

Now, those who have followed Kuhn (Gilbert and Mulkay 1984; Lynch 1985) subsequently make a distinction between idealistic notions of how a scientific community works, and how scientific communities actually conduct their work. In other words, not how the scientists themselves think they work, nor how they might claim to others that they work, but what they actually do, how a community of scientists conducts itself.

Kuhn argues that when faced with things that do not fit the dominant paradigm, scientists do a variety of things. First of all they assume that the paradigm works. In other words, they do not immediately say, This factor does not fit our rules, our ways of thinking. The overriding reaction is to fall back on the quasi-religious faith that their way of thinking 'works'.

Second, the scientists assume that any anomalies are due to mistakes in design. So if the scientists find what, according to their paradigm, they are not 'supposed' to find, then the explanation of events they advance is that their paradigm is correct, but that the methods used in the particular study must have been flawed. Subsequently there may be an increasingly frenzied search for methods that do indeed yield results that fit the predictions.

Third, even if the flaw in the methods cannot be found, the belief persists that the paradigm still works, and it is assumed that the explanation of the anomalies will be revealed later but in a way that still will ultimately fit within the paradigm. The scientists, argues Kuhn, develop modes of thinking as follows. Our results do not make sense, we are confident about our methods, we know of course that the paradigm works, so what must be happening is that there is something complex going on that will eventually be revealed to us by continuing experiments. These future results will not only explain why we got our wrong results but will confirm the ultimate legitimacy of the paradigm.

However, fourth, and perhaps most controversially, Kuhn argues that one of the reasons that people ignore factors that do not fit the paradigm is that it is in the interest of their own scientific career to ignore them. If you are a young scientist who wants promotion you do not question the professor's deeply held belief in her paradigm. If you want your papers published in the journal that top scientists edit, you don't write papers which fundamentally challenge the paradigm. If you want to obtain research grants from auspicious scientific bodies, then you don't step out of the dominant paradigm, in order to make sure you get the research grant. So in a whole variety of ways it becomes in the interest of young scientists not to rock the boat, not to fundamentally challenge the paradigm. However, what Kuhn argues is that eventually the accumulation of factors which disturb the paradigm becomes so great that there is a major shift in thinking in which the scientific community as a whole abandons the old framework, and moves on to a new paradigm.

So we have this period of normal science but anomalies increasingly seeming to question the paradigm until there is a major shift and most of the scientific community then move over and subscribe to the new paradigm and there is an abandonment of the old framework and adoption of the new one. And sometimes, argues Kuhn, that may only happen when the old generation die or retire, when they are no longer part of the scientific community and can no longer block the careers of other scientists.

There are two examples we would like to use to illustrate this notion of scientific revolution. A very good political example of this type of phenomenon is the occasion of the resignation of the British Prime Minister Margaret Thatcher in 1990. If you take Thatcherism as the paradigm that dominated the 1980s one might say that all her ministers subscribed, or at least they said they subscribed, to her political ideals. But gradually, through the late 1980s, she began to oversee the resignation of several of her key ministers, people who had previously been at the heart of the Thatcherite paradigm. At one point it had seemed that she was always going to be there; she was almost unchallengeable and the parameters were unchallengeable. Yet suddenly, when there was the challenge to her leadership, the aura of invincibility seemed to collapse very quickly. Suddenly many ministers who previously had been Thatcherites were lining up against her. And there was an abandonment of the support for Thatcher and a wholesale shift to a new order, lining up behind new leadership, when only a month or two before she seemed unquestionable and completely dominant.

The other example that we would like to draw your attention to is a piece of research from Festinger *et al.* (1956), a study called *When Prophecy Fails*, which was a study of religious cults who believed that the end of the world was coming. It is also an interesting study from a methodological viewpoint because Festinger and his co-researchers infiltrated a particular cult that believed that the end of the world was coming, attended their meetings and conducted covert participant observation research by joining in meetings. The devotees of the cult were arguing that the end of the world was coming, and occasionally there would be dates set for this to happen, and the designated dates would of course pass by. Here you have a parallel to Kuhn's notion of anomalies challenging the paradigm. You have a situation where you think that in 1960 the end of the world is going to come but of course 1960 comes and time marches on. So what happens to people within cults when anomalies arise that ought to shake the very foundations of their beliefs? What happens, Festinger argues, is that under those circumstances people do not, as you might expect, abandon their beliefs; rather they cling to them even more firmly. So the cult members who were disappointed did not suddenly stop believing in the principles of the cult; they held to them even more strongly and they explained away the continuation of the world by saying that it was because of the faith of their group that the world had been saved. Equally, other groups might say that the time must not be right, or something must be wrong: not that their paradigm was wrong, but that there must be other factors getting in the way of the paradigm working as it was 'supposed' to do. You can begin to see the parallel with Kuhn talking about scientific communities: that when things happen that ought to shake the very value system, the very paradigm of the scientists, what they tend to do is not to abandon their framework and acknowledge that it is wrong but to cling even more fiercely and protectively to it and explain away the anomalies.

The critique of scientific communities

The first critique of how scientists, social scientists and, by implication, contemporary health services researchers actually work is derived from the work of Kuhn who argues that the scientific world is shaped by social interest and not by evidence alone. This has important consequences for judging the quality of scientific and social scientific work. First, the language of scientific work can be understood as partly having a rhetorical function to persuade us to a point of view held by the authors. Second, the passive language of science hides the human agency of the researcher and makes it seem as if the natural or social world reveals itself to researchers, rather than that they work within theoretical frameworks. This type of argument about how scientific communities actually work can also be said to contribute to an overall criticism of positivism and empiricism.

A second example comprises one of many studies in which social scientists have joined communities of natural scientists and, on occasion, social scientists, and looked at not how they claim to do science, but how they actually do science. Such studies have conducted naturalistic ethnographic observations of how scientists in real laboratories actually work, and one such example is Lynch (1985). Lynch was looking at a psycho-biological laboratory in which they were studying the brain tissue of rats. The work of the laboratory involved taking the brain tissue of rats, slicing through a cross-section with a knife, staining that very thin cross-section with chemicals to amplify certain features and make them visible under the microscope, placing the slide under the microscope and then looking at the results. However, when they looked under the microscope at these cross-sections of the brain tissue of rats, the scientists found artefacts; they found features of the rat's brain that according to their paradigm 'ought not' to be there.

In studying how this community of scientists worked, Lynch was able to identify that they explained away such anomalies, just as Kuhn would have predicted. The paradigm suggested that certain features ought not to be there, so of course they must have done something wrong. The scientists 'knew' that the marks that were there, but that ought not to be, were due to either staining errors or to knife marks. The actual process of cutting the cross-section of the rat's brain had led to marks that then appeared on the slides: they weren't part of the rat's brain, but a consequence of the method that had led to the setting up of the process. However, interestingly, the scientists didn't examine their own lack of logic. The scientists did not treat as a problem of illogical thinking how the phenomenon that they were studying, the rats' brains, could be distorted by the very same technical procedures that made them observable. In other words, you can't look at a rat's brain just by taking it and holding it in your hand, so what the scientists were doing was working with certain technical procedures to make the rat's brain visible. Those procedures were cutting it into cross-sections with a knife, staining it with chemicals and putting it under the microscope. But how could the very same technical procedures which were necessary to reveal the natural world be revealing reality, but also distorting it at one and the same time?

The scientists resolved this conundrum in a very pragmatic way. They became concerned with practicalities. If there were marks there that there shouldn't be, did they have time to do another slide? Would the particular slide they generated be good enough to get into the journal; would it be good enough for publication? Whether or not the slide was accepted as legitimate knowledge became a process of the scientists discussing and negotiating between themselves. Therefore Lynch argues that 'scientific knowledge' is not just about scientists uncovering a naturally recurring reality that is 'out there' but scientific knowledge is based on the work of making judgements in the context of everyday social life in the laboratory.

As a more general conclusion, and a third critique, Giddens (1976) has argued that of course any scientific community, natural scientific or social scientific, is based on language and communication, so it can never be just about revealing reality. It can never just be about natural scientists finding the world out there. To apply it to the health service, it can never just be about the 'evidence'-based practice that is out there. Science is always about the particular community negotiating, based on language and communication, negotiating both within itself and with the outside world.

A fourth critique of the naïve conception of how scientific communities work is to go back to the famous metaphor introduced by Popper about 'all swans are white'. The problem, Giddens (1979) argues, is that if you had a group of scientists who were arguing that all swans were white, when they came across a black swan they wouldn't call it a swan; they would call it something else. In other words, the framework with which they were work-ing, which assumes that all swans are white, would lead them to miss the point. What they saw in the future would already have been shaped by their prior beliefs.

The fifth criticism comprises a piece of logical analysis from the philo-sopher Lakatos (Lakatos and Musgrave 1970; Lakatos 1978) who subjects the falsification principle to close scrutiny. 'The falsification principle is that something constitutes a scientific statement if in principle it can be shown to be false.' The problem with this statement, argues Lakatos, is that that statement is itself not falsifiable. That statement is not written in such a way that you could ever disprove the statement. Hence, argues Lakatos, the statement is itself not scientific and therefore we should not feel bound to accept it. Instead, Lakatos developed a notion of a more sophisticated falsificationism, in which the core of research programmes cannot be refuted by a single counter-example. The link between core or 'deep' scientific theories and concrete empirical tests cannot be made dir-ectly but involves intermediate level ('auxiliary') hypotheses. In this way, one cannot *isolate* a deep theoretical principle in such a way as to test it on its own. Moreover, since auxiliary hypotheses are linked, as if in a network, neither can a particular hypothesis be sufficiently isolated that it can be disproved by one empirical test. Thus scientific theories are not disprovable by one empirical counter-example (naïve falsification), but they may be so disconfirmed by cumulative examples over a period of time.

If we turn to the work of Silverman (1993: 201), he reports perhaps the most famous of all the sociological studies of how science actually works (Gilbert and Mulkay 1984). They were looking at a scientific dispute between particular groups of chemists and again they found very similar problems to those identified in the work of Lynch (1985). However, what they found was that in the discourses of science, the chemists used both Popper-like and Kuhn-like explanations of scientific practice. In other words, on some occasions the scientists would say, Well of course what we are doing is being neutral and detached and using the purest experimental method and of course we never let our moral and career interests get in the way of the search for the scientific truth. In other words they would talk in a discourse which clearly reflected the Popper account of how science works. On the other hand they would also have another repertoire of speech that they would sometimes use which acknowledged a position more aligned with Kuhn.

One way in which Gilbert and Mulkay identified that these scientists at least were aware of the Kuhnian notion of how things worked was that the scientists had a little joke list pinned up on the laboratory wall. On the left hand side of the list were scientific phrases from the Popper discourse, a typical phrase that you might find in an empiricist research report. On the right hand side of the list was a corresponding phrase which deconstructed the reality behind that claim. So an example might be 'Many competent observers have agreed that this is the case' (left hand side) and a corresponding joke 'A man in a pub told me' (right hand side), or 'These procedures were carried out with scrupulous attention to the accepted scientific method for this form of analysis' (left hand side) and 'I did it this way because my Professor told me to' (right hand side).

In other words, scientists themselves alluded to the Kuhn-like notion of how they were working. So the problem, for Gilbert and Mulkay, becomes slightly more sophisticated. It no longer becomes a question of merely exposing the fact that scientists do not work in a Popperian way in reality. Rather the problem becomes why it is that sometimes when you talk to scientists they will give you the Popperian version of how they perform their tasks and on other occasions they will talk to you in a more Kuhnian way in which they more readily acknowledge how social interests are affecting and guiding their research.

Confusingly, Gilbert and Mulkay's scientists used both quasi-Kuhnian and quasi-Popperian explanations of scientific practice. Understandably, however, they were much keener to invoke the Popperian ('sober refutation') account of how they worked and the Kuhnian ('community context') account of how certain other scientists worked.

Were these accounts to be treated as a direct insight into how scientists do their work or experience things in the laboratory? Not at all, at least in any direct sense. Instead this interview data gave Gilbert and Mulkay access to the vocabularies that scientists use. These vocabularies were located in two very different discourses:

- a 'contingent' discourse, in which people were very much influenced by political considerations, such as institutional affiliations, ability or inability to get big research contracts, etc.
- an 'empiricist' discourse, where science was a response to data 'out there' in the world.

Neither discourse conveyed the 'true' sense of science.

(Silverman 1993: 201)

Both the contingent and the empiricist discourses of science are situated in particular contexts. It no longer becomes a debate between whether scientists work in this pure Popperian way or whether they constantly let career interests and other factors shape the development of their knowledge. Rather, it becomes a problem of why scientists talk about their science in some instances in a Popperian way and in some instances in a Kuhnian way, and why they draw different discourses of different times and different occasions. For example, in dismissing the work of rival scientists, the scientists in Gilbert and Mulkay's study would react as follows:

For instance, factors adduced to explain scientific error include: failure to understand, prejudice, commitment to one's own theory, dislike of the new theory, extreme naivety, narrow disciplinary perspective, threat to status, insufficient experimental skill, false intuition, subjective bias, accepting the views of an authoritative figure, being out of touch with reality, personal rivalry, emotional involvement, general cussedness, being too busy, living in a country where theory is not popular, stupidity, pig-headedness, being American and therefore thinking in a woolly fashion!

(Gilbert and Mulkay 1984: 78)

Thus we have the answer to the question of why and when scientists invoke the different discourses. They use the 'contingent' discourse when they wish to criticize rival scientists; and they invoke the 'empiricist' discourse when they wish to assert the quality of their own work. We can see this switching between discourses if we examine sociological studies of scientists associated with the 'new genetics'.

The new genetics and flexible discursive boundaries

The work on mapping the human genome has been associated with large scientific grants in biotechnology, government support to exploit the potential commercial opportunities of genetics research, and media coverage of the claims of what has been termed the 'new genetics'. The work of Kerr *et al.* (1997) examines the claims of scientists associated with the 'New Genetics' and looks in particular at how the scientists talk, first, about their science, second, about how their place in society influences the production of scientific knowledge, and third, about how the scientific knowledge they produce is used by them to promote their place in society.

One image of scientists that the lay public hold, but which the scientists do not themselves like, is that they or the products of their work (GM crops or genetic cloning techniques) are, like Frankenstein's monster, out of control. For the scientists, this reflects the public's ignorance of technical scientific matters, for example ignorance of the technical aspects of genetics. However, as Kerr *et al.* (1998) demonstrate, people in the community have an embarrassingly good grasp of the Kuhnian version of science. They may not know anything about the technicalities of Mendelian patterns of dominant and recessive inheritance. But they do show awareness that, first, scientists have career interests to which they harness their scientific endeavours, second, scientists want to be feted for their achievements in the media and consequently sometimes make grandiose claims for the potential of their work and third, they do not involve communities in decisions about scientific direction or priorities and consequently some science seems pointless to the general public.

In their study of scientists from the field of the new genetics, Kerr *et al.* (1997) argue that scientists face the constant problem of how to maintain their authority in the public sphere, and that to preserve this authority science must be presented as objective and neutral, as akin to Popper's version of science. But as we have seen, both the scientists and members of the wider community know that science has a social context and is socially influenced, in other words akin to Kuhn's version of science. In the face of this knowledge, how do scientists construct their discourses to attempt to preserve their status as experts who can arbitrate on claims to knowledge?

According to Kerr *et al.* (1997), the genetic scientists achieve this through a series of discursive devices:

1 The genetic scientists attempt to draw a distinction between a micro-level where science operates in an objective, value-neutral manner uncontaminated by social context, and the broader macro-level where the direction and application of research are subject to social influences.
2 No definition is offered of the boundaries of this distinction. This means that the scientists can move the boundaries contingently, that is as it suits them, in each individual conversation to suit their purposes in that argument.
3 Thus, in some contexts, the boundaries are impermeable when the scientists wish to establish their right to speak authoritatively (because these boundaries have by definition to be impenetrable if their science is, in

their own terms, to be objective, neutral and uncontaminated by social factors).

4 However, in order for scientists to exercise this authority the boundaries have by definition to be permeable, so that scientists can assert their right to influence the course that society takes.

5 Thus the principles by which scientists seek to establish their authority and to exercise that authority are inherently logically contradictory.

6 The flexible boundaries of what influence society has on science can then be moved so that their own science is uncontaminated by social influence but those of rivals with whom they disagree is contaminated.

7 The flexible boundaries of what influence society has on science can then also be moved to take the credit for effects of science judged good by the public mood, and to distance them from any blame or loss of status associated with the effects of science judged bad.

8 The flexible boundaries, between allegedly pure uncontaminated science and science in its social context, enable the genetic scientists to take variable approaches to their own responsibility for matters. This may entail disclaiming any responsibility for the social impact of the new genetics by shifting this responsibility to government or 'society'. At other times they assert the importance of 'guiding' politicians and government (because of course ultimately the government funds and regulates the work of scientists). At still other times they are prepared to give individual 'neutral' social advice to a client (such as to check insurance before undergoing genetic testing), since the adverse effects of genetic discrimination by insurance companies would curtail their own professional genetic practices.

In summary, argue Kerr *et al.* (1997), the new genetics scientists are successfully manoeuvring to position themselves in a powerful strategic position within society, a position that accords them maximum power with minimum responsibility. In short, they are:

> negotiating a position of disinterested concern, which allows for a direct interface with society (government, education, patients) but ignores their own social location and vested interests.
>
> (Kerr *et al.* 1997: 300)

Re-thinking the assumptions of science

If the way scientists work in communities is not quite as it seems, then perhaps there are other aspects of the scientific endeavour that would benefit from being conceptualized in new and different ways. A key assumption of the parameters of experimental scientific design is that such designs are based around control. Variables are controlled; confounding factors are controlled out; randomized trials have control groups and so on. More recent debates in the sociology of science suggest that science proceeds *not* by effecting control over the natural world but by effecting the conditions of near absolute freedom, the freedom for the 'things' being studied to strike back (Latour 2000).

However, it is not clear what, in social research, might be taken as the equivalent of 'things', for there are several constituencies. If social science is to proceed by giving the object of its study as much freedom as possible, the subjects of research must be reconceptualized as participants. What might this freedom of research participants consist of? This may involve the researched being involved in the research process from the outset, where subjects are involved in the setting of the agenda (Oliver 1992). They may be involved in funding the research (Lawson 1991), or in collecting the data (Dyson 2000), or disseminating the results (Rice *et al.* 1994). This approach has been consolidated within 'social action' research in which subjects participate in many stages of the process (Mullender and Ward 1991).

However, in applied social research, constituencies can be difficult to delineate. Lawson (1991) asks what sides were being taken when social researchers in her university were funded by a powerful patient self-help group for multiple sclerosis to conduct research. In such a case the researchers were reliant for grant payments on the group, who had in some senses become the superordinates. The reality of the project was more complex still and entailed stakeholders who included rebellious local groups who wished to break away from the central group funding the research and not send their monies in to the centre; the central MS group who did not want doctors to have any influence over the research process; medical practitioners who still had the potential to restrict or deny access to patients; wider university departmental relations that because of scarce resources made meeting the goals of the MS group important in order to secure that funding for the university department, whilst not upsetting the medics with whom another joint grant was being negotiated.

We might envisage a future research programme in which the subjects/ participants set the agenda, pose the research question, construct the research designs, carry out the data collection, execute the data analysis, write up the findings, and publicize the results. But the research participants are, as has been said, only one research constituency. How would one accord the freedom to 'strike back' to the sponsors, gatekeeper, subjects, readers, or members of research communities? Would the result be, as Foucault might claim, that providing the conditions of absolute freedom for researching the social is an extension of surveillance, a new technology of the self by which people are increasingly required to re-present themselves to the world through research? Is this perhaps why, as Hammersley (1995) points out, not all people who share social characteristics in common that draw them into the ambit of social research may wish to play such a major role and foreground research in their lives. This non-participation might also be conceptualized as resistance to a new technology of the self, a new technology of the self we might call the participatory research form of governmentality.

Conclusion

In this chapter we have reviewed some of the insights that emerge when we consider researchers not as isolated individuals but as part of scientific communities, and indeed as part of the society they are studying. We have seen that the arguments as to whether social research can be scientific largely depend upon what you mean by science. We have reviewed the claims for scientific certainty that rest on the falsification principle advanced by Popper. We have seen too the arguments that science is shaped by the career interests of scientists, by their communication practices. Scientists draw upon different vocabularies in different situations in order to advance their own work, or to downplay the importance of the work of others. They also draw upon different discourses to assume authority for educating an ignorant public and guiding government on the one hand, but distancing themselves from the negative consequences of scientific knowledge on the other. Social research could try to be scientific by denying its own location within social influences, and assert a boundary between social 'facts' and what people and policy makers should do with these facts. But it could also be a very different kind of science in which social location of the researcher is acknowledged and in which research directions and priorities are more democratically shared.

Further reading

Schiff, M. (1995) *The Memory of Water: Homeopathy and the Battle of Ideas in the New Science*. London: Thorsons. (An account of the French Scientist Jacques Bienveniste who claimed his experiments demonstrated that water has memory-like qualities, and was subsequently ostracized by the scientific establishment.)

Shilts, R. (1987) *And the Band Played On: Politics, People, and the AIDS Epidemic*. New York: St Martin's Press. (An account of how various political factors, the social rivalries of scientists included, prevented earlier and more decisive intervention in the field of HIV prevention.)

Sykes, B. (2001) *The Seven Daughters of Eve: The Science That Reveals Our Genetic Ancestry*. New York: W.W. Norton and Company. (An account, though a one-sided account, of the rivalries of scientists underlying the production of genetic knowledge.)

(7) Validity and reliability

Validity: the very idea?

Thus far in the book, we have examined a number of key analytic dualisms. We have also suggested that each philosophical stance implicitly adopts a form of methodological criteria concerning what positivists refer to as internal validity, reliability and generalizability (see Tables 2.1, 3.1 and 4.1). Indeed, these methodological criteria are so deeply entrenched that it is not usual to find them questioned or problematized. In this part of the book, we encourage the reader to look at these taken-for-granted ideas a little more sceptically. It is important to be aware that they are controversial and debatable ideas whose presence in applied research in the social or health sciences is by no means inevitable.

Just to remind ourselves, validity is often defined in textbooks in the following kinds of terms: 'Did we measure what we were trying to measure?' or perhaps a little more floridly: 'Validity is how close what is being measured in practice is to what we intend to measure in our theory. Thinking about validity enables us to judge how close our conclusions based on the measurement results are to the truth.' Reliability is a term used to refer to the 'repeatability' or 'consistency' of a measure. A measure is considered reliable if it would yield the same result over and over again. That, at any rate, is what we might learn from an introductory textbook.

However, it is our intention to try to encourage some critical thinking about the ideas themselves. The role of validity and reliability in applied research is not simply to do with their being characteristics of good research; neither is their presence in the health care research inevitable or natural. In their present form they originated in other disciplines such as psychology, sociology and educational research, with medicine adopting them rather later (Nanda *et al.* 2000). Prior to that, these concerns about the truth of our observations have their origins much earlier, and can be traced back to very ancient dilemmas and strategies indeed, in Ancient Greek theology, poetry and statecraft.

Concerns about reliability and validity have insinuated themselves into the health care disciplines from elsewhere in the social sciences and, as we have noted, this can also be related to political and economic concerns. In Western medicine there are a variety of policy initiatives such as evidence-based practice and clinical governance which have forced a whole range of health care personnel to become scientifically literate, from consultant surgeons to volunteer care assistants.

Some of the new-found concerns with validity and reliability have involved rethinking a good many ideas. With the demand for evidence and measurement comes the demand for reliability and validity. There has been a considerable amount of work over the last decade, reformulating constructs in the health disciplines so that they have become quantifiable entities which can be measured in a reliable and valid manner. For example, Zernike and Henderson (1999) describe the development of a 'constipation risk assessment scale' addressing variables such as the fluid intake, fibre intake and activity level of patients. As the authors envisage it, once certain numerical thresholds of risk are achieved, bran and prune juice will be administered. Now, ensuring that patients avoid constipation might well be a valuable aspect of nursing care. What is interesting to us is that it is now something that one can measure with some degree of reliability and validity, rather than being something that practitioners deal with in an intuitive manner with patients individually.

This stampede to scale everything is not just limited to the traditional British concern with constipation. For example, a brief tour through some recent papers with an emphasis on the validity of something in their titles include an account of the testing of scales to measure the impairments suffered by stroke patients (Edwards and O'Connell 2003); the development of an instrument for measuring the outcomes of prostate hyperplasia (Lamping *et al.* 1998) and the validation of the McGill pain questionnaire after having been translated into Spanish (Masedo and Esteve 2000).

Concerns about validity and reliability, then, have proliferated along with the developing concerns with measurement in health care. This in turn, in the West at least, is connected with the growing vogue for evidence-based practice and the search for aspects of practice that can be measured and thus rendered researchable. The experience of pain or 'quality of life' are not inherently quantitative entities, but they can be made so via the construction of an appropriate rating instrument. Notice also that social and health scientists have borrowed a powerful lexicon of 'scales' and 'instruments' to describe what are effectively self-report questionnaires or interview guides. This spirit of quantitative enquiry in health care has foregrounded validity and reliability concerns, and has enabled them, complete with their vocabulary of 'instrumentation', to migrate from the disciplines where they originated to the health sciences.

The ideas of validity and reliability become even more curious when we consider that the origins of the concern with validity and reliability do not lie in the empirical sciences at all, but in disciplines such as history. Storytellers and politicians in ancient societies were well aware of the importance of cataloguing events for the purposes of statecraft and collective memory and identity. The problems of compiling histories and telling stories which provided a more or less faithful rendering of happenings loomed large on the Ancient Greeks' intellectual horizon.

For example, let us consider the phenomenon of toxic shock syndrome. This illustrates the difficulty of observing the state of a field of observations and making inferences about what may be happening to cause the pattern of events in question. In the late 1970s a number of bodies, especially the Centers for Disease Control in the USA, were noting a relatively new phenomenon. Female patients were being reported with a novel cluster of symptoms including fevers over 102°F, diffuse red rashes, shedding and death of skin cells, sudden drops in blood pressure, vomiting, diarrhoea, muscle aches, kidney dysfunction, liver failure, elevated blood clotting and platelet formation, mental confusion and loss of consciousness. Some cases even appeared to be lethal. As usual when a new problem is presented in health care contexts, there was at first some confusion. These cases were especially problematic because the symptoms were not necessarily consistently displayed and because the culprit, staphylococcus aurea, that was invading tampons, had been known about for decades. This familiar bacterium is generally found on people's skin, is responsible for impetigo and MRSA and its capacity for mutation keeps it one step ahead of most antibiotics. This familiar microbe had learned to exploit the tampon environment so as to completely overwhelm the body's ability to cope.

Toxic shock syndrome is interesting from our point of view because of the difficulty in identifying the problem. The inconsistency – in other words, lack of reliability – of the various symptoms made it very difficult for researchers and clinicians to make the imaginative leap to suspect that these were all indications of a common underlying problem. Imagine also this additional difficulty: individual doctors and nurses might only see a few cases, even at times when the syndrome was rife.

This lies at the heart of the problems of validity and reliability. Scientists have to make the jump from the indicators to the underlying construct in order to do anything about it. At first, one cannot see the pattern or make the jump and it is only gradually once a large number of cases have been considered that one is able to make the inference from indicators to underlying constructs that might be causing the problem. In measuring variables this is what Trochim (2001) calls 'true score theory'. This supposes that there is an underlying true value for the entity or variable and our observations of the various indicators are informed by this, plus a kind of random error. In quantitative measures it is this random element which is believed to produce the variance. The underlying variable is often presumed to be relatively constant.

This idea of accounts, measures and indicators varying widely but there being an underlying true variable, event or entity is a bit like saying 'there's no smoke without fire'. The smoke may blow in different directions but it generally tends to indicate fire, and, if we are fortunate, allows us to infer the size and location of the fire, or even what is being burned.

This approach to establishing the veracity, validity and reliability of accounts has in some form or other been deployed by historians and policy makers for the last 2500 years. In the health sciences, the concern with validity and reliability has arrived more recently. It has been accompanied by some important shifts in how we see ourselves as human beings. That is, the proliferation of validated measures for experiences which were once intensely private has made social science and health care into what a Foucauldian would call distinctly confessional enterprises. Nowadays, for example, we can find articles concerning the validation of measures relating to the severity of physical and sexual abuse suffered in childhood (Langeland *et al.* 2003) and its relationship to addictive behaviours in adulthood. More extraordinarily still, we find the expectation that people will collaborate and incriminate themselves as they participate in these meticulously validated questionnaires and structured interviews. For example, Rice and Harris (1997) describe the validation of a device intended to predict recidivism in 'child molesters and rapists'. Here, by answering the questions, the offenders themselves are involved in predicting their own future riskiness, and, depending on their answers, presumably prolonging their incarceration. Thus, in the face of an appropriately validated measure it is believed that people will not only confess personal matters but will even incriminate themselves.

Indeed, there seems to be very little that a properly validated measure cannot do, at least judging by the published literature. Given the powers attributed to this mysterious process of validation it behoves us to investigate a little more about what it means.

In doing research in health care we might make a great many different inferences and arrive at a plethora of conclusions whilst conducting research. Many of these are related to the process of doing research and are not the major hypotheses of the study. Nevertheless, like the bricks in a wall, these intermediate processes and methodological propositions provide the basis for the eventual conclusions that we wish to address. For instance, nearly all research in health or the social sciences involves measurement or observation. Even tasks like reviewing literature are now approached as if they were a piece of fieldwork, where authors tick off the characteristics of the work they are considering on rating scales, checklists or protocols. Whenever we measure or observe anything we are concerned at some level with whether we are measuring what we intend to measure or with how our observations are influenced by the circumstances in which they are made. We make assumptions about the quality of our measures which will play an important role in addressing the broader substantive issues of the study.

Most ideas about validity are grounded in a foundationalist, or naïve realist ontology. That is, talking about validity often assumes that there is a real world out there which we are trying to capture through our scholarly activity. This has sometimes been referred to as a 'death and furniture' epistemology (Edwards *et al.* 1995). In other words, the sort of vision of nature invoked when people bang the table – 'There you go: there's nothing socially constructed about that!' The death and furniture epistemology bypasses any inconvenient uncertainties as to what nature is 'made of' and establishes the external world as being full of solid objects. 'Validity' is often about trying to make our measures look as much like the solid objects they are trying to describe as possible. In a sense there is also an ethical undercurrent to these foundationalist claims about the world outside. Understanding this external reality, so the argument goes, enables us to save lives, challenge injustice, and substitute science for superstition. This goes back to what Trochim (2001) calls 'true score theory' in the study of measurement, where our observations are comprised of a true underlying value plus an element of random error. There is, in this logic, a true score under there somewhere.

Epistemologically – that is, in terms of their theory of knowledge – this desire to see what is really there can be traced back to the ancient Greeks who tended to privilege seeing as the most authentic way of knowing or mode of knowledge. To see an event, to see it for oneself, and to know it were very much the same thing. Ontologically, their own presence in the world as observers was not a problematic question for them (Hartog 2000). To be present, to be there, to see, and to know all went together for the Greeks (Clay 1983: 12–13). This arguably represents the origin of what Donna Haraway (1991) has called the 'God eyed vision' or the 'god trick', in Western science. Health sciences researchers see everything, but somehow as if they weren't there themselves, rather like the sense of surveillance over patients which we outlined in Chapter 4. Modern researchers, then, even if they are not necessarily aware of the history of the idea, are in a sense trying to see nature like a god.

Privileged visions: looking and the subject of scientific research

This prioritizing or privileging of vision has its parallels in the present where cameras are inserted into the body's recesses in order to facilitate investigation and repair. Contemporary technologies have allowed cardiovascular surgeons to insert video cameras into the blood vessels of the heart (Antona *et al.* 1998) so as to be better able to identify sites for surgery and check on the progress of healing. Seeing inside, then, is an important part of many of the more heroic treatments of the modern age. Yet the reason why the patient is on the operating table undergoing this procedure was not because anyone noticed a change in the blood vessels of the heart at all. It would much more likely be because of chest pains, shortness of breath, fatigue and sundry other symptoms suggesting poor cardiovascular condition. In health care, then, seeing the source of the pathology often occurs at a much later stage in the process than the first intimation that something is wrong.

Visualization and video are, as we might expect, especially favoured for the examination of that most visible of the body's structures, the skin, where dermatology and parasitology have been transformed by the video revolution (Micali *et al.* 2004). The skin and its flora and fauna are emblazoned for inspection by the scientist and patient as well as the clinician. As Micali *et al.* (2004: 154) say, videodermatoscopy:

> enhances the monitoring of clinical response to treatment and allows determination of the optimal timing of drug application. This may be particularly important in minimizing risk of over-treatment, reducing the potential for side-effects, and enhancing patient compliance.

Seeing, and the process of surveillance itself perhaps, can not only optimize health care or social interventions but can make people comply with them too. Seeing, then, is believed to be powerful. If people can see the good it is doing them they'll use the medication as directed. Getting people to comply with medical advice is an important concern. In the UK the annual NHS drugs bill is widely cited as £5.7 billion (Petit-Zeman 2003). Amongst clients, less than half may be complying with medical advice or treatment regimes (Cramer and Rosencheck 1998), thus leading to major concerns about waste or adverse consequences from misuse of medication. Seeing it at work, then, might encourage patients to follow the directions. In this sense, what is at stake in establishing the validity of research is also social and political because it creates an implied obligation for us to comply with professionals' directives.

To draw out the important implications of what we have covered so far, the idea behind most contemporary notions of validity is that there is some sort of split or dualism between the realm of ideas and the realm of observations. We may never be able to see exactly like a god but there are a variety of procedures we might be encouraged to undertake as researchers so as to come as close as possible to an all-knowing view of the world. Science and technology, if they are correctly applied, will allow progressively better approximations to that reality to be accomplished. In the next section, then, we will examine how the notion of validity can help us interrogate the truth of a contentious idea.

Validity and virtue: making sense of evidence

There are two realms involved in research. The first of these is the land of theory. In other words, it is what goes on inside our heads as researchers. It is a repository of ideas about how the world operates. Some of them are explicitly formulated scientific theories and others may be barely conscious. The second realm is the land of observations. It is the 'real' world of sensory data, into which we translate our ideas – our interventions, treatments, measures and observations.

As we conduct research, we are continually moving back and forth between these two realms, between the realm of theory and the realm of what is going on out there in nature – or at least what we think we can see in it. When we try to investigate a causal relationship, we usually have a theory (sometimes this is only implicit) of what the cause is. Let us call this the cause construct. For instance, if we are testing a new health educational programme, we might have an idea of what it would look like ideally. We might have ideas about the cognitive structures or attitudes that we must effect if we are to persuade people to give up smoking, eat less fat or wear condoms more frequently. Similarly, on the effect side, we have an idea of what we are ideally trying to influence and measure, in the form of an effect construct, perhaps in terms of a measurable reduction in smoking, fat consumption or frequency of high-risk sex. In order to perform interventions or do research each of these, the cause and the effect, has to be translated into real things, into a programme or treatment and a measure or observational method. The term operationalization is often used to describe the act of translating a construct into some sort of measurable manifestation. In other words, we take our idea and describe it as a series of operations or procedures. Once it is defined in terms of measurements or observations it becomes a public entity that can be looked at by any competent stranger. It is one thing, for instance, to say that we believe that a person's sense of self-efficacy (the cause construct) may be related to their success at giving up smoking (the effect construct) (Bandura 1999). But once you have defined self-efficacy in terms of a self-report questionnaire and giving up smoking in terms of a count of cigarettes smoked in your sample in the month following a decision to quit, then others can look at it and understand more clearly what you intend by the terms 'self-efficacy' and 'giving up smoking'.

Validity, in the modern era, may be divided into four broad types (Trochim 2001). Each of these types addresses a specific methodological question, as can be seen in Box 7.1.

The kinds of validity build on one another, with two of them – conclusion validity and internal validity – referring to the realm of observations and sensory experiences, one of them – construct validity – emphasizing the linkages between the observations and experiences and the theory, and the last – external validity – being primarily concerned about the range of our theory and what else it can be applied to.

This highlights the difficulties of inferring the presence of a causal construct. The imaginations of enthusiastic researchers can lead them to infer the presence of a culpable virus when other observers cannot see one. Gradually, the weight of evidence accumulates to suggest that the observed phenomena do not uniquely or exclusively point to an underlying viral pathogen. As we have seen, however, scientific truths, at least in health care, are likely to be provisional rather than permanent, so it is difficult to tell what insights the future will bring. For example, for the time being at least viral hypotheses where leukaemia is concerned have fallen into disuse.

Returning to the types of validity we mentioned above, notice how the question that each kind of validity addresses presupposes an affirmative answer to the previous one. This is what we mean when we say that the validity types build on one another (Trochim 2001). However, Trochim's (2001) typology of construct, conclusion, internal and external validity does not exhaust the question of validity and many others have addressed the issue too. Indeed, decisions about the validity of a measure, index or research procedure might well involve some entirely different issues.

This additional complexity can perhaps best be introduced by consider-

---

Box 7.1 The types of validity

Trochim (2001) distinguishes:

1 *Construct validity* – In what way can we claim the construct exists?
2 *Conclusion validity* – In our study is there a relationship between the two (or more) variables?
3 *Internal validity* – Assuming that there is a relationship in this study, is the relationship a causal one?
4 *External validity* – Assuming that there is a causal relationship in this study between the constructs of the cause and the effect, can we generalize this effect to other persons, places or times? This is often the most difficult issue to establish yet it is the one in which people are the most interested generally.

ing how the questions of validity, reliability and bias found their way into the social science canon. They did so relatively recently, and through a somewhat unlikely portal. The contemporary era of concern with reliability and validity was through the discipline of educational studies.

Reliability and validity become topics of concern in the social sciences

The question of validity received its most famous lengthy airing in a book by educational researcher Lee J. Cronbach published just over thirty years ago, which has implications for research in the health and social sciences today that are worth unpacking. The most obvious kind of validity is 'face validity' (Cronbach 1971). Face validity means the validity at face value. For example, in the school systems that Cronbach and his colleagues studied, the validity of items on tests was often established by showing them to teachers who judged whether they were suitable for what was being taught, and made suggestions for modification. This kind of procedure, whilst intuitively appealing, fell into disrepute amongst educational psychometricians. However, outside the educational measurement arena, face validity has come back in another form. Whilst discussing the validity of a theory, Lacity and Jansen (1994) define validity as making common sense, and being persuasive and seeming right to the reader. For Polkinghorne (1988), validity of a theory refers to its relationship to results that have the appearance of truth or reality.

In health care there are a whole variety of measures which appear to have some sort of 'face validity' and which are regularly sought from patients but on closer inspection may not tell the clinician very much. They are taken because they make sense in terms of the clinicians' and patients' folk understanding of medical consultations.

Doctors carry stethoscopes as a kind of relic of a bygone age when many of their patients would have had tuberculosis or perhaps, a little later, poison gas injuries from the First World War (Martin 1996). A report in one of the earliest 'classics' of respiratory medicine, the *Treatise on the Diseases of the Chest*, published in 1818, suggests that its author, a physician called Laennec (1781–1826), invented the stethoscope. Despite the fact that today chest X-rays, blood gas assays and other measures may be better guides to the processes and structures of respiration, listening to patients with a stethoscope has a great deal of 'face validity' as a procedure in the clinical consultation. This example could be multiplied across a whole range of monitoring and investigative procedures.

To place the issue of face validity and its relation to the underlying notion of construct validity on a more rigorous footing, some authors advocate thinking about it as a quantitative issue. Hunter and Schmidt (1990) take this position. In their work, construct validity is a quantitative question rather than a qualitative distinction such as 'valid' or 'invalid'; it is a matter of degree. In this view construct validity can be measured by the correlation between an *intended* independent variable or 'construct' and the *proxy* independent variable – the indicator or sign – that is actually used.

In contrast to this approach advocated by Hunter and Schmidt, other authors (for example, Cronbach and Quirk 1976; Angoff 1988) have argued that construct validity cannot be expressed as a single coefficient; there is no mathematical index of construct validity and instead it represents a qualitative judgement.

Sometimes when multiple indicators of a construct are measured they can be subject to a more thorough analysis to see if they are all measuring the same thing, or at least all varying together.

Dissenting voices: the critique of validity

Having taken this tour through the issue of validity and reliability it is perhaps appropriate to end on a critical or provocative note. The constructs which we learn about in introductory research methods courses and whose definitions so many students are taught to repeat by rote have not entered the health care arena because it is their natural home. They have found their way in because people have put them there. It is arguably no coincidence that challenges to medicine (Gabe *et al.* 1994) and to the medical profession (Freidson 1970; Illich 1977) have been followed by incorporation of methodological criteria into health services research to the point where, unless knowledge is generalizable, it is not held to be legitimate knowledge at all (Department of Health 1994). There are thus political reasons why such methodological criteria have rapidly gained a taken-for-grated status in the field.

However, some critiques of the concept of validity have emerged over the last couple of decades. A critical view of validity was expounded by Pedhazur and Schmelkin (1991). They argued that content validity is not a type of validity at all because validity refers to inferences made about scores, not to an assessment of the content of an instrument. In their view, the very definition of a 'construct' implies a domain of content. They argued that there is no sharp distinction between the content which our measures address and the construct they are aiming to uncover. This highlights the way that a good deal of the preceding discussion has been carried on as if the constructs which we are trying to measure could be defined in relatively content-free terms. However, many issues in social science and health are defined largely through their content. With some issues, like attention deficit hyperactivity disorder, researchers and concerned parents are frantically trying to establish a plausible neurological explanation, but with others, like 'quality of life', it is difficult to imagine a brain region, genetic marker or chemical substrate that underlies our measure. In other words, it is defined in and through its content.

This kind of critical discussion of the idea of validity was extended by Messick (1995) who says the conventional account of validity, which splits it into different kinds – content validity, criterion validity, construct validity and so on – is fragmented and incomplete. It is incomplete especially because it does not take into account the values inherent in the measurement process, and the social implications of these. After all, evaluations, assessments and measurements are usually undertaken because human beings want to do something. They want to evaluate the effectiveness of a drug, decide whether someone has special needs, decide whether a person is ill or not and so on. In Messick's (1995) view, validity is not a property of the test or assessment, but rather of the meaning of the test scores. Therefore Messick has added the idea of consequential validity to the list of validity types, relating to bias, fairness and justice; the social consequence of the assessment to the society.

Validity, then, is embroiled in human social, political and ethical action. What we try to find out about nature has a lot to do with what we would like to achieve with it and what we would like it to do. It is informed by a whole range of tacit theories about what happens, how it happens and what matters (Gitlin 1980). It is informed both by scientific notions of rigour and folk-epistemologies. It even has touches of vitalism in that some incarnations of validity have an implicit mission to uncover the germ of a construct hiding somewhere behind the indicators and measures. Validity, then, links modern science with much older traditions.

From validity to reliability

Validity is often to be found with its handmaiden 'reliability' in many methodology textbooks, and it is to this concept which we will now turn. Nearly everyone who has studied introductory research methods would be able to say that it has something to do with the consistency with which a particular result is obtained. Perhaps it might have something to do with whether two observers or two measurements agree, or whether an observation is inconsistent over time. Conventional views of reliability (AERA *et al.* 1985) see it as being detectable through one or more of the following characteristics: temporal stability, form equivalence and internal consistency, as detailed in Box 7.2.

According to most authors who have touched upon the subject, reliability is a **necessary** but not **sufficient** condition for validity. By analogy with a set of scales, if the needle of the scale is five pounds away from zero, the people weighed might always over-report their weight by five pounds. Whilst the measure might be consistent, it is consistently wrong and would not be considered valid and perhaps would readily be challenged by people who

---

Box 7.2 Characteristics of reliability

Temporal stability – Under this criterion, a test is reliable if the same form of a test given on two or more separate occasions to the same group of participants yields the same result. Repeated measurements may require costly and time-consuming visits to field settings, where it may not be easy to locate the original respondents anyway. Repeated testing is also likely to change the participants.

Form equivalence – This is based on the idea that two or more different forms of test, based on the same content can be used.

Internal consistency – This relates to tests, measures and questionnaires with a large number of items. We can correlate the items together in various ways so as to see whether they are related. This principle underlies measures of internal reliability such as Cronbach's Alpha, or Spilt-half.

(Based on AERA *et al.* 1985)

---

felt it had done them a disservice. A scale which weighed them five pounds lighter would probably not be challenged so readily.

Even if we accept the idea that there is an underlying true value to the factor we are measuring, there may be many sources of error. This is especially so where there may be differences in the tests, measures or tasks carried out. For example, in educational assessment, the reliability of a writing skill test score is affected by the raters, the mode of discourse and several other factors (Parkes 2000). Or, for example, there are concerns that one of the tests used to identify antibodies to HIV, the Western Blot Test, is interpreted according to different criteria in different countries. Different numbers of bands of response on the Western Blot's nitrocellulose strip are required in Africa, the United States and Australia (Turner and MacIntyre 1999) to establish a positive result, such that a person who is deemed to be HIV positive in, say, Africa is not deemed to be so in Australia. Thus, a lack of reliability can be introduced by differences in policy and conventions of laboratory practice too.

This, then, is the conventional view of reliability. The picture is complicated somewhat by a number of writers who have sought to define matters differently. The conventional view is that the reliability of a measure or observation is a prerequisite for validity. In a modified view of reliability, Moss (1994) claims that, on the contrary to what we have described above, there can be validity without reliability if reliability is defined as consistency among independent measures. In this view, reliability is an aspect of construct validity. As an assessment or measure becomes less standardized, distinctions between reliability and validity blur. In many situations, such as identifying mental health problems like 'personality disorder', different clinicians may not agree, and this blurs the boundaries of the category itself, or even leads some to question its existence (Caixeta 1996). In some cases, however, we might want to argue that inconsistency in observations does not invalidate the underlying construct. Inconsistency in a person's state of confusion does not necessarily mean that they have not got Alzheimer's disease, for example, and there may be other good reasons for presuming that they do so. Inconsistent performance across tasks or over time does not necessarily invalidate the diagnosis. Rather it becomes an empirical puzzle to be solved by searching for a more comprehensive interpretation. Initial disagreement amongst clients, clinicians and carers in responsive evaluation would not invalidate the assessment. It would provide an impetus for dialogue.

Equally, there are a number of calls from researchers and methodologists who argue for a return to the classical notion of reliability. For example, Li (2003) argues that the preceding view – which is 'soft' on inconsistency – is incorrect. According to Li, the definition of reliability should be in terms of the classic measurement model in the behavioural sciences model – reliability relates to a statistic. This represents the squared correlation between observed and true scores or the proportion of true variance in obtained test scores. In this sense reliability is a unit-less measure expressing a proportion of variance.

This leads us on to a view of reliability and validity promoted by Salvucci et al. (1997). They dissent from the conventional view that 'reliability is a necessary but not a sufficient condition of validity'. These authors conceptualize reliability as invariance and validity as unbiasedness. If we take a number of samples from our population, the sample statistic we are interested in may have a value which averages out to be very close to the population parameter (unbiasedness), but have very high variance, especially if the samples are small. Conversely, a sample statistic can have very low sampling variance but have a central tendency very different from the value we would obtain if we surveyed the whole population.

The question of 'bias' in measurement is an important one. It is a notion that has been refined by workers in psychology and other behavioural sciences. If we have a measure of depression, say, it may well show more depression amongst women than men (Nazroo and Edwards 1998). Now, this could be because the measure has 'bias' in that it more readily detects depression in women than in men. Thus, to detect whether that is the case or not researchers might be interested in looking beyond the measure itself to see if there is more evidence. That is, we might look at occupational or social impairment, suicidality, rates of use of anti-depressant medication and so on to see if there really is a difference or whether it is just our questionnaire. This would generally find that women in developed nations at least show more depressive symptoms than men (for example, Culbertson 1997). The test shows a difference but it is not 'biased'.

Now let us imagine we had another kind of questionnaire that showed no gender differences in depression. Despite this, if we looked at all the other signs of depression we would probably find more in women than in men. So, even a test or measure which appears to be scrupulously fair may mask underlying differences. Assessing 'bias' then depends on what we can find in the outside world against which to gauge our measure. Test bias is believed to be a major threat to construct validity, and therefore test bias analyses should be employed to examine the test items (Osterlind 1983). In Osterlind's view, the presence of test bias definitely affects the measurement of the underlying construct. However, the absence of test bias does not guarantee that the test possesses construct validity. In other words, the absence of test bias is a necessary, but not a sufficient condition.

With something like depression, the answer to the question of what it feels like is putatively hiding away inside people's heads. We will probably never see it directly in a research study. All the variables we might check our measures against are just indicators of this presumed underlying variable. Validation and checking for bias often involve doing research to see if all the indicators are pointing in the same direction.

This process of checking that the indicators are all pointing in the same direction is also what lies behind the notion of criterion validity. Usually, we want to measure something because it will tell us about an important issue. An examination for medical students should tell us something about whether they will make competent doctors. A measure of blood sugar should be able to tell us whether a hypoglycaemic attack is on the way. The important thing then is a criterion against which the success of our measure can be judged.

At this point the reader can probably see that we are swinging back round towards notions of validity from our consideration of reliability. This is because the two notions are closely interlinked and considering one of them is often only possible when one considers the other. They have a mutually dependent recursive relationship. As we have seen, how this is formulated depends on a variety of things such as what researchers are trying to achieve, and considerations from outside the research altogether such as history, politics and culture.

The fragility of validity

Validity is fragile and needs careful nurturing if it is to flourish in a researcher's garden. Despite all the potential disagreements that we have detailed above, it is important to note that almost all authors agree that there are multiple threats to the validity of any study. Different researchers and theorists conceptualize these differently of course, but there are common features to the set of threats they identify.

Now that we have reviewed some of the key features of validity and reliability, we are in a good position to appreciate some of these threats and how they might apply to studies in the health care disciplines. A good deal of research involves selecting, comparing or manipulating one or more variables or conditions in order to determine their effects on a measure of the well-being or behaviour of participants. For example, the relation between different levels of an independent variable like socioeconomic status and a dependent one like heart disease could form the basis of an investigation.

Validity in research is often difficult to safeguard and we might find it threatened by a variety of 'predators'. The sources of threat to internal validity include selection, history, maturation, repeated testing, instrumentation regression to the mean, experimental mortality and experimenter bias (Campbell and Stanley 1963; Cook and Campbell 1979). These are the very kinds of threats which experimental design is intended to minimize. Box 7.3 deals with these in order.

Box 7.3 Threats to the validity of experiments

Selection – Participants may find their way into different groups in a study as a result of non-random factors which influence the likelihood of being in one group or other. This may affect the outcome measures.

History – External events may influence a study's participants in the course of the investigation or between repeated measures of the dependent variable.

Maturation – Participants may change in the course of the study or between repeated measures of the dependent variable due to the passage of time.

Repeated testing – The prior measurement of the dependent variable may affect the results obtained from subsequent measurements.

Instrumentation – The reliability of the device or 'instrument' used to gauge the dependent variable or manipulate the independent variable may change over the course of a study.

Regression to the mean – Participants with extreme scores on a first measure of the dependent variable tend to have scores closer to the mean on a second measure.

Experimental mortality – In the course of a study, some participants may drop out before it is completed.

Experimenter bias – Expectations about the outcome on the part of the people running a study may significantly influence the outcome.

(Based on Campbell and Stanley 1963; Cook and Campbell 1979)

In conclusion – towards a social theory of validity and reliability

The threats to validity which we have outlined above represent a set of methodological maxims for doing good scientific work. They are the sorts of issues that can be seen in many more conventional methodology books. What is also interesting from our point of view is what they represent concerning the social processes of science. Seeing science as a kind of story-telling has been a basic staple of the sociology and philosophy of science for around thirty years. When we conduct the experiment, distribute the survey or plan the interviews we don't necessarily know what the results will be. If we did, there would not be much point in doing the research. When there are only a few explorers in a new piece of intellectual territory you can only trust your observations if you believe your exploratory technique is sound. One legacy from David Bloor's sociology of science is the so-called 'symmetry thesis' (Bloor 1976, 1981). That is, whether a belief turns out to be true or false, the social processes involved in creating it and sustaining it need to be studied in the same way. In this view the sociology of science should be impartial concerning truth or falsity, rationality or irrationality, and success or failure (Barnes *et al.* 1996). Both sides of these dichotomies will require explanation; we cannot take it for granted that one side is real and the other unreal, because that involves 'going native' in the local community of scientists in question, and the student of science should remain disinterested.

In this context, then, the kinds of methodological maxims listed above as threats to validity represent a way of making sense of how things go wrong. They are a sort of theoretical basis for understanding the mortality of ideas.

The idea of validity and its fragile status are an important plank in both naïve realist and scientific realist views of science and nature. Even though individual scientists and scientific projects may fail, we still have some glimpses into that reality if practice has fortuitously fallen into alignment with the methodological maxims. Nature, as it is disclosed through every-day seeing, is untidy. It is this special kind of seeing, disclosed through the contemplation of validity, which will reveal perfectible, regular and perhaps reliable facets of reality. The tale of validity is thus rather like a quest-myth. In this way the realist project in the philosophy of science can anchor itself to a reality which is rarely and imperfectly seen. This is the position of 'scientific realism' or 'critical realism', which contends that the job of science is to improve our perceptual or measurement processes, separate illusion from reality, and achieve the most accurate description and understanding of the phenomena in question (Hunt 1990).

The idea of validity and the presumed threats to it help to preserve the faith we might have in other researchers. If results subsequently turn out to be misleading they provide a readily available set of accounts of what might have gone wrong. Most good belief systems have a way of accounting for errors (Knorr-Cetina and Mulkay 1983).

Discussions of validity and the threats to it also serve a social function within science itself so we can examine the work of others critically and with the benefit of hindsight so it might appear that we ourselves would do better work and not be so foolish or credulous. Thus, it facilitates the maintenance of a flattering image of ourselves and our discipline despite disappointing or inconsistent findings.

Validity, then, is part and parcel of the social fabric of scientific enquiry, serving to manage the potentially vast and epistemologically untidy realm of scrutiny. Like primordial myths and stories, the maxims of validity provide a comforting image to the community of scholars and vouchsafe their collective project. Modifying Clausewitz's famous maxim, the sociologist of science Bruno Latour asserts 'science is politics pursued by other means' (1983: 168).

Further reading

William Trochim has provided an extensive textbook and associated website relating to this, in which there are some extensive discussions of validity and reliability from the perspective of mainstream social science. The book is:

Trochim, W. (2000) *The Research Methods Knowledge Base*, 2nd edition. Cincinnati, OH: Atomic Dog Publishing.

And the website is:

Trochim, William M. *The Research Methods Knowledge Base*, 2nd edition. Internet WWW page, at URL: <http://trochim.human.cornell.edu/kb/index.htm> (version current as of 16 August 2004).

There are two classic works on research design in applied settings:

Campbell, D. and Stanley, J. (1963) *Experimental and Quasi-Experimental Designs for Research*, Chicago, IL: Rand-McNally.
Cook, T. D. and Campbell, D. T. (1979) *Quasi-Experimentation: Design and Analysis Issues for Field Settings*, Boston, MA: Houghton Mifflin Company.

(These publications between them yielded the definitions of validity and the threats to validity that we have discussed in this chapter.)
The sociology of science literature drawn upon here includes:

Bloor, D. (1991) *Knowledge and Social Imagery*, Chicago, IL: University of Chicago Press.

(Bloor and his colleagues were amongst the first to try to understand knowledge generation and the beliefs that accompany this as social processes.)
A useful summary of social approaches to understanding scientific activity is

provided by Steve Fuller who says that the aim of social studies of knowledge is to 'employ methods that enable them to fathom both the "inner workings" and the "outer character" of science without having to be expert in the fields they study' (p. xii).

Fuller, S. (1993) *Philosophy, Rhetoric, and the End of Knowledge: The Coming of Science and Technology Studies*, Madison, WI: University of Wisconsin Press.

Another prominent theorist of the relationship between science and social processes is Bruno Latour:

Latour, B. (2004) *The Politics of Nature*, Cambridge, MA: Harvard University Press.

8 The implications for strategy and method

Introduction: making sense of dilemmas in practical research contexts

In this chapter we continue to outline the implications of some of the analytical dilemmas we have described in relation to practical research. The researcher or practitioner who is involved in research in health care is in a 'dilemmatic' position right from the outset. We have attempted in the earlier chapters to identify the kinds of theoretical and philosophical issues that inform research activity, and it should by now be clear why we think they are important. An explicit awareness of theoretical issues in research strategy and the existing theory underlying the research topic itself will invariably aid a researcher in making sense of the matters in hand, and will enable him or her to identify what aspects are interesting and relevant to the purposes of the inquiry. Equally, on the other horn of the dilemma rests the possibility that a researcher could become so dominated by a particular theory or line of inquiry that interesting material is discarded in favour of issues that fit the theory.

This latter pitfall could be summed up in the proverb 'to the man with a hammer everything looks like a nail'. In more academic terms, other authors have talked about 'epistemic enslavement' (Fellows 1995: 10–13) to describe a similar process, where the theory or technology deployed tends to determine one's view of 'reality'. Epistemic enslavement occurs when the technologies, forms of knowledge and techniques for problem solving form a kind of conceptual cage from which the individual or the scientific community cannot break out. That is, once medical science has come to be understood as a matter of randomized controlled trials, then it becomes difficult for researchers and clinicians to see the generation of more medical knowledge in anything other than these terms.

In the light of these competing dilemmatic positions, it is argued that neither a theory-blind nor a theory-determined approach is sustainable. Rather, we will suggest that researchers begin with methodological decisions at a strategic level (Denscombe 2003). Furthermore, the nature of their method, data collection and data analysis can be informed by critical reflection on the part of the researcher. Thus researchers and practitioners will always aware of whereabouts in the field of possibilities their decisions are taking them. An eminently practical decision may lead to limitations in the research which one might regret later.

Reflecting on strategy in a field of possibilities

Researchers then need to be aware of where their practical, pragmatic decisions leave them within a field of possibilities. Moreover, as the reader might anticipate given what has been covered so far in this volume, we believe it is important to reflect on both the theoretical and philosophical issues raised by the research strategy as well as the practical issues of using particular methods to collect data.

Given the chapter title's emphasis on strategy, we shall begin our discussion with consideration of the notion of strategy in research and why this is important before moving on to discuss the kinds of strategic dilemmas and decision making in some research studies so as to illustrate what is meant and why it is important.

In the early twenty-first century it seems that the phrase 'research strategy' is everywhere. In the UK there are some specific commitments to undertake research in the National Health Service as well as growing demands for research literacy which are placed on practitioners. The health care worker of today is as often expected to be an amateur researcher and, under evidence-based practice initiatives, is supposed to be able to build research findings into his or her practice. In this chapter the term strategy will be used in the sense of being concerned with a framework guiding those choices that determine how to attain the objective – to answer the question, solve the problem or, in other words answer the question, 'Are we doing the right things?' What the right thing is, of course, is rather more debatable. However, we shall attempt in this chapter to identify some aspects of research activity which we hope the reader will agree are worthwhile and desirable and which might yield more socially useful and trustworthy outcomes.

As a first step to illustrate the value of some sort of empirically grounded critical reflection on research designs and the process of planning and evaluating research strategies, let us consider an experimental design such as a randomized controlled trial. Here, it would be instructive to check participants' and researchers' perceptions of some of the key features of the design. For example, after the trial has started, the people involved may become aware of which condition the participants have been allocated to. This might involve them having penetrated the 'blinding' strategies used in the study, but even if they were simply guessing better than chance, it might still have a bearing on the results. Participants and researchers might well be highly motivated to work out which experimental group they might be in. This was made particularly apparent to one of us (BB) on visiting a relative in hospital who had acquired a soft tissue infection whilst undergoing an appendectomy. He had agreed to take part in a trial of different regimes of infection control and wound management and was continually speculating about which group he was in, comparing the containers and the colours of the medicaments, reading the expressions on the consultants' faces and asking nurses, especially the younger looking ones because, as he put it, 'it's easier to con the information out of them'. Whether any of this divination was successful in unlocking the secret of the trial is only part of the story. Also significant is that the patients' experience of suffering and healing is intimately intertwined with these very speculations and deductions. Study participants will almost certainly have something to say about the meaning and experience of the experimental manipulation. Even an apparently scientific enterprise like a randomized controlled trial is balanced upon, yet conceals, this complex human drama. This process of abstraction to move from the human drama of the clinic to the research findings in the scientific literature is an important one and we shall return to it later.

Equipoise – justifying clinical trials and creating 'good science'

Now, medical researchers do have a theory about some of this. The notion of equipoise has been a guiding principle of clinical experimentation for the last half century. According to Freedman (1987: 141): 'The ethics of clinical research requires equipoise, a state of genuine uncertainty on the part of the clinical investigator regarding the comparative therapeutic merits of each arm in the trial.' There is some debate as to whether equipoise in its strong form is possible. As Enkin (2000) reminds us, human beings almost invariably have preferences for particular treatments or ideas about how to cure an illness. Equipoise, with its connotations of an equal balance between or amongst the alternatives to be tested, is, Enkin continues, a theoretical ideal, which is almost always impossible to achieve in practice. Freedman (1987: 142) recognized that if we were to adhere to a strong notion of equipoise, the concept would 'present almost insuperable obstacles to the ethical commencement or continuation of a controlled trial'. Freedman then solved this problem by discarding what he called 'theoretical equipoise', which is almost unattainable, and impossible to maintain, and redefining 'clinical equipoise' as a failure of consensus within the clinical community. Moreover, it is not just any kind of breach of consensus. It involves a breach of consensus between peers of roughly equal authority and respectability. Here is how Fuks *et al.* (1998: 69) define the situation:

> Competent medical practice is defined widely as that which falls within the bounds of standard of care – that is, practice endorsed by at least a respectable minority of expert practitioners. The innovation of clinical equipoise is the recognition that study treatments, be they the experimental or control treatments, are potentially consistent with this standard of care. Thus, a physician, consistent with his or her duty to the patient, may offer trial enrolment when there 'exists . . . an honest, professional disagreement among expert clinicians about the preferred treatment.'

The model then is rather like a civilized discussion between colleagues over lunch of the relative merits of different available treatments – the kind of dispute that might otherwise be settled by the toss of a coin or turn of a card.

The purpose of this chapter – indeed this volume as a whole – is to encourage readers to be able to challenge these kinds of complacent accounts of the research process in two major ways:

1 By enabling reflection on the social context of research, it should be possible to gain some critical leverage on the claims made by the researchers and the advocates of particular research methodologies. For example, here the notion of equipoise only addresses a part of the complex social drama of the clinical trial. It conceives of researchers and clinicians as having a rather detached curiosity, far different from the strong opinions and educated guesses of actual people.
2 Second, we would hope to encourage a reflection on the kinds of world views, paradigms, philosophies and meta-theoretical commitments involved in research and how they influence the research strategy and have an impact on the concepts and methods used.

Despite our attempts to encourage this sort of stance, however, it is noteworthy that in the vast majority of cases where randomized controlled trials are reported, these kinds of issues are not mentioned. This is not simply a matter of careless omission, however, nor because researchers are simply not aware that the issues exist. To understand the substance, style and focus of scientific literature, one needs to understand how conventions, norms and situational etiquettes of publishing are successful in informing what gets into print.

Deepening our understanding: psychosocial issues in research

To pursue the question of psychosocial aspects of the research process a little further, let us consider likewise a survey strategy. It may be asked if debriefing interviews were conducted with data collectors or to what extent it is reported that data collectors were involved in the design and amendment of the design, the interpretation of results, as this may yield a number of useful insights as to what the questions mean in practice and how the research process itself is understood by participants. Indeed, there may be a number of ways in which the fieldworkers respond to the perceived awkwardness of certain issues by saying things like 'some of the questions might seem a bit silly' or 'I have to ask you, it says here, do you use tampons for your period at all?', thus phrasing the question so as to mitigate the potential intrusion. The social setting of the research then may have an impact on the results and the fieldworkers are a valuable source of insight into how this might have happened. This process has implications for approaches such as ethnography; case studies; action research and grounded theory as we shall see as we go on to discuss some examples of research in practice.

At the level of method, Pawson (1989) has suggested that concepts may be regarded as relatively external or relatively internal, and that, for example, external constructs set the limits as to what may be legitimately asked of respondents in questionnaires. For interviews, or indeed other methods that rely on the accounts given by social actors, the notion of setting the accounts into a context derived from unobtrusive measures or non-reactive measures (Webb *et al.* 1966; Lee 2000) is claimed as a methodological benefit. This usage of a variety of different yet related methods is claimed to be of benefit irrespective of the assumptions made in the research and whatever stance we ultimately take towards our data.

Having read this far into the text the reader will not be surprised to learn that we do not see research strategy as being about a choice of methods in any simple sense. Research reports typically proceed as if the research questions had simply suggested themselves as following logically from the problems or issues suggested by prior research, and the choice of methods and strategies could be said to be logically related to the kind of question in a robust manner. Thus, questions about which of two or more treatments is more effective seems to demand some sort of randomized controlled trial, a question about patients' experiences, demands, interviews and so on.

Yet the availability of a particular research method itself encourages researchers to see the world in terms of empirical questions that can be addressed by this kind of research. Hence the field of health care research becomes reconfigured as a set of comparisons which need to be made.

Questions of strategy are also determined by the grander socio-political framework within which the researcher operates. The kind of knowledge we generate as researchers is partially determined by the kind of projects that are successful in obtaining funding. In a sense, the knowledge we have is brought into being. Yet the manifest strategy is often one of scientific enquiry and sponsorship is often relegated to a footnote.

A further aspect of our exposition here is to encourage the reader to see the links between strategies and philosophies of research. The strategy or method we adopt often brings with it certain kinds of assumptions. Let us take the apparently straightforward matter of selecting a random sample of people for participation in a study. This makes a number of assumptions about the social protocols of the communities which are being sampled. That is, it is most viable in the sort of society where nothing wrong is seen in being approached and asked to participate in research by a stranger, and where records of the population of sufficient quality are kept as to make sampling from these a possibility. In some cultures the records might not be appropriate to allow this and it might be considered a breach of protocol or etiquette to approach strangers – an introduction from a trusted friend or relative might be the customary means of doing business. The adoption of an appropriate strategy then might depend on how the assumptions of the methods fit in with the social conventions of the culture within which they are applied.

The questions generally addressed in books about methodology usually relate to technical matters of research strategy. One may read a good deal about representative samples, normal distributions, F ratios, confidence intervals and so forth, but in the tradition established by Sir Ronald Fisher in his landmark publication (1925) there is little discussion of the psychosocial, philosophical, existential and ethical issues involved in research strategy. In contrast, our intention in this book is to promote an awareness of the underlying philosophical issues in research and to highlight how even mundane aspects of research strategy are underpinned by a complex choreography of theoretical and social issues which methodology specialists are only just beginning to explore.

Technical preoccupations in late modernity

This focus on technical issues at the expense of philosophical and ethical ones is a characteristic a number of authors have identified as being pervasive in the modern era. Giddens (1990, 1991) and Bauman (1993) argue that modernity is characterized by an unwillingness to confront major moral and existential issues. Furthermore, Giddens argues that this reluctance to address philosophical questions has something to do with the sheer pace of social and technical change. This is allied to an increasing global scope of change and proceeds in tandem with increases in the complexity of institutional frameworks that render modern society discontinuous with its pre-modern forms. These tendencies can be seen in health care research, inasmuch as the explosion in publications in the health sciences in the last fifty years has been accompanied by ever more complex problems and a growing pace of revolution in health care organizations as well as the communities they serve.

Zygmunt Bauman (1993) points to the pervasive experience of what he calls 'fragmentation'. In working life equally complex systems of expertise have come to predominate, and under regimes of evidence-based practice these generate truth claims that cannot be accessed or challenged by everyday lay understanding. So it is increasingly difficult to reflect on what our knowledge and our scientific practice mean in any broader sense. Thus most existing accounts of methodology contain very little of the philosophy from which they are derived. As secularization strips away spiritual truths and their moral imperatives, ethics too become focused on the narrow technical sense of the rights of participants and less on the role of our enquiry in the grander body politic. In Bauman's view, modernity seeks certainty in universality and foundations. Hence evidence, research and faith in science have an increasingly central role in modern life.

'Disembedding' and community participation

The process of singling out phenomena in the field of experience and calling them 'findings' and then attributing meaning to these research findings is one which anthropologists have sometimes described as 'disembedding'. That is, the research process enables certain findings to be taken out of their original context and used to set the agenda for practice and further research elsewhere. To explain this let us take the example of General Custer's jockstrap. An undergarment worn by the ill-fated General, resembling what we would now call a jockstrap, is on display at the Little Big Horn National Park Museum. This item, having been removed from its context, is given new meaning in the process. By stripping away the usual contexts of use of the item, and by giving it a celebrity status, the banality and unsavouriness usually associated with soiled underwear is taken away and the item is almost rendered sacred by becoming an exhibit. Moreover, it becomes emblematic of a life which was suddenly made important and posthumously grander than anything else in the routine skirmishes between troops and Native Americans. In short, Custer's jockstrap has been made special, and part of this process has involved taking it out of context. In an important way, research findings are somewhat like Custer's jockstrap. The research questions or findings are taken away from the murky, morally ambiguous questions of commercial interest or financial patronage and repositioned in a morally disinfected realm of epistemological purity.

In science, as in many spiritual traditions, selected everyday objects are rendered sacred. Fragments of wood are pieces of the true cross, and pieces of bone are the relics of saints. These comparisons are not entirely frivolous. Our point is that research transforms the meaning of experience and the nature of the strategy employed by the researcher plays an important but often unacknowledged role in helping to create that meaning. For example, in mental health care, the recent enthusiasm for cognitive behavioural interventions in schizophrenia has been promoted by a number of influential researchers and clinicians (Kuipers *et al.* 1997; Wykes *et al.* 1999; McCann 2001). However, it is possible to detect a growing sense of scepticism amongst practitioners who are not seeing the same positive results with their clients. Perhaps the results that are obtainable with carefully selected clients in prestigious teaching hospitals staffed by talented, dedicated and ambitious staff are not so easy to achieve with poor resources, demoralized staff and high caseloads. The efficacy of the therapeutic regime is sustained therefore by this process of disembedding – the findings from selected published research being granted an epistemological and practical privilege because of the way they are generated. The process of selectively focusing one's research on a particular part of the whole phenomenal field of human research – this highly specific group of clients undergoing a highly specific and meticulously occasioned intervention – more or less guarantees that the findings will be significant.

The research process then can be considered a disembedding mechanism whereby the findings of science and the science and expert knowledge can be excerpted from the often untidy natural habitats where it is originally found and interrelated across time and space. The process rests upon a shared trust in the validity of findings obtained by appropriate, agreed-upon strategies, and they form a kind of abstract steering system.

To counter this tendency of scientific enquiry to abstract or disembed the issues, persuading the community under study to participate in the design and execution of research is often identified as a desirable feature. This might especially be the case when the aim of the research in health care is to identify people in need of service or treatment who might not ordinarily come forward. An example of this is a piece of research described by Stratford *et al.* (2003) who undertook a study of conditions such as tuberculosis and HIV in a rural area of Florida. There have been well documented increases in both conditions in the USA over the last twenty years and they disproportionately affect poorer people.

The investigation was successful in that it identified previously undisclosed cases of the conditions as well as raising awareness of the problems in the neighbourhoods studied. Stratford *et al.* (2003) report that the enterprise was successful because the topic of the investigation was of immediate concern to the people involved. The communities concerned were troubled by a legacy of previous unhappy experiences of medical care and research and the involvement of local community members in planning and managing the study served to build confidence in the project. The high level of participation of all the socioeconomic and ethnic groups in the neighbourhood was achieved through a campaign that involved local press and broadcast media, local primary care workers and personal contact between friends and acquaintances. This was responsible for the relatively high (85 per cent) participation rate and the high level of participants (73 per cent) undergoing the necessary diagnostic testing. Whereas only three participants were identified as having active tuberculosis a much higher proportion (25 per cent) showed some presence of the disease and of these most had chest radiographs, and about a third went on to undertake further treatment.

A further interesting twist to this piece of research is that it was published in the *Journal of General Internal Medicine*. This in itself is significant, as a publication of this kind might, in years gone by, have been the place where one might usually find socially disembedded investigations of the body's major organ systems. This, then, is a sign of the times. Even in the case of investigations of disease and immunity the participation of community members was considered to be important and the discipline of 'internal medicine' considers this of sufficient interest and merit to publish.

The implications for strategy are twofold. First, this represents an acknowledgement that the participants in most health care investigations are sentient self-aware entities and we may take a variety of stances towards the research process. On the one hand we might adopt the oppositional stance sometimes found in randomized controlled trials where the intention is to try to outwit their tendency to guess what is going on in the study, with randomization and placebo treatments, as is the case in many randomized controlled trials. The other approach, as we have seen here, is to try to harness participants' inventiveness, resourcefulness and desire to take part in the study not only as 'subjects' in the traditional sense, but as workers and managers, and providing creative and scientific impetus too. It is perhaps this quality of the research of Stafford *et al.* which led to their high participation rate and the success of the study in identifying so many cases.

This leads to the second point. The high proportion of the sample showing some evidence of infection approaches the rates one might have found in a European city in the nineteenth century and is rather higher than one would expect to find in a conventional sample survey of the US population. The involvement of people themselves in the research discloses different layers of reality. These may be difficult to replicate formally and are often dependent on a particular set of social relationships which the researcher is able to cultivate at the time. Nevertheless, as this investigation demonstrates, they may have very important implications for health. Often health problems cluster amongst socially marginalized and hard-to-contact groups in the population and this kind of emphasis on community involvement and participation can bring the issues to the surface.

Robust strategies and the art of anticipating criticism

A robust research strategy is one which is able to anticipate any likely process of scrutiny and which will produce knowledge fit for the social purpose to which it might be put by the researcher or those who use the findings. Strong claims about causal mechanisms or significant policy commitments may well need appropriately bullet-proof evidence. Moreover, it is often difficult as a researcher to anticipate just what direction the assaults will come from. Epistemology, as Clausewitz didn't quite say, 'is the continuation of politics by other means'.

Part of developing a robust strategy, as we have indicated, might involve using a variety of strands of data collected in different ways yet all bearing on the question.

It is in this context that some authors have recommended the strategy of triangulation in research in order to gain some strength from the synergy of a number of methods or sources of evidence which can be brought to bear on the problem in question. To take an example from a project one of us (BB) has been involved in, we were interested in how staff in community mental health had taken up the idea of evidence-based practice. At the end of a period of fieldwork we had a number of formally conducted interviews, some completed questionnaires and a wide range of experiences of talking to people in corridors, car parks and common rooms. In addition there were a number of experiences we had shared with our informants as they had tried to access information about problems they were trying to resolve with their clients. The formal electronic and paper-based sources of scientific information were seldom used (Crawford *et al.* 2002), but great use was made of informal contact with colleagues, organizational and occupational folklore, articles in *Nursing Times* and popular magazines and TV programmes. These wide-ranging observations, people's accounts and our own sense of custom and practice in the discipline were all sources of 'data'. The task then was to make sense of these confusing and sometimes contradictory strands of evidence.

Triangulation is a way of making sense of this. By combining multiple observers, theories, methods and empirical materials, researchers can hope to overcome the weakness or intrinsic biases and the problems that come from single-method, single-observer, single-theory studies. Often the purpose of triangulation in specific contexts is to confirm findings in the hope that through convergence of different perspectives the point at which the perspectives converge is seen to represent 'reality', or at least a sufficiently robust version of it to publish.

More recently, one of the most prominent enthusiasts for the strategy in the social sciences has been Norman Denzin (e.g. 1989), who has written in glowing terms about it:

Triangulation, or the use of multiple methods, is a plan of action that will raise sociologists above the personal biases that stem from single methodologies. By combining methods and investigators in the same study, observers can partially overcome the deficiencies that flow from one investigator or one method.

(Denzin 1989: 42)

Triangulation is believed to offer solutions to a variety of research questions (Foss and Ellersen 2002) and may take several forms, for example as shown in Box 8.1.

Triangulation, then, has been the subject of considerable practical and theoretical interest in health care research and, especially in nursing, has often been advanced as a desirable goal. For example, Adamsen and Tewes (2000) describe how they examined nursing records, nurses' own knowledge and patients' subjective reports of problems. As we might anticipate, patients' reports contained the most problems, reporting especially that they had difficulties with pain and sleep. Overall, only 31 per cent of the problems reported by the patients were mentioned in the records kept by the nurses. On the whole nurses appeared more knowledgeable about the patients' problems than was apparent from the records, yet still fell short of the level of difficulty actually reported by patients. This kind of finding then

---

Box 8.1 Types of triangulation

1 *Data triangulation* – may involve sampling data over time, in different settings or from different people.
2 *Investigator triangulation* – involves the use of multiple, rather than single observers. In quantitative research this might involve calculating values to indicate the proportion of agreement, or in qualitative research it might involve comparing field notes and narrative records.
3 *Theory triangulation* – involves using multiple theoretical schemes in the interpretation of the phenomenon. This might yield consistency or perhaps different theories might illuminate different aspects of the phenomenon.
4 *Methodological triangulation* – involves using multiple methods and may consist of within-method or between-method strategies. For example, one may compare the results of different questionnaires (within method) or compare the results of a questionnaire study with those of focus groups (between method).
5 *Multiple triangulation* – the researcher combines, say, multiple observers, theoretical perspectives, sources of data and methodologies.

(Based on Denzin 1989; Foss and Ellersen 2002)

---

reinforces the need for a triangulated approach to the study of concepts, issues and problems in health care. The example given here could be multiplied over a variety of different fields of social research.

Thus we can see that addressing the problem using different strategies for eliciting reports of abuse can yield different pictures. Different kinds of data collection yield different results and a shrewd researcher might well want to exploit different kinds of method to identify the best one for his or her purposes. Indeed, even if we decide that we would rather have the data from a standardized checklist to facilitate statistical comparisons, it might be advantageous to know how far this departs from the kind of data you might get from depth interviews.

If we take the issue of domestic violence as an example, we can also illustrate the potential controversies surrounding theory triangulation. Denzin (1989: 75) claims that 'pitting alternative theories against the same body of data is a more efficient means of criticism – and it more comfortably conforms with the scientific method'. In the case of domestic violence we can see how this has a number of implications for research strategy and also has implications of an ethical and political nature.

In the contemporary era a good deal of research and awareness raising on domestic violence has stressed men's responsibility and culpability as batterers. Early work by Dobash and Dobash (1979) was in this mould. However, the nature of the problem and the means by which responsibility can be attributed have raised a number of controversial issues. For example, family systems theorists have proposed that the process of violence can be conceived of as a circular process in the family system, with reciprocal interactions between partners leading to an escalation of violence (Magill 1989), or have an assumption that the victim has somehow provoked the abuse. Alternatively, some thinkers and therapists have supported the notions of 'co-responsibility' or 'co-dependency'. For example, Minuchin (1984: 175) says 'focusing on the male as monster makes people experience their individual separation and perpetuates defensive aggression. The goal should be to explore and improve people's independence.' Equally, there is a suspicion that these kinds of perspectives are complicit with 'blaming the victim' in focusing on her role and downgrading the responsibility that lies with the batterer. For example, as Hansen and Harway (1993: 81) argue, 'Only when we recognise that battering is solely the responsibility of the man and that no woman deserves to be beaten and that the social/political context has a direct impact on the maintenance of the behaviour is the family system likely to change.' Or more bluntly: 'family systems don't abuse women – men do'.

In this example, then, we can see that different kinds of theories not only illuminate different aspects of the problem but also have important ethical and even legal implications, in terms of how we might intervene and where we might look for solutions.

Taking this further and working through the implications for practice and further enquiry might seem difficult. The theories are at an impasse because they point to fundamentally different things and are also in important senses opposed to one another and exist so as to discount one another. This impasse, then, might present a rather difficult case for theory triangulation.

However, there have been some recent attempts to develop ways of understanding domestic violence which are at once systemic and also focus attention on the batterer as the responsible individual on whom rests the onus for change. One such attempt is described by Rivett and Rees (2004), whose approach to interventions with violent men attempts to retain the focus on the batterer as the prime site of change, and yet also retain an awareness of the broader family and social systems within which the violence is embedded. The larger scale patterns of misogyny provide the languages, conceptual tools and techniques of martially violent men and afford some legitimation to their beliefs.

As Milner (2004) notes, applying a gender 'lens' to research on domestic violence in the last thirty years or so has highlighted the extent to which previous analyses substantially underestimated men's violence in intimate relationships (Bograd 1990). As with the Stratford *et al.* example above, once the right kind of strategic 'lens' is deployed, a great deal comes into the purview of the social or health care researcher that might not otherwise have been disclosed. In the case of domestic violence, says Milner (2004), there were increasingly strong arguments emerging in the literature that the roots of violence lie not in individual pathology or family conflicts but in men's domination and control over women.

Once again, however, the approaches, theories and strategies of researchers and practitioners generate a great deal of controversy. The pro-feminist perspective on domestic violence services has proved particularly controversial (Harway and O'Neil 1999). Some commentators believe that this perspective both undervalues the incidence of the abuse of men by women and effectively treats men as inherently 'bad' whilst ignoring the trauma experienced by many batterers (Dutton 1995; Rivett and Rees 2004). Mankowski *et al.* (2002) also note that whichever kind of model is used in therapy it runs the risk of missing significant complexities involved in domestic violence. Especially, they say, what it missed is the 'collateral damage' – the effect on other people in the household and beyond such as children, other family members, friends and neighbours.

There is another aspect to the theory and strategy here which we should note. It is remarkable how bounded this thinking and action concerning domestic violence is. That is, no one seems to be suggesting that we should abandon couple-oriented heterosexual relationships entirely and instead undertake more communitarian or polyamorous liaisons. This might sidestep the issues of ownership and control which underlie a good deal of domestic violence. There seems to be an underlying belief that, rather like a romantic story, the institutions of monogamy and heterosexuality can somehow be recuperated and absolved of responsibility if only these men would 'take responsibility for themselves' and stop beating their partners. The theoretical perspectives involved in research or practice, then, are often bounded, even when they appear to be diverse. Of course, it is easier to convince people to be less violent in relationships than it is to convince them that they don't need relationships *per se* at all.

The examples above show how problems and topics can be looked at from different angles and how this might lead to fresh insights. Moreover, if we are lucky, it will lead us to understand the subject matter in a manner which gives us more confidence about the trustworthiness of our observations, findings and conclusions.

However, despite its popularity, triangulation raises a number of problematic methodological and philosophical issues. Several critical voices have been raised against this popular strategy (Sim and Sharp 1998). Broadly, the criticisms of triangulation fall into four categories. First, it is argued that triangulation is not always a necessary ingredient of a research project, as some questions, framed in fairly specific terms, may be adequately answered with the use of a single method. For example, if the intention of a proposed study is to understand the subjective perceptions and experiences of individuals suffering from a particular chronic illness, an approach based upon an ethnographic strategy would seem suitable.

Second, triangulation is often argued to be a means of ensuring the validity of data. For example, Brewer and Hunter (1989) maintain that 'multiple measurement offers the chance to assess each method's validity in the light of other methods'. In relation to nursing research, Carr (1994) proposes triangulation as 'a valuable means of discovering the truth about nursing' – a very grand claim indeed! Bradley (1995) argues that 'methodological triangulation offers the researcher greater confidence in the validity of results'. Sim and Sharp (1998) argue, however, that these are dubious claims, especially as many authors are not necessarily clear about the definition of the sort of validity the triangulation in question is enhancing. If our different observations agree, or if they diverge, how are we to decide which is the more trustworthy? In a good deal of research on validity, one of the various measures is designated the criterion measure. In other words, it is granted a privileged status as being more likely to be 'true' – however that is defined. However, in many health care situations, if, say, our questionnaire does not yield results which agree with our interviews and these do not concur with our field observations, how do we adjudicate between these different sets of data? Can we easily say whether one is more worthy of being taken seriously than the others? As Sim and Sharp (1998) warn, often researchers make unwarranted assumptions about the criterion status of one method in relation to others. To the extent that triangulation does secure validity, this is more likely to involve content validity relating to the scope of findings.

However, it is sometimes implied that triangulation, perhaps by virtue of its connotations of surveying, can lead to criterion-related validity, that is, it can enhance the accuracy of the findings.

Third, the bringing together of different methods in triangulation tends to ignore fundamental questions as to whether the divergent methods share sufficient epistemological common ground for this to be meaningful. To what extent can we bring together data derived from a technique associated with making strong foundationalist claims, such as a sample survey, with one which is highly constructivist, such as conversation analysis which usually sees realities as being constructed by the social actors concerned?

Finally, the use of different theoretical frameworks is often advocated in the form of theory triangulation, as mentioned above. Many authors are enthusiastic:

> There would seem to be value in approaching empirical materials with multiple perspectives in mind. Data that would refute central hypotheses could be collected, and various theoretical points of view could be placed side by side to assess their utility and power.
>
> (Denzin 1989: 127)

Furthermore, Fielding and Fielding (1986) advance the view that theory triangulation is a fruitful enterprise in social research. However, the use of theories to illuminate data from different perspectives tends to mask a number of important differences between different theoretical perspectives that may be less straightforward. Theories often contain distinct epistemological assumptions about the status of data that determine how particular data should be interpreted. For example, symbolic interactionist theory would lead an investigator working in this tradition to take a particular view of data that might not be shared by a phenomenologist. On visiting a friend in hospital recovering from an operation to have a tumour ('the size of a grapefruit', as it was described at the time) removed from one of her ovaries, one of us (BB) was rather disturbed at the size of the air bubbles travelling down her drip feed tube into the vein in her arm. Fearing that she would have to endure an attack of the bends, or might even die, he attempted to summon assistance. The nurse who eventually arrived explained that a small number of air bubbles 'shouldn't be much of a problem' and it would only be dangerous 'if she was a baby or something'. Now, from a phenomenological point of view we might pursue this in terms of the nurse holding a representation of how the human circulatory system worked and the impact on this of different kinds of hazards. On the other hand, a symbolic interactionist might have focused on her management of the situation so as to minimize the seriousness of the events and minimize the potential culpability of herself and the hospital. The honest soul of phenomenological enquiry contrasts with the impression manager of symbolic interactionism, even though these two approaches are often thought of as being quite similar.

In the case of the nurse and the bubbles in the tube, her reassurances contrasted oddly with her frantic flicking of the tube so as to make the bubbles rise rather than descend into the vein. Perhaps all was not quite as well as she maintained. However, triangulation by itself does not provide clues as to the relative weight to assign to the various items of data. The theories make different kinds of claims about social and medical realities. Theory triangulation makes assumptions about the compatibility of theories which may not be warranted and underrates the distinctiveness and incommensurability of different theoretical perspectives.

Thus, as a result of these limitations perhaps researchers should approach triangulation in a cautious and critical way, with due regard to the rather dubious assumptions upon which it frequently rests (Sim and Sharp 1998). Perhaps one solution is to re-evaluate what triangulation can achieve for social researchers:

> Different methods have emerged as a product of different theoretical traditions, and therefore combining them can add range and depth, but not accuracy. In other words, there is a case for triangulation, but not the one Denzin makes. We should combine theories and methods carefully and purposefully with the intention of adding breadth or depth to our analysis, but not for the purpose of pursuing 'objective' truth.
>
> (Fielding and Fielding 1986: 87)

Triangulation may still be a useful strategy, but for rather different purposes than are sometimes claimed. It may be that announcing its death, as Blaikie (1991) does, is a little premature. Triangulation may be more valuable if it is applied more specifically to the problem of securing content validity when exploring complex social phenomena. We would advocate instead a greater attention to the often implicit assumptions entailed by the use of particular methods, and their implications for how we understand the phenomena we investigate.

Turning strategy upon ourselves

Finally, let us consider the strategies that researchers may use upon themselves. Strategy involves reaching outwards to the world beyond the would-be scientist's own personal boundaries, but it also involves changes in consciousness. The researcher may be said to undergo 'research training' and acquire disciplines of mind, yet there are equally significant personal changes in the process of enquiry. In some disciplines, such as philosophy in classical antiquity, the enquirer's own personal journey is the most important part of the enterprise. In any event, the management of ourselves as human actors and the personal strategies involved are often experienced, yet many textbooks neglect the thorny question of the effect the research has on the researcher.

There have, however, been some attempts to make sense of this. Kelly and Conner (1979) characterized the personal journey through the research process as an emotional cycle of change, involving reflections about one's practice. Five stages in this emotional cycle are identified (Lancaster 1982; Croom *et al.* 2000), as identified in Box 8.2.

We have tried to highlight areas of controversy in this volume, but even so we have merely scratched the surface of the potential for disagreement. The kind of reflective critical awareness of methodological and philosophical issues in research which we are advocating may form part of a self-validating cycle of knowledge generation (Doyal 1993; Croom *et al.* 2000). From the point of view of qualitative methodology, the concept of

---

Box 8.2 The 'emotional cycle' of research experience

Stage one, 'uninformed optimism', tends to be present at the beginning of the research process, perhaps when it is felt that research can solve the problems.

Stage two, 'informed pessimism', is reached when difficulties emerge. This may occur because of the problems in implementing research, or when the researchers feel overwhelmed by the data and have difficulty in making sense of it in relation to the original research questions. Research may make solutions even more difficult to find.

Stage three, 'hopeful realism', becomes apparent once the researchers analyse their concepts and data. Here frustration may abate and instead awareness of the complexities of social or health care settings supervenes. This involves realizing that it is not simply the research that has made an apparently simple and intuitive situation more complex, but pre-existing complexity may have been revealed and labelled by the research process.

Stage four, 'informed optimism', is achieved when the application of the evolving analysis to current problems starts to organize researchers' understanding. Sometimes research might suggest a solution in line with the original questions but, equally, researchers may be able to develop a shared language for describing the problems.

Stage five, 'rewarding completion', occurs towards the end of the research when the analysis is developed into a tool for use in practice, perhaps recorded in documentary form. Here a variety of constituencies must be satisfied, some of whom might be actively antagonistic.

(Based on Lancaster 1982; Croom *et al.* 2000).

'anthropological strangeness' (Garfinkel 1967) – as the world of work might seem to non-practitioners – might augment the findings and analysis of researchers by recognizing in the research situation the history, values and beliefs which have perhaps become too familiar to practitioners to be explicated.

Further reading

Brewer, J. and Hunter, A. (1989) *Multi-method Research: A Synthesis of Styles*, Newbury Park, CA: Newbury Park.

Denzin, N.K. (1989) *The Research Act: A Theoretical Introduction to Sociological Methods*, 3rd edition. Englewood Cliffs, NJ: Prentice-Hall. (A classic text by one of the leading enthusiasts for triangulation and one of the leading theorists of qualitative methodologies.)

Maxwell, J.A. (2005) *Qualitative Research Design: An Interactive Approach*. London: Sage Publications. (Provides a step-by-step guide to planning qualitative research in practical settings.)

Thomas, W.I. and Znaniecki, F. (1918) *The Polish Peasant in Europe and America*. Chicago, IL: University of Chicago Press. (One of the earliest works to employ triangulation as a research strategy, this book helped to define social science as we know it today.)

9   The implications for analysis

Introduction – the meaning of analysis

An awareness of analytical dilemmas, and the implications of choices they presuppose, may also inform the analysis and presentation of data, and this forms the subject of this, the third of the chapters that deal with the implications of thinking about where one sits, as an applied researcher, in the field of possibilities identified in Chapters 2–6.

In making sense of the key concepts of this chapter it might first be appropriate to identify what analysis might mean in health care research. Many of us first encounter the concept in the form of statistical analysis but there is far more to it than that. Analysis involves a whole range of choices, decisions, ideas and ideologies which go far beyond anything presented in most introductory textbooks about research methods. In this volume, as the reader will have appreciated by now, we are seeking to create a different kind of awareness about methodologies. We shall be encouraging the reader to reflect on the ways in which analysis subtly – and in some ways not so subtly – constructs the meaning of the results and hence helps to construct the meaning of the larger scale world of health and illness. Even methods which apparently offer the opportunity for objectivity, or those which claim an apparently rigorous or systematic basis, are themselves lurid with values, ideologies and tacit theories about what matters which the critically aware researcher would be well advised to understand.

Our aims in this chapter, then, are to try to pick apart some of the traditions and conventions in presenting analysis and to try to make the reader aware of some of the things that formal research reports rarely express. We will do so via some extended examples worked through in detail and via a series of shorter examples intended to illustrate the role of researchers' commitments, values, discursive resources and cultural contexts throughout the research process. It is our intention, then, to reformulate the research process as a kind of dialogue, of researchers with one another, with their socio-political context and with their participants, where they make use of culturally available technologies and concepts to formulate a defensible version of reality.

'Imposition': the researcher's role in analysis

The imposition problem relates to the way in which a researcher's values, frameworks and commitments insinuate themselves into the analysis and presentation of data. For example, in presenting descriptive statistics of data, researchers very rarely disclose to the reader their agency in constructing the data. Even in this simple context an acknowledgement of the 'imposition' problem (Pawson 1989) might be enlightening and would involve an exposition of who counted what, for what purpose and under what contextual circumstances (Dorling and Simpson 1999). Let us examine this imposition problem in a little more detail because it underlies a great many analyses in the health and social sciences, and, whether the researcher is using qualitative or quantitative techniques, the issue of the researcher's own frame of reference and how it informs the analysis will have to be addressed by any reflective or thoughtful investigator. It may well be that researchers are addressing questions where their own values are in conflict with those of the people they are researching. The imposition problem was highlighted most famously and forcefully by the Brazilian educationalist Paulo Freire (e.g. 1972) from his experience with adult literacy schemes in South America. In his work he was concerned that the views of the people that adult literacy schemes were intended to help were being subsumed beneath the views of more powerful groups such as educators and policy makers. This 'imposition' is both epistemological and political, in that it means that the world view of the élite groups is privileged and that it is imposed over the sometimes more subtle and nuanced appreciation people have for the world around them. Freire highlighted dilemmas over the kinds of texts used to teach people to read, the form that this education should take, and the extent to which this education reinforced the notion that the unequal societies in which they lived were just and rational. To avoid this imposition of a world view, Freire advocated an approach where researchers study with and work with a group of people so as to learn what is important to them and how their social and physical world works. By means of discussion with people who live in the situation under study in what he called 'culture circles' it is possible to grasp the key features of that situation. Thus, the emphasis on participative enquiry that he foregrounded has important implications for whose view of the world we impose on the raw material of experience. Indeed, in important respects it makes a difference to what that experience looks like in the first place.

Thus, shifting the frame of reference so as to be more ethnographically informed can help us understand the persistence of practices which educators and health care workers might be trying to change and understand also why efforts based on legislation and conventional health education are unsuccessful. The approaches, theoretical frameworks and tacit value systems we impose upon the phenomena in question bring to light different phenomena and lead to very different courses of action.

To return to the question of 'imposition', then, it is possible to argue that it is not simply a matter of imposing a framework or way of seeing the world and 'distorting' the data or 'forcing the pieces to fit' in any simple sense, but instead about appreciating the use of different theories or frameworks in bringing to light different aspects of the situation.

Sometimes, analysis involves bringing different perspectives together which have not hitherto been juxtaposed. For example as mentioned earlier in Chapter 4, a number of scholars such as Peckover (2002) have described how health visiting, which has usually been seen as involving the support of mothers with young children, can also be seen in terms of its disciplinary, policing and governing functions. That is not to say that health visitors do their rounds telling people what to do in any obvious sense (though they may sometimes offer advice) but it means that they encourage a particular implicit model of good child care practice and offer an opportunity to survey what mothers are doing. The process of analysis here involves taking some of the insights from the work of Foucault (for example, 1973, 1979) and Rose (for example, 1989) and applying them to health visiting. Thus everyday practices in health, education and welfare can be seen not merely as supportive or caring activity but in terms of how it shapes conduct and leads to new forms of consciousness on the part of those involved.

Analyses in the health and social sciences

Analyses in the health and social sciences can encompass a wide variety of activities. Thus it is difficult to define exactly what analysis involves. However, where analysis is performed, whether this be conceptual, or empirical, qualitative or quantitative, there are some common themes in the activity. Analysis tends to emphasize a clear, precise approach with particular weight being placed upon argumentation and evidence, avoidance of ambiguity and attention to detail. This approach owes a great deal to the foundation laid in the tradition of analytic philosophy begun by Gottlob Frege at the beginning of the twentieth century. Originally, in philosophy, there was a great deal of emphasis on the analysis of language or meaning. However, throughout the disciplines in which we are interested, analysis is characterized by its effort to clarify issues, theories or data through careful enquiry and logical rigour using methods which can be agreed upon by a community of scholars. Analysis may well involve a critical evaluation, usually made by breaking a subject (either material or intellectual) down into its constituent parts, then describing the parts and their relationship to the whole.

In addition to the usual meaning in the health sciences of analysis, referring to the statistical analysis presented in many research reports, the whole question of analysis might well involve conceptual formulation, redefinition and clarification. Indeed, using the term 'analysis' in a literature search in the health field may well turn up a great many items that involve conceptual or philosophical analyses too.

It might involve specifying a style of enquiry, for example in the form of community health needs analysis which can be defined as the process of identifying needs, opportunities and resources involved in initiating community health projects (Haglund *et al.* 1990). Harvey (cited in Billings and Cowley 1995) considers community needs analysis to be an illustration of factors that must be addressed to improve the health of a population.

Conceptual analysis, on the other hand, can liberate concepts and variables which are believed to have a bearing on health and illness yet whose immediate relevance might be unclear. For example, Maijala *et al.* (2000) provide such an analysis of the concept of envy. From the viewpoint of health care science, the analysis of envy can aid the process of understanding human beings from the perspective of subjective health and illness and thus may lead to important insights for health promotion. Envy was conceived of by the authors as a dimension of a person's health and illness and was therefore a meaningful constituent of a person's well-being. It describes a phenomenon which enables us to deepen our understanding in a way relevant to health care science and practice. As a result of their deliberations, the authors come to understand envy in the following terms:

> Envy is a painful and contradictory emotion based on an experience of lacking and comparison, which includes a distinctive desire to obtain something good the other possesses and the envious person is lacking. The things important to oneself determine the object of envy, which the other represents. Envy may include feelings of injustice, shame, guilt, grief as well as admiration and hopes for identification. It is modified greed, suggestive of the emotional state of jealousy.
>
> (Maijala *et al.* 2000: 1348)

The authors argue that this sense of subjective envy and its understanding can facilitate the identification of one's own wishes and appraisal of one's limitations, which they believe to be valuable. Maijala *et al.* (2000) are convinced of the pertinence of this kind of analysis to the development of personally valuable qualities such as self-awareness and the ability to reflect on oneself and one's relationship with one's milieu. In their view such an analysis makes it bearable to accept one's feelings and to grieve over one's faults. This also, they say, allows envy to be countered with gratitude, generosity and happiness. Thus, although Maijala *et al.* proffer a 'conceptual analysis', as we can see, the analysis itself draws deeply upon the humanist model of persons as potentially self-aware, unitary beings who are hosts to predictable and perfectible emotional states. In other words, this analysis has embedded within it the values of essentialism discussed in contrast to the work of Foucault and others in Chapter 4.

In conceptual analyses like the one featured above it is sometimes clear that the value base of the authors has insinuated itself into the text. However, even in activities such as inferential statistics, one may also uncover a number of complex and deeply ingrained ways in which social values are embedded in apparently neutral techniques (Irvine *et al.* 1979; Dorling and Simpson 1999). To pursue this point, let us consider how this is reflected in different kinds of statistical inference, and consider the contrasts between 'Bayesian' and 'frequentist' methods as described in Box 9.1.

Let us begin to delve into this question of analysis, prediction and the selection of an optimal course of action with an example, helpfully supplied by Holdsworth and Dodgson (2003). As Dr Johnson famously remarked nearly 250 years ago, whenever two Englishmen meet, their first topic of conversation is the weather. Now, despite intuitions to the contrary, the UK's Meteorological Office 24-hour weather forecast is more than 80 per cent

---

Box 9.1 Contrasting 'frequentist' and 'Bayesian' statistics

Frequentist approaches – These encompass the vast majority of statistical techniques taught in research methods courses. They could be described as 'frequentist', in that they are concerned with what would happen if a very large number of observations were made, and estimate the likelihood of the current results occurring by chance. Hence the interest in identifying whether the likelihood is less than 0.05.

Bayesian approaches, by contrast, examine the likelihood of occurrence of an event on previous occasions and use this as a way of estimating its likelihood in the present. Bayes' theorem is a means of quantifying uncertainty. Based on probability theory, the theorem defines a rule for refining an hypothesis by factoring in additional evidence and background information.

accurate in predicting the occurrence of rain. Part of the reason for this accuracy is what's called the 'base rate'. That is, the probability of rain in the UK in any hour is very low – a mere 0.08. Therefore, predicting whether it will rain during any hour during which one may want to undertake certain practical activities such as drying washing, painting one's house or holding a barbecue is twice as likely to be wrong as it is to be right; thus, as Matthews (1996: 766) claims: 'basing our decision on Met Office forecasts . . . the base-rate effect makes cheerful disregard of rain the optimal strategy'. Rain, whilst it may be personally distressing, is rarely catastrophic. However, this strategy of ignoring low frequency or probability events may be more problematic if one applies it to floods, suicide attempts or deaths.

As Holdsworth and Dodgson (2003) remind us, weather forecasts are rarely based on probability alone. Meteorological calculations of the probability of rainfall at particular times and places are routinely augmented by informal estimates of local conditions and informally estimated trends in order to arrive at specific forecasts (Meteorological Office 2001: 8).

All this talk about the weather has some important implications for how we make sense of the task facing health care researchers and clinical professionals. Base rate statistics concerning many of the common conditions which we wish to understand can only tell us so much.

The dilemmas facing the weather forecaster who analyses the patterns of air flow, temperature and pressure over the globe are similar to those faced by workers in health care. On the one hand, as Holdsworth and Dodgson (2003) argue, it is believed to be important for clinical practitioners to base their practice on evidence. Increasingly judgements as to the optimal course of action have to be justified by evidence. The kind of evidence which is most favoured is the sort of material that is published in the technical journals of the discipline or is summarized in systematic reviews of the research in a particular field. Throughout this process, researchers, editors and referees attempt to apply the most rigorous standards. Generally, with the quantitative results of these studies, the most concise way of expressing them is by quoting the frequency with which certain outcomes occur following certain specifiable initial conditions. This is what is sometimes referred to as the 'frequentist' approach.

For example, it is on the basis of studies like these that it can be stated with some confidence that around 50 per cent of people who are prescribed the antidepressant drug Imipramine show some improvement in their condition (Bollini *et al.* 1999). For those interested in the outcome of depression, we can assert on the basis of research by Morgan *et al.* (1998) that depression carries a lifetime risk of suicide of 15 per cent, that 1 per cent of people who have deliberately self-harmed eventually complete suicide (Gunnell and Frankel 1994), and that, according to Jick *et al.* (1995), 2.8 per cent of people who repeatedly indulge in deliberate self-harm will complete suicide within eight years. These are 'evidence-based' statements, often based on large-scale studies conducted over a number of years, or on the accumulated wisdom of a whole tradition of research.

Even here, in the face of studies whose scale and rigour are beyond the grasp or the wit of most of us to undertake ourselves, one must sound notes of caution. Data from the USA do not necessarily translate well into the UK context and vice versa. It is useful to know a bit more about where the data came from. Moreover, patterns of distress change over time both in terms of their incidence in the population and in terms of the clusters of symptoms which co-occur (Taylor and Field 2003; West and Sweeting 2003).

However, the clinical practitioner is usually faced with an individual and wishes to shape interventions for the good of that specific individual. The most highly valued evidence available to the practitioner then becomes of limited value. This is because most evidence is concerned with statistical frequencies; that is, the frequency with which a particular outcome might be expected in specified circumstances. When applied to an individual seeking help in the consulting room what any such relevant evidence asserts, applied to that individual, is: this individual belongs to a large class of individuals, 50 per cent of whom improve if taking Imipramine, 15 per cent of whom complete suicide eventually, 2.8 per cent within the next eight years, and so on. There is thus an epistemic gap between what the evidence warrants and what the clinician seeks for each individual patient. This is because the evidence relates to classes of individual and their shared features; but the clinician relates to individuals and to their idiosyncratic character-istics and circumstances. Probably nowhere is this epistemic gap between evidence and applicability more evident than in the area of clinical risk assessment and management. The clinician is faced with an individual with a depressive illness who has commenced an antidepressant medication, but not before being admitted to a general hospital for treatment of a Paracetamol overdose. That individual discloses continuing thoughts of sui-cide. What evidence-based risk assessment is the clinician to arrive at? On the evidence: that this patient's depressive illness has a 50:50 chance of showing an improvement in the next two to three weeks; that the patient belongs to a group in which one in 100 complete suicide, and simul-taneously belongs to another group in which 15 in 100 complete suicide eventually, at some time in the indefinite future. This is also to assert, equivalently: that there is a 50:50 chance that there will be no improvement in depressive symptoms in the next two to three weeks; that 99 times out of 100 an individual in these circumstances does not complete suicide; and 85 times out of 100 an individual who has had this illness will eventually die of something other than suicide. In fact, because very serious outcomes such as suicide or homicide have such a low base rate, that is they occur very infrequently, quantified evidence alone will never rationally justify interven-tions designed to avert such rare but serious outcomes. Thus, the problem that low base rates represent for classical frequentist statistical prediction of rare events may lead to the pessimistic conclusion that it is not possible rationally to justify reasonable judgements about the risk of adverse events.

However, this is to suppose that a frequentist approach to the estimation of risk exhausts the process of rationally justifiable estimations of risk. This is not a supposition that is generally accepted in other areas where practical reasoning about future contingencies is required. For example, Caelli *et al.* (2003) deal with concept networks, inference and decision support via reasoning with probabilities and so, right from the start, build into their research design the flexibility to handle and combine evidence under uncertainty. Indeed, such techniques have already been used extensively in medical reasoning systems (Szolovits 1995).

Notions of risk: in the abundance of rigour, controversies multiply

Howson's (1998) analysis of documentary sources such as medical journals and official reports concerned with the development of cervical screening is followed by an analysis of women's accounts of their experience of cervical screening. Howson observes that whilst expert discourse constructs 'objective risk categories' related to age and lifestyle, the women themselves articulate personalized risks which emerged from their own experience of screening participation, including timing, reliability and trustworthiness of the process.

In a landmark paper published in 1964 the Nobel prizewinning scientist Sir Peter Medawar famously argued that the scientific paper was 'fraudulent'. By this he meant that the conventional format for presenting research misrepresented the process of enquiry. Having a structure with an abstract, introduction, method, results discussion and conclusion did not adequately represent the process of research. In particular he felt that the hypothetico-deductive story told in many papers was deceptive in that deductions did not necessarily flow from prior research and theory and that hypotheses were not necessarily tested in the manner originally proposed by Karl Popper. Often, the hypotheses were made up after the scientist had performed the experiment rather than before.

Even when apparently objective and numerically based analytic procedures are employed, the potential for controversy is still substantial. Let us take the technique of meta-analysis. This is often advocated as a relatively objective means of summing up the results from a number of similar studies.

However, meta-analysis can open up controversies as well as help to resolve them. Judgements involved in the presentation of findings by researchers can be crucial in affecting the way that readers are led to make sense of the field of findings relating to a particular topic of enquiry. To illustrate what we mean, we will consider a debate which has been unfolding in the field of breast cancer screening over the last few years. Now, it is not our intention to come to firm conclusions about what the true position is. Rather, we want the reader to be aware of how disputes and debates are conducted and how decisions made about analysis and the presentation of findings can make a big difference to the kinds of conclusions people draw. Moreover, in the case of breast cancer screening it can potentially make a substantial difference to policy and to participants' survival itself.

Through the 1980s and early 1990s the practice of 'mammography' – screening for breast cancer by X-ray examination – came to be widely accepted as a result of a number of clinical trials demonstrated a substantial reduction in risk. This kind of screening came to be advocated on a number of fronts, because it was argued that early detection, before the disease 'spread', permitted therapy that was less invasive and more effective. Questions that remained were largely about the efficacy for younger women and optimal frequency for older women. At the turn of the new century this consensus was challenged in a series of interventions by two researchers at the Nordic branch of the Cochrane Collaboration, Gøtzsche and Olsen (for example, Gøtzsche and Olsen 2000; Olsen and Gøtzsche 2001a, 2001b, 2001c). They argued that the studies which had indicated a positive effect of mammography in terms of the improvements in longevity and well-being were methodologically poorer than the studies which showed a negative effect or a null effect. Olsen and Gøtzsche achieved some notoriety for their claim that instead mammography exposes women to a good deal of risk and leads to them having surgical procedures whose beneficial effect is dubious.

There are a number of complicating factors. What exactly is a breast examination? In categorizing, coding and examining the studies and screening practices some important ambiguities arise. There may be important differences between the kinds of examinations carried out by women on themselves and those carried out by trained and experienced professionals.

> Any effect of physical examination is likely to be small. A study of 122471 women found no effect of regular self-examination of the breast on breast cancer mortality after 9 years of follow-up, even though twice as many of the intervention group consulted an oncologist.
>
> (Gøtzsche and Olsen 2000: 135)

However, Freedman *et al.* (2004) state, in contrast to this, that whereas self-examination may be of little value, breast examination by an expert is effective at cancer detection and may even show up lumps that are not detected by mammography. There are thus contrasting rates of effectiveness depending on how and by whom an examination is performed.

Now, one might think that a mammogram itself, and what happens to the participants taking part in the study, are relatively unambiguous. However, here there are a number of complicating factors too. People in the experimental group assigned to the condition where regular mammograms were undertaken did not always turn up for their appointments. About 20 per cent did not appear for appointments, whereas some of those in the control condition 'defected' to the treatment group and had mammograms anyway.

There may also be biases and inconsistencies in the way mammography studies were selected and interpreted for review. Freedman *et al.* (2004) detect a consistent bias in the way that Gøtzsche and Olsen critique. Studies that found a benefit from mammography were discounted by Gøtzsche and Olsen as being of poor quality. The remaining negative studies were combined by meta-analysis into the overall conclusion that mammography is useless in saving lives or reducing morbidity.

The conclusions reached by Gøtzsche and Olsen therefore are challenged by Freedman *et al.* (2004: 43) who claim that the old consensus on mammography was correct and that Gøtzsche and Olsen have arrived at biased conclusions 'based on misreadings of the data and the literature'.

The point we are making, then, is that even where we have apparently 'objective' ways of combining the results of studies into larger scale analyses through the technique of meta-analysis, this by no means ends controversy. Even experienced researchers dispute one another's readings of the literature and accuse one another of biased selections amongst the available research. Ironically, when Gøtzsche and Olsen reached their contentious conclusions they were involved in the Cochrane Collaboration, whose mission includes providing up-to-date, accurate information about the effects of health care and applies rigorous quality standards to its conclusions. We are not suggesting that any of the authors have 'made mistakes' in any simple sense. Instead, the point is that even where there is an emphasis on rigour and quality control in analysis, there may still be controversy. Indeed, it may even be more likely under such circumstances.

That source of controversy, relating to the conclusions of meta-analyses, is only part of the problem, however. Even in an area like breast cancer and mammography, where one might expect scientific controls to be sufficient to guarantee valid and reliable conclusions, the picture is muddied considerably once one considers the picture which emerges from the everyday practices of screening and the identification of suspicious lumps or shadows.

Even with a mammogram itself, there may be inconsistencies in the way the results are interpreted. According to Baines *et al.* (1990), 93 centre radiologists only agreed with the reference radiologist 30–50 per cent of the time. 'Observer error and technical problems' led to delayed detection in 22–35 per cent of cancers. Suggestions – for instance, don't mark up the film with a grease pencil – 'were sometimes resisted by centre radiologists' (Freedman *et al.* 2004: 50). Thus, there may be considerable inconsistency, and the tendency of practitioners to mark the films themselves may lead to additional diversity in any subsequent interpretations. Scientific procedures do not necessarily yield the consistent and reliable results of the kind needed to base robust research findings.

A further complication arises from the fact that in some cases it is difficult to make sense of important data such as cause of death. If it is recorded, say, as 'heart failure', there may be a lot of difference between 'heart failure' in the context of a long battle with cancer, and heart failure where the victim enjoys apparently perfect health and suddenly falls over in the street. Likewise, a death in an oncology ward may well be attributed to cancer, even though it might primarily involve the heart ceasing to beat and the failure of resuscitation attempts.

There are a number of implications here for the critical scholar concerned with analysis. The overall results of any analysis often subsume and mask a whole range of contingent and idiosyncratic decisions which are themselves the product of an occasioned, socially embedded process of evaluation, inference, custom and practice. Once the data have been incorporated into an individual study or meta-analysis of several studies, these considerations drop below the line of sight, but it behoves critical readers to scan the literature for signs of how these crucial issues were decided. Moreover, as we have seen, there is often some argument over the appropriate inclusion of studies. This could, in rational terms, be addressed by greater explicitness over inclusion criteria and by a movement towards more widely agreed protocols for making this decision. We suspect that the problem is more fundamental than this, and meta-analysis may have had the effect of displacing the argument away from the findings of research and centring it instead on decisions about inclusion of research and its treatment in the meta-analysis itself.

So far, we have considered the issue from the point of view of detection of potential tumours and the possible ambiguities concerning interpretation of the raw data relating to their presence, and the outcome of the process. This ambiguity is compounded rather than reduced when we attempt to combine studies together in the form of meta-analysis.

Folk analysis: towards an ethnography of cancer risk

Given the theme which we have returned to many times in this volume, of clients' or patients' perspectives on the research or therapeutic procedures to which they are subject, one might well ask what it is like to undertake this kind of process. The experience of this has been illuminated by a variety of academic and popular accounts. The kinds of understandings which participants in mammography screening programmes exhibited were addressed by Silverman *et al.* (2001), who interviewed forty-one women selected to represent a variety of age, demographic and ethnic groups in the USA.

There were a number of intriguing differences between the participants' views of cancer and those of the medical and research communities. For example, women tended to view breast cancer as a progressive disease which was relatively easily cured at an early stage, but deadly and devastating if it went undetected for any length of time. Participants distinguished between benign breast disease and breast cancer, but there seemed to be a recurrent theme amongst some women that even 'benign' abnormalities in the breast such as cysts had the potential to develop into cancer. As one participant put it:

> At first it's benign, and then it reaches some point where it goes crazy . . . like a malignancy. And the malignancy kills you . . . During the early window when it's benign . . . it can be removed . . .
>
> (Silverman *et al*. 2001: 235)

This contrasts with most medical models of the progress of disease where cancers are seen as distinct from benign abnormalities and the latter are generally not seen as a precursor to the former. In nature, too, disease is not inevitably or uniformly progressive, with some cases apparently remaining stable or even reversing (Silverman *et al*. 2001). In the light of this perceived threat the participants were generally favourable about having scans. For example, 'I feel every woman should have one', or 'If someone objected to having it done, why they're taking their own life in their hands I guess' (Silverman *et al*. 2001: 234). Participants were generally convinced of the accuracy of the scans – a rather optimistic position compared with some of the findings mentioned above – and the possibility of surgical intervention as a result was seen as a kind of necessary hazard in order to combat cancer. In the medical community there are concerns that routine screening might lead to over-diagnosis and over-treatment, yet amongst the respondents there was no such caution. Indeed, 'false positive' results (and related downstream consequences) were typically seen as an acceptable consequence of screening but not as a harm. In essence, the utility of learning one did not have cancer outweighed the disutility of the false alarm. Moreover, since many women felt any abnormality had malignant potential, no biopsy was really 'unnecessary' (Silverman *et al*. 2001: 238). Despite medical caution, then, the participants were inclined to try to find abnormalities early and treat them as aggressively as possible. Hence, perhaps, the reports in the UK press of people such as 'Becky Measures' who was said to have had a double mastectomy at the age of 22 as a preventive measure, because there was a history of breast cancer in her family, even though she had not yet developed any symptoms (Blake 2004).

In making sense of such accounts, the researcher might proceed in terms of content analysis, thematic analysis or discourse analysis. For example, the strength of content analysis is argued to lie in the extent to which it is located within a theoretical framework, as for instance Saks (1991). Silverman (1998) has questioned the integrity of much 'qualitative health research' that claims to 'tell it as it is'. Such research does not often present the question that generates the answer; it does not self-locate within a coherent theoretical framework; and insufficient use is made of electronic presentation and archiving of data for reanalysis. Analysis of data by themes also fragments the data and ignores such features of talk as narrative chaining. Silverman (1998) also cautions against the over-reliance on accounts at the expense of, say, observation. The caution we are advising concerning participants' accounts places the researcher in yet another dilemmatic situation. It is usually considered desirable to respect the integrity of what one's informants say, yet this must be interpreted sceptically. Such a dilemma lies at the heart of much qualitative enquiry. Here is what two founders of the contemporary qualitative research movement in the social sciences had to say about the issue:

> We have no grounds for dismissing the validity of participant understandings outright: indeed they are a crucial source of knowledge, deriving as they do from experience of the social world. However, they are certainly not immune to assessment, nor to explanation. They must be treated in exactly the same manner as social scientific accounts.
>
> (Hammersley and Atkinson 1983: 234)

What this amounts to is that researchers' appraisal of participants' testimony involves much more than simply checking that they are telling the truth or 'triangulating' by looking at other sources of data. Rather, it entails examining the processes that shaped their views and assessing the extent to which they may be constructed by the ideological context in which they are embedded. The intention is not to 'weed out' unreliable accounts, but to use historical analysis and sociological theory to get beneath the surface of everyday 'common-sense' assumptions in order to arrive at a deeper level of understanding. Often, the analyst's intention is to go beyond mere description to develop an analysis that does not simply replicate what is found in field settings or interviews or will only be of academic interest to the researcher, but will also contribute to either improved practice or even, more grandly, towards the development of critical consciousness amongst disadvantaged groups.

However, the synthesis of ethnography and the sort of critical social research that attempts to locate the accounts from participants in a theoretical framework is not an easy one. Making the links between qualitative data and theories involves the researcher or analyst in a number of additional dilemmas, the resolution of which might require us to rethink notions of validity and reliability. This may need to be done in a form quite different to that adopted by traditional ethnography or positivist empiricism. Originally, participant observers, ethnographers and early grounded theorists were concerned to analyse the actual language, thought and accounts of people, and the aim was to record observations in a 'raw, untheorized manner'. In this way they were rather like positivistic scientists, with the exception that they did not use numbers. In the last twenty years some authors have attempted to reformulate what it is that qualitative methodologists do, for example in the 1980s Potter and Wetherell (1987) and Willis (1980) began this task.

> In fact there is no untheoretical way in which to 'see' an object. The object is only perceived and understood through an internal organisation of data, mediated by conceptual constructs and ways of seeing the world. The final account of the object says as much about the observer as it does about the object itself.
>
> (Willis 1980: 90)

The purpose here is to commence this reconceptualization, and in so doing reclaim qualitative methods for a critical sociology.

Making sense of health beliefs

With some of these approaches the questions we wish to raise concern the focus of what we are attempting to analyse too. Analytic decisions in work about the subjective content of what we think, do or say about health are connected with what we wish to analyse as well as the precise analytic strategy we apply to our work once we have obtained the data.

To illustrate what we mean, let us spend a little time considering the ever-popular 'Health Belief Model'. This is a model of the relationship between attitudinal and cognitive variables and the likelihood of an individual engaging in some desirable health-promoting behaviour. As Finfgeld *et al.* (2003) remind us, in its original form it dates back to the 1950s, when many new public health programmes were being initiated. In spite of programmes promoting a diverse range of interventions and practices from vaccination to vitamins, health care providers became aware that many individuals failed to take advantage of widely provided low-cost services, such as polio vaccinations and tuberculosis screening. The model was thus initially developed to explain how the promotion campaigns were failing, and was subsequently extended to address existing health problems and health care interventions (Rosenstock 1974; Strecher and Rosenstock 1997).

A central tenet of this model is that health behaviour is based on a conscious process of decision making, which in turn relies on attitudes and beliefs (Janz and Becker 1984). Although this perspective has been perceived as an asset, it may also be somewhat limiting as it does not clearly take into account why individuals sometimes fail to act on their belief systems. More consideration may need to be given to physiological factors and non-volitional causes of human behaviour. For example, it may be salutary to follow up on the 1966 suggestion that emotions may play a significant role in determining behaviour (Rosenstock 1966).

Critics also comment that the Health Belief Model is value-laden (Janz and Becker 1984). Based on its 1950s public health origins, the model provides for little variance outside Western culture's health-related belief systems. It is assumed that there are appropriate and inappropriate health-related beliefs, and intervention efforts should focus on moulding perceptions to conform with the former. Although this type of autocratic mindset might have worked well within the Western health care system of the 1950s, it may be somewhat limiting within a more global health care environment. Also, based on its origins, the Health Belief Model was designed to encourage participation in one time preventive health care programmes such as polio vaccinations. From this vantage point, health behaviour change was not viewed as a long-term process. Although the model has been used in a wide range of settings and circumstances, it is questionable whether the temporal nature of many types of behaviour change can be fully accounted for within this theoretical framework. Finally, despite empirical support for the Health Belief Model, experts lament that the validity and reliability of questionnaires and other research instruments used to study the theory are problematic. All too often the concepts being measured are inconsistent with the theory, and the direct cause and effect relationship between beliefs and behaviours is not fully examined. Moreover, as alluded to earlier, relationships amongst concepts and interventions to promote behaviour change have not been adequately explored (Strecher *et al.* 1997).

As Willig (2000) describes, social constructionist critics of psychological research into health beliefs (Stainton Rogers 1991; Radley 1994) have argued that such work overemphasizes the role of cognitions and neglects the social context within which health-related behaviours take place. They argue that 'health' and 'illness' are not 'fixed entities in the minds of the people concerned' (Radley 1994: 55), nor is there necessarily a single standard of health that all communities and groups of people can agree is desirable. Moreover, health-related cognitions are not consistent, stable and predictive of behaviour. Instead, talk about health and illness may well be best seen as a social practice which is inextricably intertwined with other aspects of people's lives. Thus, in this view, people's statements about health and illness are not an expression of enduring inner thoughts on the subject in any simple sense, but rather the mobilization of culturally available explanations. What people say reflects a cultural and linguistic competence too.

To illustrate this let us consider the issue of teenagers becoming pregnant. At the time of writing it has been widely reported in the press that girls as young as 14 are seeking fertility treatment on the NHS because they have been unable to become pregnant despite the fact that they have been 'trying for ages' (Alderson 2004). According to the fertility specialist who went public concerning the teenagers' requests, Jo Heaton, girls are seeking in vitro fertilization (IVF) because they have not conceived despite up to two years of sexual activity without contraception. At this time, guidelines on when women should be given IVF on the NHS, provided by the National Institute for Clinical Excellence (NICE), say that it should be given only to women between 23 and 39 who have an identified cause for fertility problems, or who have suffered unexplained fertility problems for at least three years.

Thus, there is a distinct mismatch between what the official guidelines say (and possibly also at a deeper level concerning the professional and statutory bodies) and what young women themselves think the treatment is for. Whilst government campaigns were aimed at using contraception to prevent pregnancies, Dr Heaton urged politicians to recognize that there was a large group of young teenagers who desperately wanted to become pregnant, rather than falling pregnant by accident. Now from the point of view of the health beliefs approach, it is more or less taken for granted that youngsters and adults believe that avoiding pregnancy, rather like avoiding sexually transmitted infections, is desirable. For some, of course, it might be. Thus, ideas about informing teenagers of the risks involved, getting them to acknowledge that birth control measures are appropriate for them and so on might be effective. However, in the case of the youngsters who are keen to conceive, the whole basis of this model breaks down. Thus, as Willig (2000) advocates, careful attention to the contextual circumstances of people's lives becomes paramount in developing analytic strategies, lest we under-theorize what is happening. Conventional theorizing about people's health behaviour might lead us to see this as naïve but looked at in other ways it may appear more astute. Analysis, then, at its best, involves striving to understand how apparently novel or alien events could make sense, rather than simply imposing a pre-existing framework.

Conclusion: bringing analysis into awareness

The reflective approach towards analysis we are advocating has a good deal in common with the developing professional knowledge that has been greatly influenced by the work of Schon (1987) and Eraut (1994). Schon's argument questions the transferability of knowledge produced in decontextualized, controlled academic environments to the messy, 'swampy' world of practice. Schon based his work in the professional practice of a diverse range of practitioners to illustrate that, far from being a scientific, technical enterprise, there is a good deal of artistry involved in adapting technical knowledge to the idiosyncratic problems and contexts practitioners encounter. Schon proposed that expert practitioners were those who had developed an ability to adapt and to integrate technical knowledge with that gained from experience at the point of implementation. This process, says Schon (1987), can be brought to awareness, studied and enhanced through a process of reflection. This constitutes a process of knowledge attainment emerging in practice which he claims is well suited to solving complex practice-based problems. Thus, for us as researchers, it would be desirable if the process of deriving deductions from data, assigning relative weight to different factors in a study and knowing what information to include, or perhaps more importantly, to exclude, were brought into awareness more regularly. There are a whole variety of skills in practice and logics in use (Hawes 1977) which the beginning researcher is often ill-equipped to grasp. Thus, Croom *et al.* (2000) see the work of Schon and Eraut as having much to offer those who are attempting to make sense of research in health care.

Eraut (1985: 131), in discussing how knowledge is generated from practice, suggests that the role of the researcher must change from that 'of creator and transmitter of generalizable knowledge to that of enhancing the knowledge creating capacities of individuals and professional communities'. This is an even grander proposition than that Schon advocated in that it encourages us to try to diffuse and disseminate skills which we are still only beginning to grasp.

Further reading

Aneshensel, C.S. (2002) *Theory-Based Data Analysis for the Social Sciences.* Thousand Oaks, CA: Pine Forge Press. (Provides suggestions on how data analysis can be integrated with theory and theory development.)

Beaney, M. (1996) *Frege: Making Sense.* London: Duckworth. (An accessible book about the man who laid the foundations of 'analysis' as we knew them in the twentieth century.)

Clarke, A.E. (2005) *Situational Analysis: Grounded Theory After the Postmodern Turn.* Thousand Oaks, CA: Sage Publications. (Provides a means of integrating a variety of materials and information into one's analysis – visual media, discursive materials and maps.)

Freire, P. (1972) *Pedagogy of the Oppressed.* London: Sheed and Ward. (Possibly one of the most influential works on education of the twentieth century. From our point of view it is useful because Freire warns of the possibility of imposing one point of view upon other people. He is remembered for his emphasis on dialogue and his concern for the oppressed.)

Radley, A. (1994) *Making Sense of Illness: The Social Psychology of Health and Disease.* London: Sage Publications. (Radley attempts to make sense of our responses to illness, examining the effects of personal beliefs, relationships and stressors.)

Schon, D. A. (1983) *The Reflective Practitioner.* New York: Basic Books. (Enthusiast for the idea of reflexivity and for the notion that students learn skills by practising them.)

Stainton Rogers, W. (1991) *Explaining Health and Illness: An Exploration of Diversity.* Hemel Hempstead: Harvester Wheatsheaf.

(10) Credibility, trustworthiness and authenticity in research

Introduction: beyond validity and reliability

This chapter will review the relationship between background assumptions made by the researcher and the thorny question of how we assess the credibility of research. In Chapter 7 we covered some of the issues relating to validity and reliability and attempted to discern their origins and what they might mean. In this chapter we will attempt to explore more fully some of the issues which have been opened up for scrutiny earlier in this volume and how they might pertain to the value we set on research and whether a community of scholars and practitioners, or even we ourselves, believe in what it has to say.

It should be clear that the conventional one line definition from Cook and Campbell (1979) that validity is 'the best available approximation to the truth or falsity of a given inference, proposition or conclusion' is only part of the story. Likewise, the question of reliability, which is usually addressed in terms of whether a measure or observation is stable, is at best a rule of thumb and at worst severely problematic. As a result of unpacking some of the philosophical issues in research which we have undertaken over the last nine chapters, it is now possible to consider the notions again and broaden them out. We will encourage the reader to think critically about questions of reliability and validity and become aware of alternative approaches from different styles of research. We shall address also the somewhat more abstract question of what kind of implicit model of reality these notions contain, and we shall explore what they mean for the researcher. That is, maintaining reliability and validity, or their close relatives 'credibility' and 'trustworthiness', is about the kind of attitude that researchers maintain as well as the research procedures themselves.

The sort of attitude we are referring to can be manifested in a number of different ways so as to enhance the research process. For example, internal validity was previously defined in Chapter 7 as concerning the question 'Assuming that there is a relationship in this study, is the relationship a causal one?' In a sense it is often phrased as if we were looking backwards at the research. Yet this question might be more easily answered if at the commencement of the research the investigator had striven for a stance of detachment, reflexivity upon the research process, and an acknowledgement of how language can be used persuasively or rhetorically rather than as a simple descriptive medium. Let us illustrate this with an example. One of us (BB) obtained for research purposes a few years ago some transcripts of interviews with mental health service users about their treatment. What was even more interesting than their responses were the interventions of the transcriber. For example, one client described her consultant psychiatrist as a 'paid poisoner' yet the potentially interesting comments which ensued were editorialized as 'rambles on endlessly with largely delusional content'. This rather prim comment discloses whose side the transcriber is on. Rather than being seen as a pithily expressed lay version of the professional concerns about the side effects of drugs (e.g. Breggin and Cohen 2000; Healy 2004) the respondent's comment was used to discount what she subsequently had to say. This highlights the way in which researchers are often not disinterested, and their stake in the situation or commitment might well find its way into the research. Equally, as we have just shown, it is possible to add credentials to the speaker's position by identifying alignments with more prestigious sources. Now it is not necessary at this point to take sides and say one or other position is correct, but it is important to know that different perspectives can assist in the construction of different versions of nature.

Reformulating validity: alternative approaches

In conventional terms, the external validity of a piece of research might be enhanced if investigators have due regard for the situation, the people, the 'treatments' and other key variables, and make them as representative as possible of the broader situation to which we wish to generalize. But there are a number of other techniques for enhancing it too.

For example, a further validity enhancement strategy comes from the grounded theory tradition and involves 'saturation of categories' (Glaser and Strauss 1967). This describes how, as the research progresses, issues and themes become 'saturated' – that is, each new act of data collection does not add anything new – and the researcher is reassured that the issue has been fully explored and no longer requires detailed coverage, unless we notice that something has changed.

In addition, claims to external validity can be enhanced by attending to analytical generalization. This refers to attempts to expand and generalize theories, either by using a previously developed theory as a template with which to compare the empirical results of new exemplars of the phenom-enon, or case studies. This differs from the usual statistical generalization where inferences are made from sample to a population. Here, we are con-cerned with a theoretical process, whereby theories can be used as templates for exploring new territories, yet can also be interrogated or challenged by new data. This does not necessarily lead to the rejection of the theory, as in Karl Popper's vision of scientific enquiry, but more importantly perhaps can give some clues as to what the theory is best fitted to explain, as well as what it cannot explain.

The reliability of a study can be enhanced through the application of standardized techniques such as questionnaires whose design and reliability has already been established, recording and providing sufficient detail of what went on so as to render the research processes open to audit or replica-tion by a competent stranger. The reliability of research can be enhanced also by attempting to specify and control contextual factors, so that extraneous sources of variation are reduced.

The idea of a research report has a peculiar status in that it must continu-ally convince the reader that it is not 'merely' a piece of fiction. The rigour attached to solid empirical research allows our accounts of our enquiries to be granted the status and authority associated with scientific scholarship. Making our work credible and believable, however, has to do with how we tell the story and this has a rhetorical aspect, such that the reader is steered towards the favoured interpretation. As Paul Ricouer (1977) has argued, the process of validation often follows a logic of probability rather than a logic of empirical verification. Theory testing and the development of interpret-ations involves moving from a guess to the data and using this to explore further and develop a more refined guess. In undertaking this, we must always retain the possibility of disconfirmation of our hypotheses, in other words of 'being surprised'.

This, then, is a picture of validity and reliability in research with which many scholars would find at least some elements to agree. However, in the early twenty-first century this is not the full story, as notions of validity and reliability are increasingly under challenge.

The last twenty years: the struggle for credibility

The picture of enquiry into the social world has seen the development of a number of troubling polarizations, debates and dilemmas concerning notions of rigour, validity and reliability. On the one hand the ideas we have described concerning the hierarchies of evidence so beloved of advocates of evidence-based practice in health, social care and education have been formalized and published. Computer programs, analysis techniques and the climate of research literacy have been enhanced by a whole order of magnitude. On the other hand there has, in some quarters, been a retreat from conventional notions of validity and reliability. Thus, notions of research quality in fields of enquiry related to health and social care are in a state of flux. Within the qualitative tradition of research there have been a number of attempts to supplant conventional concerns with reliability and validity with other notions of credibility and trustworthiness. Moreover, health care researchers have been grappling with some very different philosophical traditions emerging from mainland Europe such as postmodernism and deconstructionism which yield challenging perspectives on the question of validity because of the different standpoint they take on human enquiry and disciplinary knowledge, and indeed nature itself.

Given our desire to help to create a philosophically informed and wideranging, theoretically inclusive attitude towards enquiry in the health care disciplines, it is appropriate to explore some of these differing perspectives in depth. We shall first examine attempts to integrate the different perspectives on what research is and how we can make it trustworthy, and then we shall examine some areas of divergence, particularly in and around the field of deconstructionism. At first, questions of reliability and validity were clustered around the broader question of how well we can trust researchers to give us a picture of the field of phenomena they sought to describe. However, more recent currents in philosophy have opened up the question of whether there is a field of phenomena outside the 'text' – that is, our attempts to describe them – at all. The reader should bear in mind, however, that much of what is discussed here arises from debates which originated in philosophy and does not always have immediately obvious implications for applied social research. However, as we shall argue, there are potentially important consequences for how we conduct research and make sense of our findings.

We will commence by examining exactly how the debates about reliability and validity have become fractured and how researchers have in some cases come to new negotiations of what reliability and validity mean.

Let us first rehearse the mainstream position, that is, the position which would probably be recognizable to most of those who are engaged in research as representing what they are trying to do. This is an idealization rather than a description of actual practice. It is rather like a description of the 'medical model' in an introductory textbook. It helps our thinking, but most people would claim to differ from it. From this point of view, in order to understand what validity and reliability are, and why they are important, it might be as well to revisit the question of what research is and what we are trying to do when we conduct it. It is, according to Mantzoukas (2004: 994)

> an attempt to arrange and rearrange the complexities of the reality or realities within which we live and/or study, and portray them in such a way as to connect their various (seemingly unconnected) propositions in a systematic way.

In this manner we can, it is hoped, extend the knowledge base of the discipline. Notice how abstract this definition is, and how it focuses on somewhat subjective phenomena such as seeing and manipulating patterns in the complex phenomenal field we encounter when we examine health or social phenomena. We may also be concerned in our research with trying to create patterns of knowledge which are applicable to our immediate problems (Henwood and Pidgeon 1993; Sarantakos 1998; Polit and Hungler 1999; Abma 2002; Mantzoukas 2004).

Thus, in this model of enquiry, the confidence we have in the patterns we discern is crucial, and it is this source of uncertainty that the questions of validity and reliability typically seek to address. However, as the reader may remember from Chapter 7, a good deal of the present-day technical concern about reliability and validity concerns the integrity of measures used to identify and quantify the matters in hand.

Measurement in the social and health sciences often involves the process of linking abstract concepts such as well-being, mental health or quality of life to empirical indicators (Carmines and Zeller 1979; Singleton *et al.* 1993). The data collection process, then, begins with some underlying concept of theoretical interest that is unobservable in the empirical world. Thus, as it cannot be measured directly, researchers attempt to develop empirical indicators that allow these unobservable concepts to be addressed in the referent world of observable phenomena. Assessments of validity and reliability are thus generally concerned with determining the extent to which the empirical indicators that are measured can be said to meaningfully represent the underlying concepts (McClelland 1983; Singer 1990).

In this view, determining the validity of a given measure is, in a sense, a theoretically oriented problem, because assessing validity involves determining the extent to which the indicator is useful for a particular purpose, and we cannot usually assess the extent to which it is universally 'true' or suitable. Thus, once we have established 'validity' it is only meaningful in the context of a specific underlying concept; a particular indicator can be highly valid as a measure of one concept but may have little or no validity as a measure of another (Carmines and Zeller 1979: 15–17).

For example, in cognitive neuroscience there is currently a good deal of research underway concerning the patterns of brain activity that accompany particular tasks. That is, in one such field of enquiry, researchers have interested themselves in the sort of brain activity that corresponds to lying versus telling the truth. There is a good deal of interest in this technology as it is believed to have a great deal of potential in forensic contexts. Ganis *et al.* (2003) claim to have demonstrated that different types of lies produce different patterns of neural activity depending on how well rehearsed or coherent the story is. Compared with non-deceptive stories, the lies tended to be associated with higher levels of activity in a number of brain areas, presumably reflecting a greater amount of processing needed to make them convincing.

The veteran Harvard psychologist Dan Schacter has recently been involved in a series of studies to examine the brain activity patterns associated with so-called 'true' and 'false' memories (Schacter 1999; Goldman *et al.* 2003). Rather than being about accounts of child abuse, Schacter and his colleagues conduct their work on much more mundane materials such as words. If a person has been presented with words like 'bed', 'rest', 'awake' and 'tired' they might falsely recall that the term 'sleep' was in the list too, even if it was not. The mistaken recall of words that were not on the list produces different patterns of brain activity than does the recall of words that were on the list (Phillips 2004). Schacter himself is modest and cautious about the forensic applicability of this kind of work. In addition, a *New Scientist* editorial accompanying news of these developments urges caution and reminds the reader of the sheer amount of processing the raw data have to undergo in order to yield pictures of brain activity. Moreover, arbitrary decisions in the processing algorithm concerning where the boundaries are placed and the size of the units of analysis can make a big difference to the pictures obtained (*New Scientist* 2004).

The brain research described above involves being very anthropomorphic about the brain and the neurones within it. After all, individual neurones never literally 'see outside' and cannot tell whether a story corresponds to a verifiable state of nature. Moreover, the kinds of language used to describe the brain structures is lurid with value too, for example an 'active' amygdala or a 'lazy' ventral putamen which further consolidates their inclusion in a kind of moral lexicon.

In examples like this, we can see the operation of the notion of construct validity. Construct validity refers to the extent to which a measure performs in accordance with theoretical expectations. As Carmines and Zeller (1979: 23) describe it, construct validity is fundamentally 'concerned with the extent to which a particular measure relates to other measures consistent with theoretically derived hypotheses concerning the concepts (or constructs) that are being measured'. In practice, construct validation begins by specifying a theoretical relationship between two or more concepts, followed by empirical examination of this relationship and interpretation of the results. That is, perhaps in the case of the brain scan data presented above there might be *a priori* theoretical grounds for supposing that there is a relationship between regions in the brain and particular functions, such as imagining a visual scene, telling a story or even deceiving one's opponent in a game. If we see elevated activity in those parts of the brain when that particular task is undertaken, and it is different from the pattern of activity when other tasks are performed, we might see it as supporting the idea that the part of the brain in question is doing the job in question. Moreover, if we can show the pattern of activity we observe when people say they've seen a word that wasn't there and this corresponds to the sort of activity in 'false memories' for other things, then we might claim to have validated the 'construct' of false memory syndrome – or at least redescribed one process in terms of another measurable one.

The impact of a successful case of construct validation depends on the nature of the theoretical relationship that was specified: evidence supporting a more rigorous and demanding relationship will provide greater confidence in the construct validity of the measure being assessed. Carmines and Zeller (1979) consider construct validity the most useful form of validity for the social sciences, given the weaknesses of criterion-related and content validity for many abstract social science concepts. They note, though, that a potentially serious problem in assessing construct validity involves the conclusions to be drawn when a measure behaves inconsistently with theoretical expectations (Carmines and Zeller 1979: 25–6). Thus, even when researchers and theorists are working within a paradigm where there is a strong assumption that there is something there beneath the plethora of measures and indicators – in other words a foundationalist position – determining the validity of what we have discovered is still a problematic business.

One further important dimension of validity that adds additional layers of complication is the extent to which a given measure is valid across space and time. A good indicator or measure should be applicable in a wide range of circumstances and should be useful over long periods of time so as to facilitate comparisons in longitudinal work or between studies conducted at different points in time. As Goertz and Diehl (1986) note, though, scholars are often forced to strike a difficult balance between choosing a valid indicator for one particular historical period and choosing an indicator that is comparable across multiple periods. In any case, to examine, say, depression, or even something as apparently clear cut as tuberculosis, one is usually handicapped by the fact that definitions and diagnostic techniques for the syndrome in question change, sometimes quite dramatically, and it is difficult to make precise comparisons from one era to the next even across the life span of particular patients.

Thus, in mainstream research and therapeutic opinion in the health and social sciences, there is a strong sense that validity and reliability are central to the research enterprise. In much conventional research where researchers are convinced of this importance, it is pretty much business as usual. Indeed, where a field is bedevilled with inconsistency it is sometimes suggested that it is the underlying construct, rather than the highly esteemed method, which is awry. However, in qualitative research at the same time, perhaps because it lacks the certainty of hard numbers and probability values, many researchers and theorists have expressed a crisis of confidence from both inside and outside the field. Now, there are a number of ways in which rigour can be attained in research, some of which, like triangulation, we have already described. However, rather than climb aboard this particular bandwagon in qualitative enquiry, a number of leading qualitative researchers argued that reliability and validity were terms which related exclusively to the quantitative paradigm and were inappropriate to qualitative research (Leininger 1994; Altheide and Johnson 1998). As an alternative to conventional notions of reliability and validity some suggested adopting new criteria for ensuring rigour in qualitative enquiry (Lincoln and Guba 1985; Leininger 1994; Rubin and Rubin 1995).

Beyond validity and reliability: rigour and credibility

Guba and Lincoln (1981) began this process of redefinition by starting from the relatively uncontentious position that all research must have 'truth value', 'applicability', 'consistency' and 'neutrality' in order to be worthwhile, and that the nature of knowledge within the rationalistic (or quantitative) paradigm is different from the knowledge in the naturalistic (qualitative) paradigm. Consequently, each paradigm requires paradigm-specific criteria for addressing 'rigour' (the term most often used in the rationalistic paradigm) or 'trustworthiness', their parallel term for qualitative 'rigour'.

In their original formulation of the issue in the 1980s, Guba and Lincoln argued that it would be advantageous to replace the concepts of reliability and validity with the parallel concept of 'trustworthiness'. This was said to involve four aspects: credibility (resembling internal validity), transferability (which corresponds to external validity), dependability (which is like reliability) and confirmability (which looks like objectivity) (see Box 10.1).

Subsumed within these were a number of methodological strategies for ensuring qualitative trustworthiness, such as audit trails, 'member checks' when coding, categorizing or confirming results with participants, peer debriefing, negative case analysis, structural corroboration, persistent observation and referential material adequacy (Guba and Lincoln 1981, 1982; Lincoln and Guba 1985). To put this in practical terms, one of us (SD) investigated the experience of children with learning difficulties and their parents in seeking health services, social support and education. Thus, in

---

Box 10.1 Methodological criteria: traditional concepts and Guba and Lincoln's reconceptualized version

Internal validity, which Lincoln and Guba translate as truth value, is replaced by the concept of *credibility* – whether or not the participants studied find the account true.

External validity, or the extent to which findings are more generally applicable, is replaced by fittingness or *transferability*, which is based on the idea that accounts may be transferable to other specified settings through the provision of thick description about both the sending and the receiving contexts.

Reliability, or the consistency of findings, is replaced by the notion of *dependability*, which is achieved through an auditing process called an 'audit trail', in which the researcher documents methods and decisions, and assesses the effects of research strategies, rather than being concerned about replication.

Objectivity, or a concern with neutrality, is replaced by *confirmability* – the extent to which findings are qualitatively confirmable through the analysis being grounded in the data and through examination of the 'audit trail'.

---

one case, parents' complaints that the child had been described by a health professional as a 'vegetable' were placed on a much stronger footing because in another strand of the research SD observed and tape-recorded health professionals describing their clients in exactly those terms (Dyson 1987). Involving parents, health professionals and children themselves in the research enhanced the 'structural corroboration' and 'referential material adequacy' of the research. The reader can probably see parallels here with the idea of triangulation discussed in Chapter 8 too. If different people, different angles and different kinds of investigation of the field of enquiry point in the same direction then we can be more confident about the findings than if it were a single uncorroborated complaint.

It was in this tradition too that the characteristics of the investigator as a crucial element in the research process were re-emphasized. What we can see as a result of the process of enquiry will be informed by the personal qualities and often undisclosed subtle techniques of enquiry. It was emphasized that the researcher needed to be adaptable to changing circumstances, holistic, having processional immediacy, sensitivity and ability for clarification and summarization (Guba and Lincoln 1981).

Now, the criteria outlined by Lincoln and Guba for 'trustworthiness', like the ideas of validity and reliability they sought to replace, were predicated on the assumption that there was a real world outside that we could come to know if we enquired about it in the right way. Or at least we could achieve successively better approximations to it. That is, it was more or less a 'foundationalist' view of nature and of scientific enquiry. A world view, in other words, rather like the *X Files* slogan, 'The truth is out there.'

This foundationalist position would not necessarily be appropriate for research that took a more avowedly constructivist slant. Here, research is often predicated on the assumption that the realities which the researcher discovers are created *in situ* by the various actors involved, for example the people being observed and interrogated, the investigator and the wider community of readers and writers who see the finished product. Therefore the question of credibility – or validity – is problematic, since if we were to take constructivism in a strong form we would believe that 'there is no ultimate benchmark to which one can turn for justification' (Lincoln and Guba 1985: 295). However, even here the analysis and report are believed to need to 'ring true', or exhibit verisimilitude (Garman 1996: 19). Similarly, in relation to transferability, constructivist research usually aims to explore situated patterns within particular cases, rather than producing externally valid generalizations. Transferability to other contexts is then assessable by those who read the reported cases, given sufficiently detailed description and interpretation in the research accounts presented. In relation to confirmability, it is assumed that the value-free, objective enquirer is a myth, but that researchers should be reflexive and open about their positioning, and should be able to foreground personal and cultural values and the theoretical and epistemological stances from which the research is undertaken in a way that the reader can understand and take into account (Usher and Edwards 1994: 147–53). In this view, the research report should also present a construction grounded in the 'tangible realities' of the case, such as what was said, written or observed. Thus, it is rather like the exhortations in methodologies like conversation analysis to 'anchor the interpretation to the text'.

Finally, in this perspective, it is recognized that direct or literal replicability of findings is impossible, no matter what values and methods are deployed by the researchers. However, despite the expectation of near infinite variability, it is anticipated that amongst a particular community of researchers, if they perform an investigation amongst the same community of research participants at a similar time, then the 'data sets' obtained by these researchers, and thus their emergent understandings, will be largely comparable. Even here, then, there is some expectation that the findings will be broadly similar, even where we are not working with a concept of reliability as it would appear in more positivist approaches to knowledge acquisition.

Lest the reader goes away with the impression that qualitative researchers have abandoned the notions of validity and reliability wholesale it is important to note that, especially in Great Britain and Europe, there are several prominent qualitative authors who argue that the concepts of reliability and validity taken in a broad and abstract sense can be applied to research right across the spectrum of methods because the goal of achieving credible and plausible descriptions and analytic explanations is central to all research (Hammersley 1992; Yin 1994; Kuzel and Engel 2001).

So far, then, we have seen some of the approaches to trustworthiness and credibility in research that do not rely on strictly interpreted notions of reliability and validity. So far we have presented a relatively unproblematic picture of researchers who may differ in the terminology they may use all struggling to ensure their results are trustworthy and verifiable. But the whole question is more complicated than that. If it were this simple, the kinds of processes described here that both qualitative and quantitative researchers engage in would be sufficient to complete our consideration of validity, reliability, trustworthiness and rigour. If things were as we described them in this chapter it could be supposed that there was a comfortable, essential unity to the process of human enquiry whether it is qualitative or quantitative. The researchers quoted here – even those who are departing from the quasi-scientific notion of objectivity – are haunted by notions of realism. The ideas presuppose a confirmable, trustworthy reality that lies behind the researchers' accounts. Even where constructivism is mentioned, it is still believed possible to create accounts of the research topic that 'ring true'. Therefore much of what we have reviewed above makes assumptions and uses enquiry strategies and values which are surprisingly similar to the more positivistic research they have sought to leave behind. It is, in other words, 'haunted by a metaphysics of presence' (Derrida 1976) such that notions of presence, being, stability and knowability are privileged over absence, instability and indeterminacy. Even with nods towards the idea that social realities are constructed or that society is, in Becker's famous phrase, 'people doing things together', the nature of social realities is still seen as potentially knowable by the researcher.

A metaphysics of credibility in research

In an important sense the ideas of validity, reliability, trustworthiness or credibility identified in the literature we have reviewed above are scarcely empirical at all. They are often abstractions or idealizations, and sometimes seem a long way away from the processes that scientists and social scientists use to ensure in practice the robustness of their work. At least since the late 1970s, with the publication of work such as *Laboratory Life* (Latour and Woolgar 1986), it has been apparent that naïve descriptions of the scientific method, in which theories are challenged by the outcomes of experiments, are inconsistent with actual scientific practice. Typically, an experiment produces only inconclusive data that is attributed to failure of the apparatus or experimental method, and a large, yet often implicit, part of scientific training involves learning how to make subjective decisions about what data to keep and what data to ascribe to artefact or error – a process that to an untrained outsider looks like a mechanism for ignoring data that contradict orthodox ideas. The point is not that scientists arbitrarily throw out results that don't fit the theory – far from it. Their processes of selection and sifting are nuanced, disciplined and meticulously careful. Certainly, this practice is accompanied by the rhetoric of hypothesis testing, validity and reliability, yet these ideas do not seem to grasp the process which observers of science see going on. Likewise, discounting the results from reviews of research on depression or schizophrenia as we have seen earlier do not proceed as crude acts of sabotage but by purporting a meticulous knowledge of the syndromes, the treatments and the research methods used to study them.

To sum up the story so far, we have a strong sense that researchers of all persuasions are working quite hard to make it look as though there is something out there. Whether they be constructivists or hard-nosed empiricists in the spirit of Auguste Comte, they are desperately creating accounts which are valid, reliable, credible or trustworthy and ring true. At the same time, descriptions of these constructs don't seem to offer a very good characterization of what researchers can be seen to be doing when they are observed at work.

Therefore in the closing stages of this chapter it is perhaps appropriate to consider some ideas and approaches that have attempted to prick the conceit of this approach and destabilize the certainty with which this metaphysics of presence is adhered to in much research in health care and elsewhere. To pursue this argument let us return to someone we have already mentioned briefly, Jacques Derrida, who has been a significant and controversial influence on many qualitative enquiries in Europe and the USA (Denzin 1994). Indeed, he is credited with usurping the security of research methods and findings in the social and health sciences where once qualitative methods and approaches were relatively unproblematic (Vidich and Lyman 1998). Derrida has inspired a new kind of critical ethnography that seeks to be evocative rather than explanatory (Linstead 1993), especially where the authors play with different kinds of representation and textuality; where impressions, poetry and images are as much a part of the presentation as the sober 'facts 'n' figures' approach of more traditional styles of research. In a sense it challenges the connections which have hitherto been assumed to exist between the world and the texts in which we read 'it' (Fox 1997; Parker 1997; Madigan 1999; Ronai 1999; Lather 2001; van Loon 2001).

Deconstructing text, deconstructing context

In Chapter 4 we provided a brief description of how deconstruction worked as a practical technique. In this section we shall develop some of the implications from this and examine what they mean for the conduct of social enquiry more generally. Once the presumed relationship between a text and the facet of nature it purports to describe is challenged, this has profound implications for notions of validity and reliability, partly because the simple reflections of nature in language upon which these notions of validity or credibility are built have been disrupted, but also because there are implications here for what we do with the texts themselves. As Kilduff and Kelemen (2001: 58) said, 'The practical relevance of the deconstruction of a foundational text involves the effort to permanently change the way the text is used.' In a sense the outcome of a deconstructive experience is to teach us something about how the text is composed that we cannot unlearn: in a phrase beloved of cyberpunk science fiction authors, one becomes 'incurably informed'. In the case of validity and reliability discourses in the social and health sciences, the role of deconstruction is to encourage us to wonder what would happen if we did not so diligently guard the trust-worthiness of our research enterprise. Would there be a sudden prolifer-ation of dangerous fictions masquerading as science? If so, this is pretty much what many authors in debates about scientific issues accuse each other of anyway, as we have seen.

This then leaves us with the question of why people involved in health-related research are so concerned about the distinction between the arts and sciences, between fiction and truth, and why they place so many stipulations in place to constrain the investigative manoeuvres which are considered legitimate. This is especially odd in a field where personal accounts, the arts and fictional portrayals have had such an important place.

For Derrida (1981), a text has no controlling centre for its meaning, so rigorous reading or deconstructive analysis will always reveal that a text contains suggestions that are contrary to the overt message. This may also be contrary to the author's intention or our common-sense interpretation of it. Texts that are full of rigour and order have a barely contained chaos hiding just beneath the surface, which perhaps would be liberated if the rituals of objectivity were not followed to the letter. The idea that nature is a tidy, lawful, regular place is undermined by the implication that if we do not follow the methodological protocols it will not look so tidy at all. The deconstructive spirit encourages us to look for this kind of implicit contra-diction. A deconstructionist reading of a text focuses on those aspects that disrupt, exceed and resist singularity. Furthermore, ambiguities are not something that can readily be eliminated but, as Derrida (1981: 220–1) argued, 'undecidability is not caused . . . by some enigmatic equivocality, some inexhaustible ambivalence of a word in "natural" language', but instead these points of ambiguity 'mark the spots of what can never be mediated, mastered, sublated or dialecticized'. The ambiguities, plays on words and apparent contradictions to which Derrida often draws attention are not themselves of crucial importance. However, they are useful as they mark the spots where fault lines in the deeper logic of the text's arguments can be most easily discerned.

As we have hinted, a fundamental idea in this approach is the idea of 'conversion' (Alvesson and Sköldberg 2000: 191), that is, showing how a certain meaning is 'dependent upon a repressed opposite' is believed to be a fruitful way forward for this kind of empirical enquiry into how texts sustain their meaning. However, as Alvesson and Sköldberg note, 'A problem [for the approach] is that this appears best suited to fairly limited empirical materials' (2000: 191) and has not so far been widely applied to longer texts reporting detailed scientific enquiries. The situation is complicated by the difficulty in characterizing deconstructive analysis in clear enough terms that it can be deployed by others. Some authors have gone against the original spirit of Derrida and have tried to provide itemized instructions for doing deconstructive readings (Martin 1990; Boje 2001; for an exception, see Rhodes 2000).

Deconstructive analysis is perhaps well suited to the task of understanding how it is that certain things come to be seen in nature or become truthful. Once we start looking at the mechanics with which a text operates as a guarantor of truth we are equipped to see how texts have a curious autonomy from the nature they purport to describe. To illustrate this let us consider a couple of examples of phenomena that appeared to be perfectly valid in the past and were reliably observed, yet are all but forgotten nowadays.

The approach to examining the nature of validity and trustworthiness we are developing in this chapter is allied in some ways with the principles of deconstruction. Derrida has explicitly encouraged us to turn the process of scholarship upon itself in the 'university of tomorrow', where he wanted researchers to study how truths were established in academic disciplines. At the end of the twentieth century he unveiled a bold and ambitious plan for the revision of the traditional academic disciplines so that they would come to study themselves in this way (Derrida 2001). That is, the study of history was to be about how historical knowledge was created and given legitimacy rather than the study of the events themselves. Although it was not his primary concern, perhaps in line with this spirit the proper study of the social sciences as they are applied to health should be how knowledge about health care is created, legitimated, disseminated and used.

The deconstructive approach in the social and health sciences, then, urges us to undertake a close and critical reading of the texts of the discipline in order to uncover the ways of thinking that constrain our impressions or conceptualizations of the world. A deconstructive approach to texts, practice or form of knowledge is not necessarily a destructive one. Derrida's original aim was not to destroy, merely to point out hidden assumptions and contradictions that shape a text and the account of nature it seeks to construct.

In practical terms, the message for researchers themselves from this chapter is that validity, credibility or trustworthiness need to be seen in a wide-ranging and inclusive way. In a very narrow sense it is possible to hear people talking about 'validating a measure' when all they are doing is piloting a questionnaire. However, we would hope to have encouraged the reader to consider the questions raised by notions of validity, credibility and rigour more broadly. They have links with concerns about trustworthiness and authenticity in qualitative research and have connections with research strategies such as triangulation and multimethod approaches which we have described elsewhere in this volume. Moreover, we have tried to highlight the relationship between validity and theory. Measures, indicators and data which may be perfectly valid for one theoretical purpose may be entirely invalid for another.

In practice we might try to tackle problems we encounter in research systematically using these tools and strategies. For example, one might wish to address concerns over variability in meaning to assess the *extent* of such variability (Hindess 1973). If independent coders, observers or raters disagree, this is often seen as a problem. But we can see this as an interesting challenge to be solved. We can find out how far they disagree and why they do so. Or, if we are concerned that a study is overly reliant on self-report interview data, there may be ways and means of building in further checks on its authenticity by recording other aspects of the interaction in the research setting, or by participant observation. This might also serve as a way of evaluating participants' accounts. People may tell a story to achieve moral goals, that is, to present them in a good light, express a grievance or position them in a network of rights, duties and responsibilities. However, as part of a more comprehensive research strategy, it might also be possible to check out other evidence that might relate to what they are talking about. People's accounts often refer to a physicality or state of nature that may require testing by the researcher. Indeed, in some kinds of action research the researcher and participants may work together to check it out.

A further aspect of the discourses of validity and credibility we have highlighted is the insight possible from the deconstructionist approach. Notions of validity form part of a suite of devices for authenticating and legitimating clams to knowledge.

This last point leads to a final possibility. Perhaps one way of rethinking the ideas of validity and credibility is to begin looking at how these discourses are used by researchers. Maybe the interesting aspects of validity and credibility involve what you can see researchers doing with the concepts as they discuss their own – or more particularly, each other's – work. Here perhaps we can see how these discourses and rhetorics might be deployed to produce and police the boundaries of knowledge, and might involve granting legitimacy to some studies, techniques and ways of knowing over and above others. As we have attempted to illustrate, there are some ideas, concepts and observations that have not withstood the test of time, no matter how well supported and valid they might have appeared in the period where they originated. Therefore it behoves us to take seriously the strategies people use to convince others of the truth of their 'reality'. As Schegloff (1997) urges, the Archimedian point of leverage should be sought in the interaction or in the text itself, rather than outside. In deciding what is relevant or what is happening, the analyst should, in Schegloff's view, look at the people to whom it matters most – the researchers themselves as they battle it out and impugn one another's work.

If we take this deconstructive thinking at face value, there are disturbing implications for the practice of health and social care (Clarke 1996). If it is impossible for researchers and practitioners to reach a satisfactory under-standing of what they do and reality is indeed indeterminate, how do they know that they are doing any good? How can researchers be assured that the data they have so painstakingly gathered will not become hopelessly outdated in a short time? Indeed, if the research is socially or politically significant it will be variously impugned and derided and its validity and credibility will be challenged anyway, whatever epistemological position one subscribes to. It is perhaps easier to anticipate this rough and tumble from the outset than to be offended by it later.

There is thus something important to be salvaged from the decon-structionist assault on scientific convention. It can sensitize us to the fact that there may be conflicting opinions about illness, unexplored dimensions and different layers of reality. What doctors know is different from what nurses know and differs again from the patient's experience. The sense that authority lies in the text itself rather than its correspondence with nature is reminiscent of Michel Foucault's connection between discourse and power. Scholars such as Richard Brown (1998) have noted, for example, how the power of language and rhetoric are crucial in establishing the legitimacy of scientific practice which is in his view grounded at least partially in narra-tive. Correspondingly, Pierre Bourdieu (1999) argues that authority is not based in research itself, but arises instead from agents' capacity to speak or write in a way that conveys legitimacy. So when we see the terms validity and credibility being used it is important to note who is speaking or writing and who has the power to define what legitimate knowledge looks like.

The choice of strategies for determining the authenticity or validity of research, like the choice of research methods themselves, is influenced by the assumptions the researcher holds about the social world and its inhabitants, as well as the nature of the study itself (Harris 1996: 318). Similarly, the question of validity and reliability are intimately connected with the mode of knowing which is privileged and depends upon the epistemological assumptions of the researcher – what nature is and whether we can come to know it. Thus, what appears in most introductory textbooks to be a simple, practical matter of checking our measures and our research design instead opens up some of the most fundamental questions about human knowledge, understanding and consciousness. And that, in a sense, is the most practical application of all.

Further reading

Atkinson, P., Coffey, A., Delamont, S., Lofland, J. and Lofland, L. (eds) (2001) *Handbook of Ethnography*. London: Sage Publications. (A useful, critical guide to ethnographic research methods and their evaluation.)

Boje, D.M. (2001) *Narrative Methods for Organizational and Communication Research*. London: Sage Publications. (The author provides some memorable ways of making sense of the plethora of different stories to be found in any human organization.)

Denzin, N.K. and Lincoln, Y.S. (eds) (2000) *Handbook of Qualitative Research*, second edition. Thousand Oaks, CA: Sage Publications. (A classic and remarkably comprehensive guide to the variety of qualitative techniques available.)

Kirk, J. and Miller, M.L. (1985) *Reliability and Validity in Qualitative Research*. Thousand Oaks, CA: Sage Publications. (Interesting approach to understanding social enquiry as a human process whilst attempting to secure quality standards.)

Lincoln, Y. and Guba, E. (1985) *Naturalistic Inquiry*. Beverly Hills, CA: Sage Publications. (This contains the statement of quality criteria in qualitative research mentioned earlier in this chapter.)

(11) Reviewing the field

In this book, we have sought not only to explain the basic outline of competing philosophies of research, but to illustrate how these concerns impinge upon applied research, with a special emphasis on research in health care since this is a field which has attracted a great many applied social researchers at the turn of the millennium. We began by considering the different levels of the research endeavour, from the research philosophies that have been the subject of much of this book, through methodological concerns of validity and reliability, through choices at the levels of strategy and method to the types of analysis of data that are possible. We may begin applied research at the level of strategy and method, but this does not mean we can ignore the philosophies of research that underpin our choices. Indeed, an awareness of those philosophical issues can, we think, lead to better research.

We have presented the main philosophical debates in the form of a series of analytic dualisms. The first of these, addressed in Chapter 2, concerned the nature of the social world we are attempting to study. To what extent can this world be characterized as material in nature? To what extent can physical bodies, architectural spaces and economic constraints be regarded as having a material existence irrespective of the internal thought processes through which we make sense of them? To what extent do these external constructs act upon us and constrain our actions irrespective of what thought processes we have?

The opposing view is one that places its faith in the realm of ideas, or, as we have termed it, idealism. From this perspective, researchers work primarily with the internal constructs of the research participants, and focus on the variability of meaning, the ways in which this meaning is constructed and negotiated in the course of social interaction. But researchers are still required to consider at what point they accord primacy to the agency of the research participants and their internal constructs, as opposed to the structural constraints suggested by the material constructs external to the consciousness of the individuals concerned.

The second of the analytical dualisms was discussed in Chapter 3. This chapter concerns a debate about the legitimate limits of social knowledge about the world. If we agree that legitimate knowledge is restricted to what we can directly know from individuals and individual consciousness, then it follows that claims to knowledge that are expressed in terms of group concepts (social class, patriarchy, institutional racism) are beyond the limits of what is possible as social scientific knowledge. This restriction does compel us as researchers to take the expressed views of individuals seriously, to validate what may be minority experiences or views, and perhaps to empathize. However, if we accept that the social world is like an onion, with layers of reality that can be peeled back in order to generate understandings of how societies operate at ever deeper levels, then we will not wish to take individual representations of the world at face value. Indeed, to do so could be deemed naïve, and a recipe for legitimizing the status quo in the face of various dimensions of social oppression such as racism or sexism. As such we have seen that for some scientific realists there is an imperative to challenge the current social order to change the lived experiences of research participants. Against this, the danger is that the researcher is then making implicit claims to know better than the participants what the nature of their experience is.

A third analytic dualism derives from a consideration of the work of Michel Foucault, and more broadly those termed postmodernists. We examined this debate in Chapter 4. The debate centres on whether the human subject can be considered as a starting point for analysing society, as a unitary, rational and consistent whole whose essence may be derived from an analysis of what they say and how they act. Against this view is that the human subject is but an historically-specific effect of power/knowledge. In this so-called anti-essentialist view, historically and culturally specific forms of power relations create different discourses. All discourses open up what may be known in certain ways, but equally close just as many avenues down. In this Foucauldian world, knowledge is always an effect of power. Power itself is always dangerous, and discourses, as the products of power, must always been challenged and interrogated for their potential for people to find them oppressive. Social research, in this scheme of things, cannot identify an unproblematic progress, cannot tell us the best we can do nor what we should do. Rather, social research can merely help us choose the form of power we wish to govern our lives.

We have also looked, in Chapter 5, at the moral and political values social researchers have adopted in applied research. We considered the applied researcher who takes the side of the underdog, of those most oppressed in our society. The problem is increasingly that in considering many dimensions it may not be clear who is the underdog and in what sense. We looked at the politically engaged researcher who asks in whose interests is what type of knowledge produced and promulgated. Postmodernism helps us expose our competing discourses to one another, helps reveal what each of us feels is at stake in the organization of social life. Positivism, as we have seen, tends to be associated with the view that social research can and should be neutral, though those who try to maintain this distinction between fact and value also try to maximize their influence on policy, as we saw in Chapter 6. In this chapter, we looked at how social researchers are not individuals but are part of scientific communities, with group behaviours, norms, allegiances and vested interests that shape the production of social knowledge. Radically new ideas tend not to be welcomed by scientific communities, who then may act in confederacy against the bringer of innovative ways of seeing the world.

In Chapter 7, we sought to raise a novel perspective on the issues of validity and reliability. Usually these are seen as being at the heart of scientific endeavour in the social sciences, yet the genealogy of the ideas is rather different. They originated in storytelling, history and politics in classical antiquity and more recently insinuated themselves into the social sciences via disciplines such as educational studies in the United States. They address the fundamental problem of how we make inferences about the constructs and explanatory entities which are believed to underlie the phenomena we study. Critical realism provides a justification for these constructs, but we are still left with the problem of working out what they might be and how we might know about them. Particularly when confronted with complex and diverse sets of indicators, it may be difficult to infer explanatory systems like 'toxic shock syndrome' or 'multiple personality disorder' at all.

Moving on from this, in Chapter 8 we attempted to outline what we might learn for our choice and implementation of research strategy. There has sometimes been a tendency for research techniques to dominate this area, where strategy exists at the level of deciding whether to do a randomized controlled clinical trial, a survey, an interview study and so on. Thus there is a good deal of often unacknowledged theoretical political and ethical work involved before we even get as far as the choice of method. We have also attempted to highlight the sheer range of issues that have an impact on strategy, from the psychosocial microstructure of research encounters, where participants may be trying to guess the purpose of the study, through to the more distal but nevertheless important impact of grander social, political and economic considerations. Moreover, on closer analysis many of the strategies which have been take for granted as useful in the past, such as 'triangulation', may yield additional problems. They may enrich the picture of what is going on but leave us with more conceptual difficulties since different methods may bring with them incompatible assumptions and world views.

In Chapter 9, we examined how the analytic dualisms discussed might help us to think about the process of analysing data. Once again there are no easy solutions, yet we would hope to have sensitized readers to some of the problems that exist in making meaning out of 'data'. The perspectives we bring to the research situation may have a substantial impact on the way we make sense of what is happening. Now, without suggesting that we abandon our humanitarian concerns, it is nevertheless important to recognize the impact of these on our analysis and on the viability of this analysis to lead to subsequent improvements in health or well-being amongst the communities we study. Even statistics and meta-analyses, although they are often thought of as reducing ambiguity, are often the precursors of even more controversy as researchers dispute the best way of making sense of the work that has already been done on, say, breast cancer screening or medication effectiveness. An additional layer of complication for us is opened up in social research on health because participants themselves have their own understanding of health, illness and risk which inform their behaviour and treatment-seeking strategies.

Finally, in Chapter 10 we return to the issues raised in the chapter on validity and reliability and discuss some alternative approaches to the dilemmas these raise. There are a whole range of other attempts to secure the credibility, trustworthiness and believability of a research programme once it emerges into the public domain. There are even more complications adduced to the picture once we examine what happens when researchers try to make sense of results which do not fit the predictions and begin to unpick the underlying constructs on which the research purports to be based. Finally, we return to the deconstructionist project which we initially outlined earlier in the book and explore what this celebration of radical uncertainty can offer to researchers concerned about the veracity of their data.

In summary, we argue that researchers will inevitably start with a series of assumptions about the nature of the world and the research process. Some of them are built in to the very research strategies we employ. We believe that researchers will be best served if they employ strategies sensitive to the contextual features of the research problem, but our sensitivity and awareness as researchers (and the ability to be critical and analytical with our data) can arguably be improved by reflecting upon where the contingent choices in the research process leave us in a field of analytical possibilities. This is surely more fruitful than approaches to research that start from a presumed philosophical position and attempt to derive strategy and method from that position. The awareness of our own position as researchers in a field of possibilities confers a number of possible benefits to the research. First, it permits appropriate caveats and cautions to be included in a discussion. Second, it allows researchers to situate themselves in the research process and at least makes possible reflection upon the effects of their activities, activities that create and make sense of data. Third, it enables researchers to anticipate criticisms of the respective scientific community, and to address those concerns within the overall strategy. But perhaps most importantly of all, a critical reflection upon where practical strategic choices have positioned us as applied researchers enables us to compensate for the inherent weaknesses in the approach we have implicitly adopted.

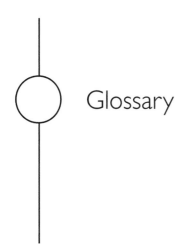 Glossary

Action research: A research strategy based around the iterative, cyclical process of a baseline assessment of a problem; a planned intervention; and an evaluation of that intervention.

Actor-network theory: This is associated with Bruno Latour and is concerned with the processes by which scientific disputes become closed or resolved, ideas accepted, tools and methods adopted. The field of enquiry is seen as a network of actors which may include scientists, but also their tools, instruments and objects of study such as bacteria, sea scallops or physical phenomena such as gravity waves.

Analytic dualisms: A set of key philosophical tensions (materialism/idealism; nominalism/scientific realism; essentialism/anti-essentialism), which researchers implicitly use to make sense of their research endeavours.

Analytic generalization: Generating ideas that are conceptual keys to other situations as well as the one being studied and using such ideas as templates with which to analyse comparable social situations.

Anti-essentialism: A view of the social world in which there are no fundamental fixed truths or essences but in which reality is a series of shifting possibilities.

Auditability: The extent to which the processes by which research has been conducted are clearly and fully documented such that an outsider can critically examine the steps taken to reach the conclusions drawn.

Background assumptions: The unthought-about and unnamed beliefs that help formulate our ideas about researching the social world, which we may not bring to the forefront of our minds. If they are not formally expressed, they cannot be challenged, and thus remain a limit on our research imaginations.

Bayesian statistics: These examine the likelihood of occurrence of an event on previous occasions and use this as a way of estimating its likelihood in the present. Bayes' Theorem is a means of quantifying uncertainty. Based on probability theory, the theorem defines a rule for refining an hypothesis by factoring in additional evidence and background information.

Bias: A systematic inconsistency in one or more parts of the research process. By contrast, **experimenter bias** is a tendency towards a lack of fairness or impartiality on the part of the researcher, based on his or her personal preferences.

Bracketing: A concept from phenomenology in which researchers attempt to discard their preconceptions of the phenomenon under study in order to understand that phenomenon at a deep level. See **phenomenology**.

Case study: A research strategy characterized by multi-method, depth study of one, or a few, cases of a situation.

Conclusion validity: The degree to which the conclusions reached by researchers about the relationships between variables within their data are reasonable.

Confirmability: The extent to which the researcher makes available the processes of research for external audit. Compare **objectivity**.

Consequential validity: The degree to which the results are commensurate with the purposes to which the results were supposed to be applied.

Construct validity: The degree to which conclusions can legitimately be made from the indicators of the study to the theoretical concepts that those indicators are held to represent.

Content analysis: A form of analysis that entails counting the frequencies of words or images and making comparisons based on these frequencies.

Content validity: The extent to which the research concepts or measures incorporate all aspects that should be included and none that should not be included.

Convergent validity: The degree to which concepts that should in theory be closely associated are actually observed to be closely associated.

Conversation analysis: Naturally occurring talk is transcribed in fine detail and the underlying patterns by which people create a sense of order are outlined. See **ethnomethodology**.

Correspondence problem: The notion that meanings attributed to social phenomena may be different at the levels of individual words, in terms of cultural meanings, and with respect to what dimensions of an issue are important for the research participants in the first place.

Counterfactual thinking: A process of thinking beyond the immediate appearances of society to consider what other possibilities could be brought into view if some or all of the current parameters of social order were changed.

Credibility: The extent to which a phenomenon can be considered authentic within the context in which it is produced. Compare **internal validity**.

Criterion validity: The degree to which a research concept accurately reflects relevant criteria external to the original context of the research.

Critical realism: See **realism**.

Death and furniture: A humorous characterization of everyday versions of foundationalism, where people stress the solidity of common objects or the certainty of death to make a point about the solidity of the 'real world'.

Deconstruction: A form of analysis associated with postmodernism. Our sense of who we are manifests itself through difference. Deconstruction exposes attempts of vested interests to deny this difference.

Deduction: The assessment of predictions of particular observable events from general hypotheses in order to test the hypotheses. Compare **induction**.

Demarcation problem: The problem of how, and where, to draw the line between true scientific forms of knowledge and other claims to knowledge.

Dependability: A focus on the reproducibility of the processes of data collection and data analysis rather than replication of results. Compare **reliability**.

Discourse analysis: An approach to analysing text and talk that emphasizes the social actions achieved through the use of language.

Disembedding: Taking something away from its original context and ascribing different meanings to it. According to Giddens, Western societies themselves are 'disembedded' in that they are not gathered in small enclosed units, in close physical and verbal proximity.

Empiricism: A philosophy of research that regards only that knowledge gained through experience and the senses as legitimate.

Epistemology: The study of how, in principle, we may gain knowledge – in the case of social research, how we gain knowledge about the social world.

Equipoise: A state of being equally balanced. In research it refers to a situation when either of two possibilities might be true and the study is intended to adjudicate between these competing claims.

Essentialism: The belief that things have invisible core properties, and that these give the thing its identity or 'nature', distinguishing it from other things. These inherent characteristics may be regarded as applying irrespective of cultural, historical or societal contexts.

Ethnicity: A shared kinship lineage, linked to a geographical territory, real or imagined, possibly also sharing common culture, religion, language, dress, diet and customs.

Ethnography: A research strategy that attempts to describe the meanings and understandings of members of a culture in graphic detail, linking particular actions to their place in the overall culture. **Critical ethnography** claims to link the particular situations studied to underlying factors not immediately evident and by doing so challenge the status quo.

Ethnomethodology: An approach to research that studies the way we achieve our sense of social order by means of conversation and interaction. It is concerned with the methods that ordinary people use to perform their occupational or social tasks and construct social realities. See **conversation analysis**.

Evidence-based practice: A policy that is becoming increasingly popular in health and social care, which encourages practitioners to ensure that the interventions they offer are supported by contemporary research evidence rather than being based on custom and practice.

Experiment: A research strategy that entails the random allocation of subjects to an experimental and a control group, and manipulation of one or more variables, in order to test a hypothesis.

External constructs: Concepts about which different respondents are likely to share similar understandings, in the view of the researcher.

External validity: The extent to which the results of the study can be statistically generalized beyond the context of the original study.

Face validity: The extent to which the measurement indicator 'looks right' or is intuitively appealing to the user or research participant. This kind of validity is treated sceptically by many researchers.

Falsification principle: A doctrine that only statements which are amenable to being shown to be false should qualify as scientific statements.

Feminist research: A collection of approaches to research that emphasize the damage done to women's interests by traditional research and the potential for research to advance the interests of women by choice of topic, style of engagement with participants, methodological criteria by which research is judged and contribution to the political emancipation of women.

Field of possibilities: The series of analytical dualisms which researchers implicitly draw upon to create their own research positions.

Frequentist statistics: These encompass the vast majority of statistical techniques taught in research methods courses, which could be described as 'frequentist', in that they are concerned with what would happen if a very large number of observations were made, and estimate the likelihood of the current results occurring by chance.

Gaze: A Foucauldian concept. The execution of a particular discourse of power that brings about a particular type of knowledge, for example the medical gaze.

Genealogy: The study of family origins. In Foucauldian theory, an approach to research that suggests a given system of thought was the result of particular socio-historical circumstances, not the outcome of some inevitable trajectory of progress.

Generalizability: See **validity, external**.

Governmentality: A Foucauldian concept. A form of exercising domination in which people position themselves in relation to expected 'norms' in an apparently voluntary manner.

Grounded theory: A research strategy that involves working with the concepts and categories of the research subjects.

Hermeneutics: The methodology and principles of studying interpretation, meaning and purpose.

Hypothetico-deductive method: The scientific method of testing law-like statements (hypotheses) of particular observed events, then seeing if the predictions turn out as expected, thus refuting or confirming the hypotheses.

Idealism: An approach to the ontological question of what the social world is made up of that centres on the meanings, understandings and interpretations of individuals. Compare **materialism**.

Ideology: The processes by which knowledge is produced that affect relations of power. Often used to refer to the way in which the system of values and beliefs of the powerful are (mis)represented as obvious, natural and unchangeable. See **reification**.

Imposition problem: The notion that asking a research question itself necessarily imposes a particular framework of thinking onto an issue, thus drawing attention to the researcher's role in creating, rather than just obtaining, data.

Induction: A form of reasoning that starts from a series of small-scale observations and builds up more general arguments from these. Compare **deduction**.

Internal constructs: Concepts that are highly likely to be understood in ways that are different and of consequence for the findings of the research. Compare **external constructs**.

Internal reliability: A property of a scale or questionnaire where all the items correlate with one another, presumably because they are all measuring the same thing; assessed with a statistic such as Cronbach's alpha.

Internal validity: A concern with whether we are actually describing what we claim to be describing, measuring what we claim to be measuring.

Interpretive phenomenological analysis: An approach that emphasizes the researcher's attempts to explore the meaning of research participants' lives through interpretation based on mutual engagement.

'Knowing better': A deliberately ambiguous phrase to encapsulate the ideas that, first, research may go beyond appearances and thus have depth and be incisive, and second, that research may be arrogant in asserting privileged knowledge beyond the consciousness of individuals studied. Compare **'taking at face value'**.

Life-world: The world as subjectively, immediately and directly experienced in everyday life, as opposed to the 'objective' scientific world. See **phenomenology**.

Lived experience: Paying attention to the experiences of research participants rather than conceptualizing, categorizing or theorizing about such experiences. See **phenomenology**.

Marxism: Following Karl Marx, who argued that much of how society operates is determined by the particular social–historical manner in which human beings come together in the process of labour.

Materialism: An approach to the ontological question which holds that the social world is material and external to the researcher. Compare **idealism**.

Member checks: The process of the researcher checking back with research participants whether the interpretation of data matches their understandings.

Meta-analysis: Putting together the results of many studies on the same issue to increase the trustworthiness of the findings.

Meta-narratives: A claim that modernist theories provide explanations of society that are too uniform and all-embracing, in contrast to the diversities and differences that exist within phenomena. See **postmodernism**.

Methodological collectivism: An approach to knowledge that permits reference to collective entities as real phenomena. Compare **methodological individualism**.

Methodological individualism: An approach to knowledge in which knowledge may only be gained through individuals and individual consciousnesses. Compare **methodological collectivism**.

Methodology: The study of how we know we have gained knowledge through social research. Methodological criteria include **validity** and **reliability**.

Modernity: Describes both a period of time, and an approach to research, that focuses on categorization, generalization and uniformity of process and purpose.

Negotiated order: A concept that reality is not fixed and stable, but is constantly created and recreated through a series of formal and informal manoeuvrings. See **symbolic interactionism**.

Nominalism: An approach to epistemology that asserts that collective structures are merely names given to those collectivities.

Objectivity: The combination of principles that hold that there is a reality independent of the researcher's interpretation of it, and that research should conform to **value freedom**.

Observation: A method of data collection based on the researcher viewing at first hand. **Naturalistic observation** is where the researcher observes the situation in its natural context, attempting to disturb the situation as little as possible. **Participant observation** entails the researcher joining in the activities observed in order to understand through insider experience the situation studied. **Structured observation** is more characteristic of positivist approaches in which a predetermined schedule of categories of behaviour is devised.

Operationalism: The argument that a research concept can only legitimately be defined in terms of the operations we carry out to prove, measure or apply it.

Operationalization: The process of turning a concept that is too nebulous to be measured into an indicator that is amenable to measurement.

Paradigm: A term from the philosophy of science that describes an over-arching (and possibly taken-for-granted) framework adopted by researchers. This framework specifies how a research problem should be constructed, what methods should be adopted, and what evidence is likely to look like.

Patriarchy: The product of those structures, ideologies and discourses that privilege and maintain a dominant male view of the world.

Phenomenology: A philosophy of research based around how people make sense of their social world. To do this, one strand of phenomenology directs researchers to exclude all their preconceptions. See **bracketing**. Another strand directs researchers to be reflexive about their role in the co-production of meaning. See **symbolic interactionism**.

Placebo: An inert substance, made to look like a real drug, which can then be used to evaluate whether any observed effect is due to the effects of the real drug or to the psychological effects of believing that one is receiving the real drug. See **randomized controlled trial**.

Positivism: A research philosophy that advocates the application of approaches equivalent to the natural sciences in the study of social phenomena.

Postmodernism: A philosophy which in terms of research focuses on the local rather than the universal, emphasizes discontinuity and difference rather than categorization and generalization, and examines the agency in the writing of results.

Power/knowledge: A Foucauldian concept that sees knowledge as an effect of power.

Questionnaire: A research method that entails the administration of a structured series of questions to a respondent.

Random error: Inconsistencies (in either direction) in the measured data due to limitations in the precision with which the particular measurement can be made. **Systematic errors**, by contrast, are consistent inaccuracies in the same direction reproduced throughout the research because of a flaw in method or measurement.

Random sampling: A type of probability sampling in which each member of the population being studied has an equal chance of being in the sample selected.

Randomized controlled trial (RCT): A particular form of the experimental research strategy originally used in agriculture, but now popular in health research. See **placebo**.

Rationality: **Formal rationality** is the trend towards the increasing predictability of society, the reliability with which we can anticipate the consequences of our actions. **Substantive rationality** is the extent to which something contributes to the realization of a specific political or moral goal held by a group.

Realism (epistemology): **Scientific realism** is a belief that social research involves identifying the underlying structures that generate the appearances of the social world. These structures need not be observable. **Critical realism** aims to identify these structures in order to expose social injustices and challenge the conditions that are said to generate those injustices.

Realism (ontology): A belief that the social world comprises material things that are independent of what the researcher thinks of those things. Sometimes called **naïve realism**.

Realms: The **observable** realm is that which a researcher can witness at first hand. The realm of the **actual** represents events taking place outside the immediate view of the researcher. The realm of the **real** refers to unobservable structures that generate the appearances of the social world. See **scientific realism**.

Reification: Regarding social structures or technological artefacts that have been created by the actions of humans as somehow natural, inevitable and unchangeable.

Reliability: A methodological criterion that assesses such factors as the extent to which the research can be repeated over time or replicated between different researchers.

Sample-oriented validity: Concerned with types of validity that relate to whether ideas are appropriately grouped together. See **content validity**.

Saturation of categories: The point where emerging concepts have been fully explored and no new categories are being generated. See **grounded theory**.

Scientific communities: The group of researchers, natural or social scientists, who work both cooperatively and competitively in creating knowledge.

Scale: In the social sciences this often refers to a self-report questionnaire which yields a single score if a participant's responses to the questions are added up. In constructing a 'scale', care is taken to ensure that all the items are correlated together, that is, it has high internal reliability or consistency.

Scientific revolution: The tipping point at which the majority of a scientific community abandon the old paradigm in favour of the new one.

Self: The personal side of an individual, which is continually reformulated as a consequence of interaction with the social side of an individual, one's **self-in-the-world**.

Self-in-the-world: The self-conscious, partial and motivated presentation of one's identity in interaction with the selves-in-the-world of others. See **symbolic interactionism**.

Sign-oriented validity: Concerned with types of validity that relate to whether proxy indicators are a good representation of a theoretical construct. See **construct validity** and **criterion validity**.

Social actors: A term emphasizing that people actively construct their social world and do not just live in it, and, like actors in drama, that they interpret their roles in society. See **symbolic interactionism**.

Social constructionism: Social phenomena and meanings do not pre-exist but are created and recreated by individuals, including researchers.

Sociology: Studying human societies.

Sociology of Science; Sociology of Scientific Knowledge; Science Studies: These are umbrella terms for an approach to the study of scientific knowledge that stresses the role of social and cultural factors in the choice of topics of enquiry, the kinds of methods used, the resolution of disputes and the dissemination of knowledge. See **Strong Programme.**

Standardized instrument: A research instrument that has been statistically adjusted on the assumption that in measuring 'reality' there are always many small fluctuations around some precise 'true' value (a 'normal' distribution), so that it may be directly compared to other similarly adjusted instruments.

Statistical conclusion validity: The degree to which conclusions, based on your statistical choices of sample size and significance level set, are correct.

Strategy: A level of research that refers to the broad organizing features of the design.

Strong Programme: A view, from those researching how communities of scientists actually work, that not only is scientific knowledge influenced by 'weak' factors such as the lives of scientists (their career interests for instance), but by 'strong' factors. This would include in particular the fact that scientific theories are influenced by the socio-cultural context in which they are formulated, that the sociology of science should be impartial or symmetrical in that it must account for both true and false scientific ideas within the same explanatory framework and that it should be reflexive and be able to account for sociology itself.

Subject positions: A Foucauldian concept in which there are no essential fixed identities, but different possible stances depending upon the social context.

Subjectivism: A general term used to cover all research approaches that emphasize the internal meanings, perceptions and interpretations of people as the basis for a study of human societies.

Subordinate: The less powerful person or group in a given social situation. Compare **superordinate.**

Superordinate: The relatively more powerful person or group in a given social situation. Compare **subordinate.**

Surveillance: A Foucauldian concept. A principle of social organization and regulation associated with the growth of disciplinary knowledge such as medicine, psychiatry and criminology.

Survey: A research strategy that comprises an attempt to collect empirical data, obtaining breadth of coverage and collecting data for both each case (research subject) and each variable (information sought of each research subject).

Symbolic interactionism: A philosophy of research based on the notion that social meaning is created through the exchange of symbols, especially language.

Taking at face value: A deliberately ambiguous phrase to encapsulate the ideas that, first, research could take people seriously and thereby validate their experience, and second, research may not go beyond appearances and thus may be superficial. Compare **'knowing better'.**

Technicism: A tendency to glorify technology as self-evidently a positive thing and as necessarily representing progress.

Technologies of the self: The range of means and techniques that people apply to themselves in order to govern themselves. See **governmentality.**

Temporal stability: The extent to which research instruments reproduce consistent results over time.

Texts: The artefacts of research (including research reports, journal articles, interview transcripts) are amenable to different readings, many unknown to the author/speaker.

Thematic analysis: Identifying common themes (often in interview transcripts) and aggregating those themes into more general categories and codes. See **grounded theory**.

Topicalize: A linguistic technique of drawing attention to an utterance of another so as to make that utterance the focus of attention and the person explicitly accountable for the logical implications of that utterance.

Totalizing fallacy: A postmodernist term used to suggest that modernist theories attempt all-embracing explanations that ignore counter-tendencies, exceptions and disconfirming factors.

Transferability: The extent to which the conceptual findings of research may be applicable in other settings. Compare **external validity**.

Triangulation: The process of bringing more than one dimension to bear on a research problem in order to increase the trustworthiness of the findings. **Data triangulation** involves putting more than one piece of data together to draw a conclusion. Triangulation may also comprise **investigator** (compares the findings of more than one researcher); **methods** (compares the findings of more than one method of data collection) and, though greatly disputed, **theories** (compares the findings of more than one theoretical position to the problem). **Multiple triangulation** entails use of more than one of these types of triangulation.

True score theory: A theory of measurement that maintains that every measurement is an additive composite of two components: the **true score** of the variable in question, and **random error**. Across a set of scores, it is assumed that the variability of a measure is the sum of the variability due to true score and the variability due to random error.

Underdog: A colloquial term for the less powerful person in any social situation. See **subordinate**.

Value freedom: A principle that research can and should be concerned with the truth and not influenced by the researcher's own moral or political beliefs.

Validity: A key set of methodological criteria, broadly concerned with the extent to which the researcher is 'getting at the truth'. See **conclusion validity, consequential validity, construct validity, content validity, convergent validity, criterion validity, external validity, face validity, internal validity, sample-orientated validity, sign-orientated validity, statistical conclusion validity**.

Variables: Especially in experimental research, the factors delineated by the researcher as the ones under study. The independent variable is the variable manipulated by the researcher, and the dependent variable is the one that is measured.

World 'in here': see **idealism**.

World 'out there': see **materialism**.

Bibliography

Abma, A.T. (2002) Emerging narrative forms of knowledge representation in the health sciences: two texts in a postmodern context, *Qualitative Health Research*, 12: 5–27.

Adamsen, L. and Tewes, M. (2000) Discrepancy between patients' perspectives, staff's documentation and reflections on basic nursing care, *Scandinavian Journal of Caring Sciences*, 14: 120–9.

AERA (American Educational Research Association). APA (American Psychological Association) and NCME (National Council on Measurement in Education) (1985) *Standards for Educational and Psychological Testing*. Washington, DC: Authors.

Alderson, A. (2004) Girls as young as 14 demand NHS fertility treatment, *Sunday Telegraph*, 4 July: 1.

Allen, D. (1997) The nursing-medical boundary: a negotiated order?, *Sociology of Health and Illness*, 19(4): 498–520.

Altheide, D. and Johnson, J.M.C. (1998) Criteria for assessing interpretive validity in qualitative research, in N.K. Denzin and Y.S. Lincoln (eds) *Collecting and Interpreting Qualitative Materials*. Thousand Oaks, CA: Sage Publications.

Alvesson, M. and Sköldberg, K. (2000) *Reflexive Methodology: New Vistas for Qualitative Research*. London: Sage Publications.

Angoff, W.H. (1988) Validity: an evolving concept, in H. Wainer and H.I. Braun (eds) *Test Validity*. Hillsdale, NJ: Lawrence Erlbaum.

Ankarloo, B. and Henningsen, G. (1993) *Early Modern European Witchcraft: Centres and Peripheries*. Oxford: Oxford University Press.

Antona, C., Pompilio, G., Lotto, A.A., Di Matteo, S., Agrifoglio, M. and Biglioli, P.

(1998) Video-assisted minimally invasive coronary bypass surgery without cardiopulmonary bypass, *European Journal of Cardio-Thoracic Surgery*, 14 (Supplement 1): 62–7.

Archer, M. (2000) For structure: its reality, properties and powers: a reply to Anthony King, *Sociological Review*, 48(3): 464–72.

Arelett, P., Bryan, P. and Evans, S. (2001) A response to 'Measles mumps, rubella vaccine: through a glass darkly' by Drs A.J. Wakefield and S.M. Montgomery and published reviewers' comments, *Adverse Drug Reactions and Toxicology Reviews*, 20(1): 37–45.

Arendt, H. (1954) *Between Past and Future*, New York: Knopf.

Armstrong, D. (1983) *The Political Anatomy of the Body*, Cambridge: Cambridge University Press.

Atkinson, J.M. (1978) *Discovering Suicide: Studies in the Social Organization of Sudden Death*. London: Macmillan.

Atkinson, J.M and Drew, P. (1979) *Order in Court: The Organization of Verbal Interaction in Judicial Settings*. London: Macmillan.

Attridge, D., Bennington, G. and Young, R. (eds) (1987) *Post-Structuralism and the Question of History*. Cambridge: Cambridge University Press.

Baines, C.J., McFarlane, D.V. and Miller, A.B. (1990) The role of the reference radiologist: estimates of inter-observer agreement and potential delay in cancer detection in the national breast screening study, *Investigative Radiology*, 25: 971–6.

Bandura, A. (1999) A socio-cognitive analysis of substance abuse: an agentic perspective, *Psychological Science*, 10(3): 214–17.

Bannister, P., Burman, E., Parker, I., Taylor, M. and Tindall, C. (1994) *Qualitative Methods in Psychology: A Research Guide*. Buckingham: Open University Press.

Barbacid, M., Bolognesi, D. and Aaronson, S.A. (1980) Humans have antibodies capable of recognizing oncoviral glycoproteins: demonstration that these antibodies are formed in response to cellular modification of glycoproteins rather than as consequence of exposure to virus, *Proceedings of the National Academy of Science, USA*, 77: 1617–21.

Barnes, B., Bloor, D. and Henry, J. (1996) *Scientific Knowledge: A Sociological Approach*. London: The Athlone Press.

Bauman, Z. (1993) *Postmodern Ethics*. Oxford: Blackwell.

Becker, H. (1967) Whose side are we on?, *Social Problems*, 14: 239–47.

Becker, H., Greer, D., Hughes, E. and Strauss, A. (1961) *Boys in White*. Chicago, IL: University of Chicago Press.

Beecham, L. (1998) Junior doctors look forward to shorter hours, *British Medical Journal*, 317: 1473.

Begley, C.M. (1996) Using triangulation in nursing research, *Journal of Advanced Nursing*, 24: 122–8.

Berg, M. (1996) Practices of reading and writing: the constitutive role of the patient record in medical work, *Sociology of Health and Illness*, 18(4): 499–524.

Bhaskar, R. (1979) *The Possibility of Naturalism: A Philosophical Critique of the Contemporary Human Sciences*. Brighton: Harvester Wheatsheaf.

Billig, M. (1979) *Fascists: A Social Psychological View of the National Front*. London: Academic Press.

Billings, J.R. and Cowley, S. (1995) Approaches to community needs assessment: a literature review, *Journal of Advanced Nursing*, 22: 721–30.

Blaikie, N. (1991) A critique of the use of triangulation in social research, *Quality and Quantity*, 25: 115–36.

Blake, C. (2004) My gamble with cancer. I didn't take the test because I knew the result, if positive, would terrify me, *Sunday Telegraph*, 4 July: 23.

Bloor, D. (1976) *Knowledge and Social Imagery*. London: Routledge and Kegan Paul.

Bloor, D. (1981) The strengths of the Strong Programme, *Philosophy of the Social Sciences*, 11: 199–213.

Bograd, M.(1990) Feminist approaches for men in family therapy, *Journal of Feminist Family Therapy*, 3 (4): [entire issue].

Boje, D.M. (2001) *Narrative Methods for Organizational and Communication Research*. London: Sage Publications.

Bollini, P., Pampallona, S., Tibaldi, G., Kupelnick, B. and Munizza, C. (1999) Effectiveness of antidepressants: meta-analysis of dose-effect relationships in randomised clinical trials, *British Journal of Psychiatry*, 174: 297–303.

Bourdieu, P. (1999) The specificity of the scientific field and the social conditions of the progress of reason, in M. Biagioli (ed.) *The Science Studies Reader*. New York: Routledge.

Bowler, I. (1993) 'They're not the same as us?': midwives' stereotypes of South Asian maternity patients, *Sociology of Health and Illness*, 15(2): 457–70.

Bradley, S. (1995) Methodological triangulation in healthcare research, *Nurse Researcher*, 3: 81–9.

Breggin, P.R. and Cohen, D. (2000) *Your Drug May Be Your Problem*. New York: Perseus Publishing.

Brewer, J. and Hunter, A. (1989) *Multi-Method Research: A Synthesis of Styles*. Newbury Park, CA: Sage Publications.

Brown, B. and Crawford, P. (2003) The clinical governance of the soul: deep management and the self-regulating subject in integrated community mental health teams, *Social Science and Medicine*, 56: 67–81.

Brown, B., Crawford, P. and Hicks, C. (2003) *Evidence-Based Research: Dilemmas and Debates in Health Care*. Maidenhead: Open University Press.

Brown, R. (1998) *Toward a Democratic Science: Scientific Narration and Civic Communication*, New Haven, CT: Yale University Press.

Browne, J. and Minichiello, V. (1995) The social meanings behind male sex work: implications for sexual interactions, *British Journal of Sociology*, 46: 598–622.

Burgess, R.G. (1984) *In the Field: An Introduction to Field Research*. London: Allen and Unwin.

Burton, S., Regan, L. and Kelly, L. (1989) *Supporting Women and Challenging Men. Lessons from Domestic Violence Intervention Programmes*. Bristol: The Policy Press.

Butler, J. (1990) *Gender Trouble: Feminism and the Subversion of Identity*. London: Routledge.

Byrne, D. (1998) *Complexity Theory and the Social Sciences: An Introduction*. London: Routledge.

Caelli, K., Downie, J. and Caelli, T. (2003) Towards a decision support system for health promotion in nursing, *Journal of Advanced Nursing*, 43(2): 170–80.

Caixeta, M. (1996) A critical look at current conceptions of personality disorder: medical and moral aspects, *International Journal of Psychopathology, Psychopharmacology and Psychotherapy*, 1(1): 43–5.

Caldwell, J.C., Orubuloye, I.C. and Caldwell, P. (2000) Female genital mutilation: conditions of decline, *Population Research and Policy Review*, 19: 233–54.

Calnan, M. (1987) *Health and Illness: The Lay Perspective*. London: Tavistock.

Campbell, D. and Fiske, D. (1959) Convergent and discriminant validity by the multitrait-multimethod matrix, *Psychological Bulletin*, 56: 81–105.

Campbell, D.T. (1969) Reforms as experiments, *American Psychologist*, 24: 409–29.

Campbell, D.T. and Stanley, J.C. (1963) *Experimental and Quasi-Experimental Designs for Research*. Chicago, IL: Rand McNally.

Carmines, E.G. and Zeller, R.A. (1979) *Reliability and Validity Assessment*. Newbury Park, CA: Sage Publications.

Carr, L.T. (1994) The strengths and weaknesses of quantitative and qualitative research: what method for nursing?, *Journal of Advanced Nursing*, 20: 716–27.

Chandler, D. (2001) *Semiotics: The Basics*. London: Routledge.

Chapman, S. and Eggar, G. (1983) Myth in cigarette advertising and health promotion, reprinted in Beattie, A., Gott, M., Jones, L. and Sidell, M. (eds) (1993) *Health and Wellbeing: A Reader*. London: Macmillan.

Cicourel, A. (1964) *Method and Measurement in Sociology*. New York: Free Press.

Clarke, L. (1996) The last post? Defending nursing against the postmodernist maze, *Journal of Psychiatric and Mental Health Nursing*, 3: 257–65.

Clarke, M. (1990) Memories of breathing: a phenomenological dialogue: asthma as a way of becoming, *Pedagogy: A Human Sciences Journal*, 8: 208–23.

Clay, S.J. (1983) *The Wrath of Athena: Gods and Men in the Odyssey*. Princeton, NJ: Princeton University Press.

Clendon, J. and White, G. (2001) The feasibility of a nurse practitioner-led primary health care clinic in a school setting: a community needs analysis, *Journal of Advanced Nursing*, 34(2): 171–8.

Collins, D. (1999) Hesiod and the divine voice of the muses, *Arethusa*, 32: 241–62.

Collins, H. (2004) *Gravity's Shadow*. Chicago, IL: University of Chicago Press.

Cook, T.D. and Campbell, D.T. (1979) *Quasi-Experimentation: Design and Analysis Issues for Field Settings*. Boston, MA: Houghton-Mifflin Company.

Cook, T.D. and Campbell, D.T. (1986) The causal assumptions of quasi-experimental practice, *Synthese*, 68: 141–80.

Cramer, J.H. and Rosencheck, R. (1998) Compliance with medication regimens for mental and physical disorders, *Psychiatric Services*, 49: 196–201.

Crawford, P., Brown, B., Hicks, C. and Anthony, P. (2002) Reluctant empiricists: community mental health nurses and the art of evidence-based praxis, *Health and Social Care in the Community*, 10(4): 287–98.

Cronbach, L.J. (1971) Test validation, in R.L. Thorndike (ed.) *Educational Measurement*, 2nd edn. Washington, DC: American Council on Education.

Cronbach, L.J. and Quirk, T.J. (1976) Test validity, in *International Encyclopedia of Education*. New York: McGraw-Hill.

Croom, S., Proctor, S. and Le Couteur, A. (2000) Developing a concept analysis of control for use in child and adolescent mental health nursing, *Journal of Advanced Nursing*, 31(6): 1324–32.

Cross, A. (2004) The flexibility of scientific rhetoric: a case study of UFO researchers, *Qualitative Sociology*, 27(1): 3–34.

Cuff, E.C., Sharrock, W.W. and Francis, D.W. (1990) *Perspectives in Sociology*, 3rd edn. London: Routledge.

Culbertson, F.M. (1997) Depression and gender, *American Psychologist*, 52: 25–31.

Culley, L., Dyson, S.M., Ham-Ying, S. and Young, W. (2001) Caribbean nurses and racism in the NHS, in L. Culley and S.M. Dyson (eds) *Ethnicity and Nursing Practice*. Basingstoke: Palgrave.

Currer, C. (1986) Concepts of well- and ill-being: the case of Pathan mothers in Britain, in C. Currer and M. Stacey (eds) *Concepts of Health and Illness*. Leamington Spa: Berg.

Daly, M. (1979) *Gyn/Ecology*. London: The Women's Press.

Dandeker, C. (1983) Theory and practice in sociology: the critical imperatives of realism, *Journal for the Theory of Social Behaviour*, 13: 195–210.

Dandeker, C. and Scott, J. (1979) The structure of sociological theory and knowledge, *Journal for the Theory of Social Behaviour*, 9: 303–25.

Davis, R.E. (2002) 'The strongest women': exploration of the inner resources of abused women, *Qualitative Health Research*, 12(9): 1248–63.

Dawis, R.V. (1987) Scale construction, *Journal of Counseling Psychology*, 34: 481–9.

Deer, B. (2004) Fresh doubts cast on MMR study data, *Sunday Times*, 25 April: 11.

Denscombe, M. (2003) *The Good Research Guide*, 2nd edn. Buckingham: Open University Press.

Denzin, N.K. (1989) *The Research Act: A Theoretical Introduction to Sociological Methods*, 3rd edn. Englewood Cliffs, NJ: Prentice-Hall.

Denzin, N.K. (1994) Postmodernism and deconstructionism, in D.R. Dickens and A. Fontana (eds) *Postmodernism and Social Inquiry*. London: UCL Press.

Department of Health (1994) *Supporting Research and Development in the NHS (The Culyer Report)*. London: HMSO.

Derrida, J. (1976) *Of Grammatology* (translated by G. Spivak). Baltimore, MD: Johns Hopkins University Press.

Derrida, J. (1981) *Dissemination* (translated by B. Johnson). London: Athlone Press.

Derrida, J. (2001) The future of the professions or the unconditional university (thanks to the 'humanities', what could take place tomorrow), in L. Simmons and H. Worth (eds) *Derrida Down Under*. Palmerston North: Dunmore Press.

DiCicco, L. (2001) The disease of Katherine Anne Porter's Greensick Girls in 'Old Mortality', *The Southern Literary Journal*, 33(2): 80–98.

Dingwall, R. and Robinson, K. (1993) Policing the family: health visiting and the public surveillance of private behaviour, in A. Beattie (ed.) *Health and Wellbeing: A Reader*. London: Macmillan.

Dobash, R.E. and Dobash, R.P. (1979) *Violence Against Wives: A Case Against the Patriarchy*. New York: Free Press.

Dobash, R.E., Dobash, R.P., Cavanagh, K. and Lewis, R. (2000) *Changing Violent Men*. London: Sage Publications.

Donzelot, J. (1979) *The Policing of Families*. London: Hutchinson.

Dorkenoo, E. and Elworthy, S. (1992) *Female Genital Mutilation: Proposals for Change*. London: Minority Rights Group International Report.

Dorling, D. and Simpson, S. (eds) (1999) *Statistics in Society: The Arithmetic of Politics*. London: Arnold.

Douglas, J.D. (1967) *The Social Meanings of Suicide*. Princeton, NJ: Princeton University Press.

Doyal, L. (1993) On discovering the nature of knowledge in a world of relationships, in A. Kitson (ed.) *Nursing: Art and Science*. London: Chapman and Hall.

Durkheim, E. ([1897] 1970) *Suicide: A Study in Sociology*. London: Routledge and Kegan Paul.

Dutton, D. (1995) *The Batterer: A Psychological Profile*. New York: Basic Books.

Dyson, S.M. (1987) *Mental Handicap: Dilemmas of Parent–Professional Relations*. London: Croom Helm.

Dyson, S.M. (1995) Interviewing by conversation, *Sociology Review*, 3(4): 21–3, reprinted in Laws, S., Harper, C. and Marcus, R. (2003) *Research for Development: A Practical Guide*. Sage Publications/Save The Children Fund.

Dyson, S.M. (2000) Working with sickle cell/thalassaemia groups, in H. Kemshall and R. Littlechild (eds) *Participation in Social Care: Researching for Practice*. London: Jessica Kingsley Publishers.

Eagleton, T. (1991) *Ideology: An Introduction*. London: Verso.

Edwards, B. and O'Connell, B. (2003) Internal consistency and validity of the Stroke Impact Scale 2.0 (SIS 2.0) and SIS–16 in an Australian sample, *Quality of Life Research*, 12(8): 1127–35.

Edwards, D., Ashmore, M. and Potter, J. (1995) Death and furniture: the rhetoric, politics, and theology of bottom line arguments against relativism, *History of the Human Sciences*, 8(2): 25–49.

Elin, M. (1995) A developmental model for trauma, in L. Cohen, J. Berzoff and M. Elin (eds) *Dissociative Identity Disorder*. London: Jason Aronson.

El Saadawi, N. (1980) *The Hidden Face of Eve: Women in the Arab World*. London: Zed Press.

Enkin, M.W. (2000) Clinical equipoise and not the uncertainty principle is the moral underpinning of the randomised controlled trial, *British Medical Journal*, 321: 756–8.

Eraut, M. (1985) Knowledge creation and knowledge use in professional contexts, *Studies in Higher Education*, 10: 117–33.

Eraut, M. (1994) *Developing Professional Knowledge and Competence*. Brighton: Falmer Press.

Evans, D. (2003) *Placebo: The Belief Effect*. London: HarperCollins.

Fabos, A.H. (2001) Embodying transition: FGC, displacement, and gender-making for Sudanese in Cairo, *Feminist Review*, 69: 90–110.

Fellows, R. (1995) *Philosophy and Technology*. New York: The Press Syndicate of the University of Cambridge.

Festinger, L., Riecken, H.W. and Schachter, S. (1956) *When Prophecy Fails*. New York: Harper Torch.

Fielding, N. (1981) *The National Front*, London: Routledge and Kegan Paul.

Fielding, N.G. and Fielding, J.L. (1986) *Linking Data*. Newbury Park, CA: Sage Publications.

Finch, J. (1984) 'It's great to have someone to talk to': the ethics and politics of interviewing women, in C. Bell and H. Roberts (eds) *Social Researching: Politics, Problems, Practice*. London: Routledge and Kegan Paul.

Finfgeld, D.L., Wongvatunyu, S., Conn, V.S., Grando, V.T. and Russell, C.L. (2003)

Health Belief Model and Reversal Theory: a comparative analysis, *Journal of Advanced Nursing*, 43(3): 288–97.

Fisher, R.A. (1925) *Statistical Methods for Research Workers*. London: Oliver and Boyd.

Foss, C. and Ellersen, B. (2002) The value of combining qualitative and quantitative approaches in nursing research by means of method triangulation, *Journal of Advanced Nursing*, 40(2): 242–8.

Foucault, M. (1971) *Madness and Civilization*. London: Tavistock.

Foucault, M. (1973) *The Birth of the Clinic*. London: Tavistock.

Foucault, M. (1978) *The History of Sexuality. Vol. 1: An Introduction* (Translated by Robert Hurley). New York: Vintage Books.

Foucault, M. (1979) *Discipline and Punish*. New York: Vintage Books.

Fox, N.J. (1991) Postmodernism, rationality and the evaluation of health care, *Sociological Review*, 39: 709–44.

Fox, N.J. (1997) Texts, frames and decisions over discharge from hospital: a deconstruction, *Social Sciences in Health*, 3(1): 41–51.

Fox-Genovese, E. (1996) *'Feminism is Not the Story of My Life': How Today's Feminist Elite Has Lost Touch with the Real Concerns of Women*. New York: Doubleday.

Fracassini, C. (2004) Study clears MMR of autism link, *Sunday Times*, 20 June: 5.

Frank, A.W. (1991) For a sociology of the body: an analytical review, in M. Featherstone, M. Hepworth and B. Turner (eds) *The Body: Social Process and Cultural Theory*. London: Sage Publications.

Frank, A.W. (1995) *The Wounded Storyteller: Body, Illness and Ethics*. Chicago, IL: University of Chicago Press.

Freedman, B. (1987) Equipoise and the ethics of clinical research, *New England Journal of Medicine*, 317: 141–5.

Freedman, D.A., Pettiti, D.B. and Robbins, J.M. (2004) On the efficacy of screening for breast cancer, *International Journal of Epidemiology*, 33: 43–55.

Freidson, E. (1970) *Profession of Medicine: A Study in the Sociology of Applied Knowledge*. London, New York: Harper and Row.

Freire, P. (1972) *Pedagogy of the Oppressed*. Harmondsworth: Penguin.

Fuks, A., Weijer, C., Freedman, B., Shapiro, S., Skrutkowska, M. and Riaz, A. (1998) A study in contrasts: eligibility criteria in a twenty-year sample of NSABP and POG clinical trials, *Journal of Clinical Epidemiology*, 51: 69–79.

Gabe, J., Kelleher, D. and Williams, G. (1994) (eds) *Challenging Medicine*. London: Routledge.

Gallagher, R.E. and Gallo, R.C. (1975) Type C RNA tumor virus isolated from cultured human acute myelogenous leukemia cells, *Science*, 187: 350–3.

Gallo, R.C., Wong-Staal, F., Reitz, M., Gallagher, R.E., Miller, N. and Gillepsie, D.H. (1976) Some evidence for infectious type-C virus in humans, in D. Balimore, A.S. Huang and C.F. Fox (eds) *Animal Virology*. New York: Academic Press.

Ganis, G., Kosslyn, S.M., Stose, S., Thompson, W.L. and Yurgelun-Todd, D. (2003) Neural correlates of different types of deception: an fMRI investigation, *Cerebral Cortex*, 13: 830–6.

Garfinkel, H. (1967) *Studies in Ethnomethodology*, Englewood Cliffs, NJ: Prentice-Hall.

Garman, N. (1996) Qualitative inquiry: meaning and menace for educational researchers, in P. Willis and B. Neville (eds) *Qualitative Research Practice in Adult Education*. Ringwood, Victoria: David Lovell Publishing.

Garrett, L. (1994) *The Coming Plague*. Harmondsworth: Penguin.

Geddes, J., Freemantle, N., Harrison, P. and Bebbington, P. (2000) Atypical antipsychotics in the treatment of schizophrenia: systematic overview and meta-regression analysis, *British Medical Journal*, 321(7273): 1371–6.

George, S. (1986) *Ill Fares the Land: Essays on Food, Hunger and Power*. Harmondsworth: Penguin.

Gergen, K. (2000) *The Saturated Self*. New York: Basic Books.

Giddens, A. (1976) *New Rules of Sociological Method: A Positive Critique of Interpretive Sociologies*. London: Hutchinson.

Giddens, A. (1979) *Central Problems of Sociology*. London: Macmillan.

Giddens, A. (1990) *The Consequences of Modernity*. Cambridge: Polity Press.

Giddens, A. (1991) *Modernity and Self Identity*, Cambridge: Polity Press.

Giddens, A. (1994) Living in a post-traditional society, in U. Beck, A. Giddens and S. Lash (eds) *Reflexive Modernization*. Cambridge: Polity Press.

Gilbert, G.N. and Mulkay, M. (1984) *Opening Pandora's Box*. Cambridge: Cambridge University Press.

Giorgi, A. (1970) *Psychology as a Human Science: A Phenomenologically Based Approach*. New York: Harper and Row.

Gitlin, T. (1980) *The World is Watching*. Berkeley, CA: University of California Press.

Glaser, B.G. and Strauss, A.L. (1967) *The Discovery of Grounded Theory: Strategies for Qualitative Research*. Chicago, IL: Aldine.

Goertz, G. and Diehl, P.F. (1986) Measuring military allocations: a comparison of different approaches, *Journal of Conflict Resolution*, 30(3): 553–81.

Goffman, E. (1959) *The Presentation of Self in Everyday Life*. New York: Doubleday.

Goldmann, R.E., Sullivan, A.L., Droller, D.J. *et al.* (2003) Late frontal brain potentials distinguish true and false recognition, *Neuro Report*, 14: 1717–20.

Goodenough, F.L. (1949) *Mental Testing: Its History, Principles, and Applications*. New York: Rinehart.

Gordon, D., Waiter, D.G., Williams, J.H.G., Murray, A.D., Gilchrist, A., Perrett, D.I. and Whiten, A. (2004) A voxel-based investigation of brain structure in male adolescents with autistic spectrum disorder, *Neuroimage*, 22: 619–25.

Gøtzsche, P.C. and Olsen, O. (2000) Is screening for breast cancer with mammography justifiable?, *The Lancet*, 355: 129–34.

Gouldner, A. (1970) *The Coming Crisis of Western Sociology*. New York: Basic Books.

Graham, H. (1976) Smoking in pregnancy: the attitudes of expectant mothers, *Social Science and Medicine*, 10: 399–405.

Graham, H. (1984) *Women, Health and the Family*. Brighton: Harvester Wheatsheaf.

Gruenbaum, E. (2001) *The Female Circumcision Controversy: An Anthropological Perspective*. Philadelphia, PA: University of Pennsylvania Press.

Guba, E.G. (1981) Criteria for assessing the trustworthiness of naturalistic inquiries, *Educational Communication and Technology Journal*, 29(2): 75–91.

Guba, E.G. and Lincoln, Y.S. (1981) *Effective Evaluation: Improving the Usefulness of Evaluation Results through Responsive and Naturalistic Approaches*. San Francisco, CA: Jossey-Bass.

Guba, E.G. and Lincoln, Y.S. (1982) Epistemological and methodological bases of naturalistic inquiry, *Educational Communication and Technology Journal*, 30(4): 233–52.

Guba, E.G. and Lincoln, Y.S. (1989) *Fourth Generation Evaluation*. Newbury Park, CA: Sage Publications.

Gunnell, D. and Frankel, S. (1994) Prevention of suicide: aspirations and evidence, *British Medical Journal*, 308: 1227–33.

Habermas, J. (1978) *Knowledge and Human Interests*, London: Heinemann.

Haglund, B., Weisbrod, R. and Bracht, N. (1990) Assessing the community: its services, needs, leadership, and readiness, in N. Bracht (ed.) *Health Promotion at the Community Level*, Newbury Park, CA: Sage Publications.

Hammersley, M. (1992) *What's Wrong with Ethnography?* London: Routledge.

Hammersley, M. (1995) *The Politics of Social Research*. London: Sage Publications.

Hammersley, M. (2000) *Taking Sides in Social Research: Essays in Partisanship and Bias*. London: Routledge.

Hammersley, M. and Atkinson, P. (1983) *Ethnography: Principles in Practice*. London: Tavistock Publications.

Hammersley, M. and Gomm, R. (1997) Bias in social research, *Sociological Research Online* 2 (1), http://socresonline.org.uk/socresonline/2/1/2.html

Hansen, M. and Harway, M. (1993) *Battering and Family Therapy*. London: Sage Publications.

Haraway, D. (1991) *Simians, Cyborgs and Women: The Reinvention of Nature*. London: Routledge.

Harding, S. (1998) Can Men Be the Subjects of Feminist Thought?, in T. Digby (ed.) *Men Doing Feminism*. London: Routledge.

Harris, R. (1996) Reflection on the role of an evaluator, in P. Willis and B. Neville (eds) *Qualitative Research Practice in Adult Education*. Ringwood, Victoria: David Lovell Publishing.

Harrison, S. (1998) The politics of evidence-based medicine in the UK, *Policy and Politics*, 26 (1): 15–31.

Hartog, F. (2000) The invention of history: the re-history of a concept from Homer to Herodotus, *History and Theory*, 39: 384–95.

Harway, M. and O'Neil, J. (1999) *What Causes Men's Violence Against Women?* Thousand Oaks, CA: Sage Publications.

Hawes, L.C. (1977) Toward a hermeneutic phenomenology of communication, *Communication Quarterly*, 25: 30–41.

Haynes, J. (2004) Antidepressants little better than placebos, *Pulse*, http://www.pulse-i.co.uk. Accessed 30 July 2004.

Healy, D. (2004) *Let Them Eat Prozac*. New York: New York University Press.

Helman, C. (1978) Feed a cold, starve a fever, reprinted in Black, N., Boswell, D., Gray, A., Murphy, S. and Popay, J. (eds) (1984) *Health and Disease: A Reader*. Milton Keynes: Open University Press.

Henderson, M. (2004) Depression drugs little better than dummy pills, *The Times*, 20 July: 6.

Henwood, L.K. and Pidgeon, F.N. (1993) Qualitative research and psychological theorizing, in M. Hammersley (ed.) *Social Research: Philosophy, Politics and Practice*. Buckingham: Open University and London: Sage Publications.

Heslop, L., Elsom, S. and Parker, N. (2000) Improving continuity of care across psychiatric and emergency services: combining patient data within a participatory action research framework, *Journal of Advanced Nursing*, 31(1): 135–43.

Hey, V. (1999) Frail elderly people: difficult questions and awkward answers, in S. Hood, B. Mayall and S. Oliver (eds) *Critical Issues in Social Research: Power and Prejudice*. Buckingham: Open University Press.

Hindess, B. (1973) *The Use of Official Statistics in Sociology*. London: Macmillan.

Hockey, J. (1986) *Squaddies: Portrait of a Sub-Culture*. Exeter: University of Exeter Press.

Holdsworth, N. and Dodgson, G. (2003) Could a new Mental Health Act distort clinical judgement? A Bayesian justification of naturalistic reasoning about risk, *Journal of Mental Health*, 12(5): 451–62.

Holme, S.A., Beattie, P.E. and Fleming, C.J. (2002) Epidemiology and health services research: cosmetic camouflage advice improves quality of life, *British Journal of Dermatology*, 147(5): 946–9.

Homer (1854) *The Iliad and Odyssey* (translated by A. Pope). London: Nathaniel Cooke.

Hopkins, S. (1999) A discussion of the legal aspects of female genital mutilation, *Journal of Advanced Nursing*, 30(4): 926–33.

Howson, A. (1998) Surveillance, knowledge and risk: the embodied experience of cervical screening, *Health*, 2(2): 195–215.

Hunt, E. (1993) On avoiding 'psychiatric' patients, *Journal of Emergency Nursing*, 19: 375–6.

Hunt, S.D. (1990) Truth in marketing theory and research, *Journal of Marketing*, 54: 1–15.

Hunter, J.E. and Schmidt, F.L. (1990) *Methods of Meta-Analysis: Correcting Error and Bias in Research Findings*. Newbury Park, CA: Sage Publications.

Illich, I. (1977) *Limits to Medicine: Medical Nemesis, the Expropriation of Health*. Harmondsworth: Penguin.

Irvine, J., Miles, I. and Evans, J. (1979) *Demystifying Social Statistics*. London: Pluto Press.

James, N. (1989) Emotional labour: skill and work in the social regulation of feelings, *Sociological Review*, 37(1): 15–42.

Janz, N.K. and Becker, M.H. (1984) The Health Belief Model: a decade later, *Health Education Quarterly*, 11: 1–47.

Jenkins, A. (1996) Moving towards respect: a quest for balance, in C. McClean, M. Carey and C. White (eds) *Men's Ways of Being*. Oxford: Westview Press.

Jick, S., Dean, A. and Jick, H. (1995) Antidepressants and suicide, *British Medical Journal*, 310: 215–18.

Johnson, T., Ashworth, C. and Dandeker, C. (1984) *The Structure of Social Theory: Strategies, Dilemmas, Projects*. London: Macmillan.

Keat, R. (1979) Positivism and statistics in social science, in J. Irvine, I. Miles and J. Evans (eds) *Demystifying Social Statistics*. London: Pluto Press.

Kelly, D. and Conner, D.R. (1979) The emotional cycle of change, in J.E. Jones and

J.W. Pfeiffer (eds) *The 1979 Annual Handbook for Group Facilitators*. La Jolla, CA: La Jolla University Associates.

Kerr, A., Cunningham-Burley, S. and Amos, A. (1997) The new genetics: professionals' discursive boundaries, *Sociological Review*, 45(2): 279–303.

Kerr, A., Cunningham-Burley, S. and Amos, A. (1998) The new genetics and health: mobilizing lay expertise, *Public Understanding of Science*, 7: 41–60.

Ketchem, A. (2004) *Mulan: The Complete Script*, http://www.fpx.de/fp/Disney/Scripts/Mulan.html. Accessed 14 February 2004.

Kilduff, M. and Kelemen, M. (2001) The consolations of organization theory, *British Journal of Management*, 12: 55–9.

Klein, M., Janssen, P., MacWilliam, L., Kaczorowski, J. and Johnson, B. (1997) Determinants of vaginal-perineal integrity and pelvic floor functioning in childbirth, *Journal of Obstetrics and Gynaecology*, 176: 403–10.

Klein, M., Kaczorowski, J., Robbins, J., Gauthier, R., Jorgensen, S. and Joshi, A. (1995) Physicians' beliefs and behaviour during a randomised controlled trial of episiotomy: consequences for women in their care, *Journal of the Canadian Medical Association*, 153: 769–79.

Knorr-Cetina, K.D. and Mulkay, M.J. (1983) *Science Observed*, Beverly Hills, CA: Sage Publications.

Kopelman, M.D. (1995) The assessment of psychogenic amnesia, in A.D. Baddely, B.A. Wilson and F.N. Watts (eds) *Handbook of Memory Disorders*. Chichester: Wiley.

Kuhn, T. (1962) *The Structure of Scientific Revolutions*. Chicago, IL: University of Chicago Press.

Kuipers, E., Garety, P., Fowler, D., Dunn, G., Bebbington, P., Freeman, D. and Hadley, C. (1997) London–East Anglia randomised controlled trial of cognitive behavioural therapy for psychosis, *British Journal of Psychiatry*, 171: 319–27.

Kuzel, A. and Engel, J. (2001) Some pragmatic thoughts on evaluating qualitative health research, in J.M. Morse, J. Swanson and A. Kuzel (eds) *The Nature of Qualitative Evidence*. Thousand Oaks, CA: Sage Publications.

Krause, S.J. and Backosija, M.M. (2003) Development of a neuropathic pain questionnaire, *Clinical Journal of Pain*, 19(5): 306–14.

Lacity, M. and Jansen, M.A. (1994) Understanding qualitative data: a framework of text analysis methods, *Journal of Management Information Systems*, 11: 137–60.

Lakatos, I. (1978) *The Methodology of Scientific Research Programmes: Philosophical Papers, Volume 1* (edited by J. Worrall and G. Currie). Cambridge: Cambridge University Press.

Lakatos, I. and Musgrave, A. (1970) *Criticism and the Growth of Knowledge*. Cambridge: Cambridge University Press.

Lamping, D.L., Rowe, P., Black, N. and Lessof, L. (1998) Development and validation of an audit instrument: the Prostate Outcomes Questionnaire, *British Journal of Urology*, 82(1): 49–62.

Lancaster, J. (1982) Change theory: an essential aspect of nursing practice, in J. Lancaster and W. Lancaster (eds) *The Nurse as a Change Agent*. London: C.V. Mosby.

Langeland, W., Draijer, N. and van den Brink, W. (2003) Assessment of lifetime physical and sexual abuse in treated alcoholics: validity of the Addiction Severity Index, *Addictive Behaviors*, 28: 871–81.

Lather, P. (1991) *Getting Smart: Feminist Research and Pedagogy with/in the Postmodern*. London: Routledge.

Lather, P. (2001) Postmodernism, post-structuralism and post(critical) ethnography: of ruins, aporias and angels, in P. Atkinson, A. Coffey, S. Delamont, J. Lofland and L. Lofland (eds) *Handbook of Ethnography*. London: Sage Publications.

Latour, B. (1983) Give me a laboratory and I will raise the world, in K.D. Knorr-Cetina and M.J. Mulkay (eds) *Science Observed*. Beverly Hills, CA: Sage Publications.

Latour, B. (2000) When things strike back: a possible contribution of 'science studies' to the social sciences, *British Journal of Sociology*, 51(1): 107–23.

Latour, B. and Woolgar, S. (1986) *Laboratory Life: The Construction of Scientific Facts*, 2nd edn. Princeton, NJ: Princeton University Press.

Lawson, A. (1991) Whose side are we on now? Ethical issues in social research and medical practice, *Social Science and Medicine*, 32: 757–67.

Learmouth, M. (2004) The violence in trusting Trust Chief Executives: glimpsing trust in the UK National Health Service, *Qualitative Inquiry*, 10(4): 581–600.

Lee, E., Clements, S., Ingham, R. and Stone, N. (2004) *A Matter of Choice? Exploring Reasons for Variations in the Proportions of Under-18 Conceptions that are Terminated*. York: Joseph Rowntree Foundation and York Publishing Services.

Lee, R.M. (2000) *Unobtrusive Methods in Social Research*. Buckingham: Open University Press.

Leininger, M. (1994) Evaluation criteria and critique of qualitative research studies, in J.M. Morse (ed.) *Critical Issues in Qualitative Research Methods*. Newbury Park, CA: Sage Publications.

Li, H. (2003) The resolution of some paradoxes related to reliability and validity, *Journal of Educational and Behavioral Statistics*, 28: 89–95.

Lincoln, Y.S. and Guba, E.G. (1985) *Naturalistic Inquiry*. Beverly Hills, CA: Sage Publications.

Linstead, S. (1993) From postmodern anthropology to deconstructive ethnography, *Human Relations*, 46(1): 97–120.

Longino, H.E. (1990) *Science and Social Knowledge: Values and Objectivity in Social Enquiry*. Princeton, NJ: Princeton University Press.

Luckács, G. (1971) *History and Class Consciousness: Studies in Marxist Dialectics*. London: Merlin Press.

Lukes, S. (1974) *Power: A Radical View*. London: Macmillan.

Lupton, D., McCarthy, S. and Chapman, S. (1995) 'Doing the right thing': the symbolic meanings and experiences of having an HIV antibody test, *Social Science and Medicine*, 41(2): 173–80.

Lynch, M. (1985) *Art and Artefact in Laboratory Science*. London: Routledge.

McCann, E. (2001) Recent developments in psycho-social interventions for people with psychosis, *Issues in Mental Health Nursing*, 22: 99–107.

McClelland, C.A. (1983) Let the user beware, *International Studies Quarterly*, 27(2): 169–77.

McKnight, A. and Merrett, J.D. (1986) Smoking in pregnancy – a health education problem, *Journal of the Royal College of Practitioners*, 36: 161–4.

MacPherson, W. (1999) *The Stephen Lawrence Inquiry: Report of an Inquiry by Sir William MacPherson* (Cm 4262-I). London: The Stationery Office.

Madigan, S. (1999) Inscription, description and deciphering chronic identities: preparation for practice, in I. Parker (ed.) *Deconstructing Psychotherapy*. London: Sage Publications.

Magill, J. (1989) Family therapy: an approach to the treatment of wife assault, in B. Pressman, G. Cameron and M. Rothery (eds) *Intervening with Assaulted Women: Current Theory, Research and Practice*. Hillsdale, NJ: Lawrence Erlbaum.

Maijala, H., Munnukka, T. and Nikkonen, M. (2000) Feeling of 'lacking' as the core of envy: a conceptual analysis of envy, *Journal of Advanced Nursing*, 31(6): 1342–50.

Mankowski, E., Haaken, J. and Silvergleid, C. (2002) Collateral damage: an analysis of the achievements and unintended consequences of batterer intervention programs and discourse, *Journal of Family Violence*, 17: 167–84.

Mantzoukas, S. (2004) Issues of representation within qualitative inquiry, *Qualitative Health Research*, 14(7): 994–1007.

Marino, R., Browne, J. and Minichiello, V. (2000) An instrument to measure safer sex strategies used by male sex workers, *Archives of Sexual Behavior*, 29(3): 217–28.

Martin, J. (1990) Deconstructing organizational taboos: the suppression of gender conflict in organizations, *Organizational Science*, 1: 339–59.

Martin, L. (1996) *The House Officer's Survival Guide: Rules, Laws, Lists and Other Medical Musings*. Cleveland, OH: Lakeside Press.

Marx, K. (1845) *Theses on Feuerbach*, http://www.marxists.org/archive/marx/works/1845/theses/theses.htm. Accessed 15 July 2005.

Masedo, A.I. and Esteve, R. (2000) Some empirical evidence regarding the validity of the Spanish version of the McGill Pain Questionnaire (MPQ-SV), *Pain*, 85(3): 451–6.

Matthews, R. (1996) Base-rate errors and rain forecasts, *Nature*, 382: 766.

Medawar, P.B. (1964) Is the scientific paper fraudulent? Yes; it misrepresents scientific thought, *Saturday Review*, 1 August: 42–3.

Merckelbach, H., Devilly, G.J. and Rassin, E. (2002) Alters in dissociative identity disorder: metaphors or genuine entities?, *Clinical Psychology Review*, 22: 481–97.

Messick, S. (1995) Validity of psychological assessment: validation of inferences from persons' responses and performance as scientific inquiry into scoring meaning, *American Psychologist*, 9: 741–9.

Meteorological Office (2001) *Annual Report and Accounts 2000/1*. London: The Stationery Office.

Micali, G., Lacarrubba, F. and Tedeschi, A. (2004) Videodermatoscopy enhances the ability to monitor efficacy of scabies treatment and allows optimal timing of drug application, *Journal of the European Academy of Dermatology and Venereology*, 18: 153–4.

Milner, J. (2004) From 'disappearing' to 'demonized': the effects on men and women of professional interventions based on challenging men who are violent, *Critical Social Policy*, 24(1): 79–101.

Minichiello,V., Marino, R., Browne, J. and Jamieson, M. (1998) A review of male to male commercial sex encounters, *Venereology*, 11: 32–42.

Minuchin, S. (1984) *Family Kaleidoscope*, Cambridge, MA: Harvard University Press.

Morgan, G., Buckley, C. and Nowers, M. (1998) Face to face with the suicidal, *Advances in Psychiatric Treatment*, 4: 188–96.

Morley, D. (2002) (ed.) *The Gift: New Writing for the NHS*. Birmingham: Stride Books in association with Birmingham Health Authority.

Moss, P.A. (1994) Can there be validity without reliability?, *Educational Researcher*, 23: 5–12.

Moustakas, C. (1994) *Phenomenological Research Methods*. London: Sage Publications.

Mullender, A. and Burton, S. (2000) Dealing with perpetrators, in J. Taylor-Browne (ed.) *Reducing Domestic Violence: What Works?* London: Home Office.

Mullender, A. and Ward, D. (1991) *Self-Directed Groupwork: Users Taking Action for Empowerment*. London: Whiting and Birch.

Munro, R. (1998) The project isn't working, *Nursing Times*, 92(42): 27–9.

Nanda, S.K., Rivcas, A.L., Trochim, W.M. and Deshler, D. (2000) Emphasis on validation in research: a meta analysis, *Scientometrics*, 48(1): 45–64.

Nazroo, J.Y. and Edwards, A. (1998) Gender differences in the prevalence of depression: artifact, alternative disorders, biology or roles?, *Sociology of Health & Illness*, 20: 1–15.

New Scientist (2004) No brainer: misplaced faith in mind reading scans is a sure route to injustice (Editorial), *New Scientist*, 183(7468): 3.

Nijenhuis, E.R.S. and van der Hart, O. (1999) Forgetting and re-experiencing trauma, in J. Goodwin and R. Attias (eds) *Splintered Reflections: Images of the Body in Trauma*. New York: Basic Books.

Oakley, A. (1981) Interviewing women: a contradiction in terms?, in H. Roberts (ed.) *Doing Feminist Research*. London: Routledge.

Oakley, A. (1992) *Social Support and Motherhood*. Oxford: Blackwell.

Okamura, J.Y. (1981) Situational ethnicity, *Ethnic and Racial Studies*, 5(4): 394–420.

Oliver, M. (1992) Changing the social relations of research production?, *Disability, Handicap and Society*, 7(2): 101–14.

Olsen, O. and Gøtzsche, P.C. (2001a) Cochrane review on screening for breast cancer with mammography, *The Lancet*, 358: 1340–2.

Olsen, O. and Gøtzsche, P.C. (2001b) *Screening for Breast Cancer with Mammography* (The Cochrane Database of Systematic Reviews). Chichester: John Wiley and Sons.

Olsen, O. and Gøtzsche, P.C. (2001c) *Systematic Screening for Breast Cancer with Mammography*, http://image.thelancet.com/lancet/extra/fullreport.pdf Accessed 1 September 2004.

Osterlind, S.J. (1983) *Test Item Bias*. Newbury Park, CA: Sage Publications.

Parker, I. (1994) Discourse analysis, in P. Banister, E. Burman, M. Taylor and C. Tindall (eds) *Qualitative Research Methods in Psychology: A Research Guide*. Buckingham: Open University Press.

Parker, S. (1997) *Reflective Teaching in the Postmodern World*. Buckingham: Open University Press.

Parkes, J. (2000) The relationship between the reliability and cost of performance assessments, *Education Policy Analysis Archives* 8(16) [online], http://epaa. asu.edu/epaa/v8n16 Accessed 6 September 2004.

Paterson, E. (1981) Food-work: maids in a hospital kitchen, in P. Atkinson and C. Heath (eds) *Medical Work: Realities and Routines*, Farnborough: Gower.

Patrick, J. (1973) *A Glasgow Gang Observed*. London: Eyre Methuen.

Pawson, R. (1989) *A Measure for Measures*. London: Routledge.

Pawson, R. and Tilley, N. (1997) *Realistic Evaluation*. London: Sage Publications.

Peckover, S. (2002) Supporting and policing mothers: an analysis of the disciplinary practices of health visiting, *Journal of Advanced Nursing*, 38(4): 369–77.

Pedhazur, E.J. and Schmelkin, L.P. (1991) *Measurement, Design, and Analysis: An Integrated Approach*. Hillsdale, NJ: Lawrence Erlbaum Associates.

Petit-Zeman, S. (2003) The great drugs lottery, *Guardian*, G2 Supplement: 14.

Phillips, H. (2004) Private thoughts, public property, *New Scientist*, 183(2468): 38–41.

Phillips, M. (2003) This baby suffered brain damage and epilepsy after the MMR jab. So why did doctors ignore warnings that it might be unsafe?, *Daily Mail*, 12 March: 36.

Polit, F.D. and Hungler, P.B. (1999) *Nursing Research: Principles and Methods*. Philadelphia, PA: Lippincott.

Polkinghorne, D.E. (1988) *Narrative Knowing and the Human Sciences*. Albany, NY: State University of New York Press.

Popper, K.R. (1945) *The Open Society and Its Enemies*. London: George Routledge.

Popper, K.R. (1959) *The Logic of Scientific Discovery*. London: Hutchinson.

Popper, K.R. (1979) *Objective Knowledge. An Evolutionary Approach*. Oxford: Clarendon Press.

Porter, R. (1987) *Mind-Forg'd Manacles: A History of Madness from the Restoration to the Regency*. New York: Continuum Publishing Group.

Porter, S. (1993) Critical realist ethnography: the case of racism and professionalism in a medical setting, *Sociology*. 27(4): 591–609.

Porter, S. (1998) *Social Theory and Nursing Practice*. Basingstoke: Macmillan.

Potter, J. (1997) Discourse analysis as a way of analysing naturally occurring talk, in D. Silverman (ed.) *Qualitative Research: Theory, Method and Practice*. London: Sage Publications.

Potter, J. and Wetherell, M. (1987) *Discourse and Social Psychology: Beyond Attitudes and Behaviour*. London: Sage Publications.

Propp, V. ([1928] 1968) *The Morphology of the Folktale*. Austin, TX: University of Texas Press.

Radley, A. (1994) *Making Sense of Illness: The Social Psychology of Health and Disease*. London: Sage Publications.

Radley, A. (1999) The aesthetics of illness: narrative, horror and the sublime, *Sociology of Health and Illness*, 21(6): 778–96.

Radley, A. and Billig, M. (1996) Accounts of health and illness: dilemmas and representations, *Sociology of Health and Illness*, 18(2): 220–40.

Rhodes, C. (2000) Reading and writing organizational lives, *Organization*, 7(1): 7–29.

Rice, C., Roberts, H., Smith, S.J. and Bryce, C. (1994) 'Its like teaching your child to swim in a pool full of alligators': lay voices and professional research on child accidents, in J. Popay and G. Williams (eds) *Researching the People's Health*. London: Routledge.

Rice, M.E. and Harris, G.T. (1997) Cross validation and extension of the violence risk appraisal guide for child molesters and rapists, *Law and Human Behaviour*, 21(2): 231–46.

Ricouer, P. (1977) *The Rule of Metaphor: Multi-disciplinary Studies of the Creation of Meaning in Language* (Translated by R. Czerny, K. McLaughlin and J. Costello). Toronto: University of Toronto Press.

Rivett, M. and Rees, A. (2004) Dancing on a razor's edge: systemic group work with batterers, *Journal of Family Therapy*, 26: 142–62.

Romm, N. (1997) Becoming more accountable, *Sociological Research Online*, 2(3), http://www.socresonline.org.uk/socresonline/2/3/2.html

Ronai, C.R. (1999) The next night sous rature: wrestling with Derrida's mimesis, *Qualitative Inquiry*, 5(1): 114–29.

Roper, L. (1994) *Oedipus and the Devil: Witchcraft, Sexuality and Religion in Early Modern Europe*. London: Routledge.

Rose, N. (1989) *Governing the Soul: The Shaping of the Private Self*. London: Routledge.

Rosenstock, I.M. (1966) Why people use health services, *Milbank Memorial Fund Quarterly*, 44: 94–127.

Rosenstock, I.M. (1974) Historical origins of the Health Belief Model, *Health Education Monographs*, 2: 328–35.

Ross, C.A. (1997) *Dissociative Identity Disorder: Diagnosis, Clinical Features, and Treatment of Multiple Personality*. New York: Wiley.

Roth, J. (1966) Hired hand research. Reprinted in Denzin, N. (ed.) (1978) *Sociological Methods: A Sourcebook*. London: Butterworths.

Rubin, H.J. and Rubin, I.S. (1995) *Qualitative Interviewing: The Art of Hearing Data*. Thousand Oaks, CA: Sage Publications.

Rushdie, S. (1985) *The Jaguar Smile: A Nicaraguan Journey*. New York: Picador.

Saks, M. (1991) The flight from science? The reporting of acupuncture in mainstream British medical journals from 1800 to 1990, *Complementary Medical Research*, 5(3): 178–82.

Salvucci, S., Walter, E., Conley, V., Fink, S. and Saba, M. (1997) *Measurement Error Studies at the National Center for Education Statistics*. Washington, DC: US Department of Education.

Sarantakos, S. (1998) *Social Research*, 2nd edn. London: Macmillan.

Schacter, D.L. (ed.) (1999) *The Cognitive Neuropsychology of False Memories*. London: Psychology Press.

Schegloff, E.A. (1997) Whose text? Whose context?, *Discourse and Society*, 8(2): 165–88.

Schon, D.A. (1987) *Educating the Reflective Practitioner*. New York: Jossey-Bass.

Seide, M. and Miller, R. (1983) The relationship between psychiatric and medical emergency services, *Quality Review Bulletin*, 9: 134–8.

Siegel, S. (1983) Brown on epistemology and the new philosophy of science, *Synthese*, 14: 61–89.

Silverman, D. (1993) *Interpreting Qualitative Data*. London: Sage Publications.

Silverman, D. (1998) The quality of qualitative health research: the open-ended interview and its alternatives, *Social Sciences in Health*, 4(2): 104–18.

Silverman, E., Woloshin, S., Schwartz, L.M., Byram, S.J., Welch, H.G. and Fischoff, B. (2001) Women's views on breast cancer risk and screening mammography: a qualitative interview study, *Medical Decision Making*, 21: 231–40.

Sim, J. and Sharp, K. (1998) A critical appraisal of the role of triangulation in nursing research, *International Journal of Nursing Studies*, 35: 23–31.

Singer, J.D. (1990) Variables, indicators, and data: the measurement problem in macropolitical research, in J.D. Singer and P.F. Diehl (eds) *Measuring the Correlates of War*. Ann Arbor, MI: University of Michigan Press.

Singleton, R.A. Jr, Straits, B.C. and Straits, M.M. (1993) *Approaches to Social Research*, 2nd edn. New York: Oxford University Press.

Skidmore, D. (1995) Risk-taking or knowing the score: a preliminary study of young males' intravenous drug use and unprotected sex, *Social Sciences and Health*, 1(1): 14–21.

Sleep, J., Roberts, J. and Chalmers, I. (1989) Care during the second stage of labour, in I. Chalmers, M. Enkin and M.J.N.C. Keirse (eds) *Effective Care in Pregnancy and Childbirth*. Oxford: Oxford University Press.

Smith, F.B. (1979) *The People's Health 1830–1910*. London: Croom Helm.

Smith, J.A., Jarman, M. and Osborn, M. (1999) Doing interpretative phenomenological analysis, in M. Murray and K. Chamberlain (eds) *Qualitative Health Psychology: Theories and Methods*. London: Sage Publications.

Smith, M.D. (1994) Enhancing the quality of survey data on violence against women: a feminist approach, *Gender and Society*, 8(1): 109–27.

Snyder, H.W. and Fleissner, E. (1980) Specificity of human antibodies to oncovirus glycoproteins: recognition of antigen by natural antibodies directed against carbohydrate structures, *Proceedings of the National Academy of Science USA*, 77: 1622–6.

Stainton Rogers, W. (1991) *Explaining Health and Illness: An Exploration of Diversity*. Hemel Hempstead: Harvester Wheatsheaf.

Stimson, G. and Webb, B. (1975) *Going to See the Doctor*. London: Routledge and Kegan Paul.

Stratford, D., Chamblee, S., Ellerbrock, T.V., Johnson, R.J.W., Abbott, D., Reyn, C.F. and Horsburgh, C.R. (2003) Integration of a Participatory Research Strategy into a Rural Health Survey, *Journal of General Internal Medicine*, 18(7): 586–8.

Strauss, A.L., Schatzman, L., Ehrlich, D., Bucher, R. and Sabshin, M. (1963) The hospital and its negotiated order, in E. Friedson (ed.) *The Hospital in Modern Society*. London: Macmillan.

Strecher, V.J., Champion, V.L. and Rosenstock, I.M. (1997) The Health Belief Model and health behaviour, in D.S. Gochman (ed.) *Handbook of Health Behaviour Research I: Personal and Social Determinants*. New York: Plenum Press.

Strecher, V.J. and Rosenstock, I.M. (1997) The Health Belief Model, in K. Glanz, F.M. Lewis and B.K. Rimer (eds) *Health Behavior and Health Education: Theory, Research, and Practice*, 2nd edn. San Francisco, CA: Jossey-Bass.

Szolovits, P. (1995) Uncertainty and decisions in medical informatics, *Methods of Information in Medicine*, 34: 111–21.

Taylor, S. (1992) Measuring child abuse, *Sociology Review*, 1(3): 23–7.

Taylor, S. and Field, D. (2003) *Sociology of Health and Health Care*. Oxford: Blackwell.

Thomas, L.M. (1996) 'Ngaitana (I will circumcise myself)': the gender and generational politics of the 1956 ban on clitoridectomy in Meru, Kenya, *Gender and History*, 8(3): 338–63.

Thomas, W.I. and Thomas, D.S. (1928) *The Child in America: Behaviour Problems and Programs*. New York: Knopf.

Thomas, W.I. and Znaniecki, F. (1918) *The Polish Peasant in Europe and America*. Chicago, IL: University of Chicago Press.

Thompson, R.S., Rivcara, F.P., Thompson, D.C., Barlow, W.E., Sugg, N.K., Maiurro, R.D. and Rubanowice, D.M. (2000) Identification and management of domestic violence: a randomised trial, *American Journal of Preventative Medicine*, 19(4): 253–64.

Thucydides (1943) *The History of the Peloponnesian Wars*, edited and translated by R.W. Livingstone. Oxford: Oxford University Press.

Trochim, W. (2001) *The Research Methods Knowledge Base*, 2nd edn. Cincinnati, OH: Atomic Dog Publications.

Tsai, G.E., Condie, D., Wu, M.T. and Cheng, I. (1999) Functional magnetic resonance imaging of personality switches in a woman with dissociative disorders, *Harvard Review of Psychiatry*, 7: 119–22.

Turner, V. and MacIntyre, A. (1999) The yin and yang of HIV, *Nexus* 6(6): 47–54.

Uhlmann, V., Martin, C.M., Sheils, O. *et al.* (2002) Potential viral pathogenic mechanism for new variant inflammatory bowel disease, *Molecular Pathology*, 55: 84–90.

Usher, R. and Edwards, R. (1994) *Postmodernism and Education*. London: Routledge.

Van Loon, J. (2001) Ethnography: a critical turn in cultural studies, in P. Atkinson, A. Coffey, S. Delamont, J. Lofland and L. Lofland (eds) *Handbook of Ethnography*. London: Sage Publications.

Vidich, A.J. and Lyman, S.M. (1998) Qualitative methods: their history in sociology and anthropology, in N.K. Denzin and Y.S. Lincoln (eds) *The Landscape of Qualitative Research: Theories and Issues*. Thousand Oaks, CA: Sage Publications.

Wakefield, A.J. and Montgomery, S.M. (2000) Measles, mumps and rubella vaccine: through a glass, darkly, *Adverse Drug Reactions and Toxicology Reviews*, 19(4): 265–92.

Wakefield, A.J., Murch, S.H., Anthony, A. and Linnell, J. (1998) Ileal-lymphoid-nodular hypoplasia, non-specific colitis and pervasive developmental disorder in children, *Lancet*, 351: 637–41.

Wallis, R. (1976) *The Road to Total Freedom: A Sociological Analysis of Scientology*. London: Heinemann Educational.

Waltz, C.F., Strickband, O.L. and Lenz, E.R. (1991) *Measurement in Nursing Research*, 2nd edn. Philadelphia, PA: F.A. Davies.

Webb, E.J., Campbell, D.T., Schwartz, R.D. and Sechrest, L. (1966) *Unobtrusive Measures: Non-reactive Research in the Social Sciences*. Chicago, IL: Rand McNally.

Weber, M. (1989) *Max Weber's 'Science as a Vocation'*. London: Unwin Hyman.

West, P. and Sweeting, H. (2003) Fifteen, female and stressed: changing patterns of psychological distress over time, *Journal of Child Psychology and Psychiatry*, 44(3): 399–411.

Whyte, W.F. (1984) *Learning from the Field: A Guide from Experience*. London: Sage Publications.

Williams, C. (1999) Doing health, doing gender: teenagers, diabetes and asthma, *Social Science and Medicine*, 50(3): 387–96.

Willig, C. (2000) A discourse-dynamic approach to the study of subjectivity in health psychology, *Theory and Psychology*, 10(4): 547–70.

Willis, P. (1977) *Learning to Labour: How Working Class Kids Get Working Class Jobs*. Farnborough: Saxon House.

Willis, P. (1980) Note on method, in S. Hall, D. Hobson, C. Lowe and P. Willis (eds) *Culture, Media, Language*. London: Hutchinson.

Wilson, H.W. (1993) What's culture got to do with it? Excising the harmful tradition of female circumcision, *Harvard Law Review*, 106: 1944–61.

Wolf, N. (1991) *The Beauty Myth*. New York: Vintage.

Wykes, T., Parr, A.M. and Lanfau, S. (1999) Group treatment of auditory hallucinations, *British Journal of Psychiatry*, 175: 180–5.

Wyre, R. (1992) The Gracewell Clinic, in W.R. Stainton, D. Hevery, J. Roche and E. Ash (eds) *Child Abuse and Neglect: Facing the Challenge*, 2nd edn. London: Batsford.

Yates, S. (2002) *Power and Subjectivity: A Foucauldian Discourse Analysis of Experiences of Power in Learning Difficulties Community Care Homes*. Unpublished PhD, De Montfort University, Leicester.

Yin, R.K. (1994) Discovering the future of the case study method in evaluation research, *Evaluation Practice*, 15: 283–90.

Yoder, L. and Jones, S.L. (1982) The emergency room nurse and the psychiatric patient, *Journal of Psychosocial Nursing and Mental Health Services*, 20: 22–8.

Young, E. (2001) Autism 'no longer a rare condition', *New Scientist*, 13 December.

Zernike, W. and Henderson, A. (1999) Evaluation of a constipation risk assessment scale, *International Journal of Nursing Practice*, 5(2): 106–9.

Index